Andreas Rentschler

Model Transformation Languages with Modular Information Hiding

The Karlsruhe Series on Software Design and Quality
Volume 17

Chair Software Design and Quality
Faculty of Computer Science
Karlsruhe Institute of Technology

and

Software Engineering Division
Research Center for Information Technology (FZI), Karlsruhe

Editor: Prof. Dr. Ralf Reussner

Model Transformation Languages with Modular Information Hiding

von

Andreas Rentschler

Scientific Publishing

Dissertation, Karlsruher Institut für Technologie (KIT)
Fakultät für Informatik
Tag der mündlichen Prüfung: 14. Januar 2015
Referenten: Prof. Dr. Ralf Reussner
Prof. Dr. Bernhard Beckert

Impressum

KIT Scientific Publishing

Karlsruher Institut für Technologie (KIT)
KIT Scientific Publishing
Straße am Forum 2
D-76131 Karlsruhe

KIT Scientific Publishing is a registered trademark of Karlsruhe Institute of Technology. Reprint using the book cover is not allowed.

www.ksp.kit.edu

Print on Demand 2015

ISSN 1867-0067
ISBN 978-3-7315-0346-0
DOI: 10.5445/KSP/1000045910

Model Transformation Languages with Modular Information Hiding

zur Erlangung des akademischen Grades eines

Doktors der Ingenieurwissenschaften

der Fakultät für Informatik
des Karlsruher Instituts für Technologie

genehmigte

Dissertation

von

Andreas Rentschler

aus Eberbach (Baden)

Tag der mündlichen Prüfung:	14. Januar 2015
Erster Gutachter:	Prof. Dr. Ralf Reussner
Zweiter Gutachter:	Prof. Dr. Bernhard Beckert

Abstract

With a ratio of an estimated 60%, maintenance costs constitute a substiantial share of the lifecycle costs of a typical software project. It is a major objective of software engineers to explore techniques that help to enhance maintainability and understandability of software artifacts. One established concept in this field is modular programming. By providing concepts to divide functionality into independent modules, modular programming helps to manage even complex programs. David L. Parnas has expanded on this idea by introducing the additional concept of module interfaces. According to Parnas, any outbound dependencies of a module must be explicitly declared in the module's interface description to foster the encapsulation of design decisions (*information hiding*).

Modularity is broadly used by modern general-purpose languages to tackle the complexity of larger programs. No need for such a high-level concept arises for most domain-specific languages, i.e., lean languages designed for compact problem descriptions. One notable exception to this rule of thumb are model transformation languages. Model transformations, together with models, form the principal artifacts in model-driven software development, a methodology of software engineering that aims to automatically generate large parts of a software from abstract models. In such a process, transformations play a pivotal role, as they assign semantics to models by means of other models and languages with already well-defined semantics, usually residing at a lower level of abstraction. Industrial practitioners report that, despite their domain-specificity, transformation programs on larger models quickly get sufficiently large and complex and at the same time less maintainable.

A multitude of specific transformation languages exist, and most of them establish some sort of modularity, but almost all of them solely have reuse in mind while they neglect maintenance issues. An interface concept to attain information hiding modularity as propagated by Parnas is supported by none of them.

This thesis presents three contributions that render maintenance of model transformations more efficient. The first and major scientific contribution of this thesis is an **information hiding modularity concept tailored to model transformations**. One novelty when it comes to model transformations is that metamodels are software artifacts that are specified independently from the transformation. Thus, interfaces must not only control visibility of methods, but also control accessibility to incoming and outgoing data types. Access control can be explicitly declared on a fine-grained level, i.e., packages and classes inside a metamodel. For obtaining maximal usability, on top of our proposed syntactical extension, a **type inference system** is defined that statically checks at design-time if interface contracts are met or if they are not. Our module concept has been initially defined for the imperative transformation language QVT-Operational (QVT-O) due to its clarity. In the scope of this thesis, it is further shown that the concept is applicable to declarative transformation languages as well. In this context, we study the semantics of the declarative transformation language QVT-Relations (QVT-R).

Legacy transformations are often monolithic or a suitable modular design cannot be determined. To improve maintenance effort in such cases, we develop a **concept for visualization of dependence information** according to the methodology of visual analytics, the second contribution of this thesis. The concept is implemented as a maintenance tool that statically analyzes dependencies occurring among mapping methods and model elements. Information is shown in an interactive graph-based view that offers cross-view navigation and task-dependent filtering.

In addition, a **software clustering** approach is adapted to the requirements of the transformation domain. It forms the third contribution of this thesis. In contrast to previously known approaches, high cohesion and low coupling is not only based on control dependencies, it can also incorporate dependencies to the classes of metamodels and their package structure. The approach is particularly suitable to find decompositions for legacy transformations.

We **evaluated** each of the three contributions in a case study based on larger transformations from the Palladio research project. For this purpose, the module concept had been integrated into two imperative transformation languages, Xtend and QVT-O.

The **first study** focuses on an Xtend transformation that maps architectural descriptions in the Palladio component model to simulation code. It is shown that locating the concerns in the modularized variant requires significantly less effort than in the previous unmodularized variant. In the study, two realistic maintenance scenarios had been examined, a bug fix and a functional enhancement. The **second case study** validates the visualization approach in an empirical experiment. Participants had to carry out realistic maintenance tasks on a QVT-O transformation for mapping the Palladio component model to a queueing Petri net model. Results show that participants using the approach spotted locations of concerns with significantly higher efficiency. The **third case study** aims to evaluate the automatic clustering approach. Two previously modularized transformations are automatically re-modularized, one QVT-O transformation that translates a set of advanced modeling concepts of the Palladio model to basic concepts, and an Xtend transformation that maps the Palladio model to simulation code. We are able to confirm a significantly higher similarity between the automatically and the manually clustered variant, when taking not only control but also model structures and dependencies into account of the automatic clustering process.

This dissertation points out that also domain-specific languages must provide appropriate structuring concepts to ensure readability and maintainability of larger and more complex programs. The particular notion of an interface highly depends on the domain and the requested level of granularity; In the case of model transformations, for example, we regard mapping methods in combination with distinct model elements as equivalent parts of an interface, thereby gaining extended expressiveness that results in significantly better maintainable software.

Kurzfassung

Betrachtet man die Gesamtkosten eines typischen Softwareprojekts über seinen gesamten Lebenszyklus, so tragen die Kosten ihrer Wartung mit geschätzten 60% zu einem wesentlichen Teil zu den Gesamtkosten bei. Softwaretechniker sind deswegen von je her an Techniken interessiert, die die Wartbarkeit und Lesbarkeit der Softwareartefakte steigern. Ein bewährtes Entwurfskonzept ist das modulare Programmieren; es sieht die Auftrennung von Funktionalität in unabhängige Module vor, und macht damit auch komplexere Programme beherrschbar. David L. Parnas hat diese Idee um einen Schnittstellenbegriff erweitert, bei dem die Abhängigkeiten eines Moduls nach außen explizit in seiner Schnittstelle zu deklarieren sind, um die Kapselung von Entwurfsentscheidungen – das sogenannte *Information Hiding* – zu ermöglichen.

Derartig ausgereifte Modulkonzepte sind jedoch bisher hauptsächlich nur in Allzwecksprachen vorzufinden, während domänenspezifischere Sprachen in der Regel nur für kleinere Programme konzipiert sind, sodass Wartungsprobleme hier eher selten auftreten. Eine Ausnahme stellen Transformationssprachen dar, wie sie in der modellgetriebenen Softwareentwicklung in Gebrauch sind. In der modellgetriebenen Softwareentwicklung geht es darum, große Teile einer Software aus Modellen generativ zu erzeugen. Hierfür werden in der Regel spezielle Transformationssprachen eingesetzt, die Modelle mit hoher konzeptioneller Nähe zur Problemdomäne auf Modelle und Sprachen mit wohldefinierter Semantik abbilden, üblicherweise auf einem niedrigeren Abstraktionsniveau. Praktiker aus der Industrie berichten, dass Transformationsprogramme in größeren Projekten schnell besonders groß werden und dabei schwerer wartbar.

Zwar sehen viele Transformationssprachen Modulkonzepte vor, diese zielen aber häufig auf eine Wiederverwendbarkeit der Module ab. Ein Schnittstellenbegriff, wie er von Parnas für eine bessere Wartbarkeit propagiert wurde, wird von keiner dieser Sprachen bisher unterstützt.

Der wissenschaftliche Hauptbeitrag dieser Arbeit ist ein **auf Transformationssprachen zugeschnittenes Modul- und Schnittstellenkonzept, das Information Hiding explizit unterstützt**. Eine Besonderheit bei Transformationen ist, dass Modelle unabhängig von Transformationen spezifizierte Artefakte sind. Daher wird an den Schnittstellen im Gegensatz zu bisher bekannten Konzepten zusätzlich der Zugriff auf ein- und ausgehende Daten geregelt. Diese Zugriffsregelung findet anstatt auf Modellebene auf feingranularer Ebene statt, den Paketen und Klassen innerhalb eines Modells. Basierend auf unserer syntaktischen Erweiterung wird ein **statisches Typsystem** formuliert, das die Konformität von Implementierungen zu deren Schnittstellen zur Entwurfszeit überprüft. Es wird außerdem gezeigt, dass das für die imperative Sprache QVT-Operational (QVT-O) definierte Konzept auch auf weitere imperative sowie deklarative Transformationssprachen anwendbar ist. In diesem Zusammenhang findet eine formale Betrachtung der Semantik der deklarativen Sprache QVT-Relations (QVT-R) statt.

Bestehende Transformationen sind häufig monolithisch oder für sie lässt sich keine vorteilhafte Modularisierung finden. Um die Wartung solcher Transformationen zu erleichtern, wird ein **Visualisierungsansatz nach der Visual-Analytics-Methodologie** vorgestellt, bei dem ein Werkzeug die auftretenden Abhängigkeiten zwischen Abbildungsfunktionen und Modellelementen innerhalb der Entwicklungsumgebung kontinuierlich anzeigt, über aufgabenabhängige Filtereinstellungen verfügt und interaktiv navigierbar ist.

Weiterhin wird der für gewöhnliche Programme verbreitete Reengineering-Ansatz des **Software-Clustering** auf Transformationsprogramme übertragen, sodass für schlecht oder nicht modularisierte Transformationen automatisch geeignetere Modularisierungen vorgeschlagen werden. Im Gegensatz zu gewöhnlichen Programmen besteht bei Transformationen die Möglichkeit, vorhandene Paketstrukturen involvierter Modelle in den Modularisierungprozess einzubeziehen.

Für eine **Evaluation** wurde das Modulkonzept in die imperativen Transformationssprachen Xtend und QVT-O integriert. Es wurden drei Fallstudien auf größeren Transformationen durchgeführt. Die **erste Fallstudie** basiert auf in Xtend geschriebenen Transformationsschablonen, die aus Architekturbeschreibungen im Palladio-Komponentenmodell Simulationscode generieren. Hier konnte im Rahmen von realen Wartungsszenarien gezeigt werden, dass der Aufwand zur Lokalisierung relevanter Codestellen bei der Verwendung von Modulen gegenüber der alten, nicht modularisierten Variante signifikant reduziert wird. Betrachtet wurde ein Szenario zur Fehlerbehebung sowie ein Szenario, bei dem um neue Funktionalität erweitert wird. Das im Rahmen einer Vorarbeit entstandene Visualisierungswerkzeug wurde in einer **zweiten, empirischen Fallstudie** validiert, bei der eine QVT-O-Transformation sowohl korrektiven als auch aufwertenden Wartungsaufgaben aus der Praxis unterzogen wurde. Das Ergebnis des Experiments ist, dass sich mit dem Werkzeug relevante Codestellen deutlich effizienter lokalisieren lassen. Die **dritte Fallstudie** basiert auf einer in QVT-O geschriebenen Transformation zur Überführung einer Gruppe erweiterter Modellierkonzepte des Palladio-Komponentenmodell in elementare Konzepte desselben Modells, und des in Xtend implementierten Generators von Simulationscode aus Komponentenmodellinstanzen. Die Transformationen werden mit dem Clusteringansatz modularisiert, und das Ergebnis mit einer händisch modularisierten Variante verglichen. In beiden Fällen ist die Ähnlichkeit zur händischen Variante signifikant höher, wenn neben den Kontroll- zusätzlich Modellstrukturen und -abhängigkeiten in das Clustering miteinbezogen werden.

Die Beiträge dieser Arbeit verdeutlichen, dass nicht nur Allzwecksprachen, sondern auch domänenspezifische Sprachen geeignete Strukturierungskonzepte anbieten müssen, wenn die Les- und Wartbarkeit auch für große und komplexe Programme gewährleistet werden soll. Der Schnittstellenbegriff kann, abhängig von der Domäne und der geforderten Granularität der Schnittstelle, jeweils ein anderer sein; im Fall von Modelltransformationen, beispielsweise, sollten Modellelemente neben Abbildungsmethoden ebenfalls als Teil der Schnittstelle berücksichtigt werden, um eine gleichbleibende Granularitätsstufe zu wahren.

Acknowledgements

It is obvious that, although a dissertation lists one individual as author, research and writing remains a communal enterprise. There are numerous pieces to the puzzle that had to come together successful for this dissertation project, and I am glad so many people have contributed to the success of this dissertation by adding one or the other piece over the years.

First and foremost, I want to express my particular gratitude to Ralf Reussner for his invitation to join the group, and for being an excellent supervisor during Lucia Happe's parental leave. It was basically his idea to elaborate on this topic, bringing together model transformations and modularity concepts to handle maintainability issues. At the same time, I thank Lucia Happe who, despite many understandable distractions after Natalie's birth, still found enough time to be a great supervisor over the last years, as she constantly brought in new ideas. I further want to say thank you to Bernhard Beckert who agreed on being the second referee of this work.

Much of the work in this dissertation was funded with support from the German Science Foundation (DFG). Without financial backing, research presented hereinafter would not have been possible.

My first major publication probably wouldn't have turned out successful without Qais Noorshams, who provided invaluable feedback and ideas for my publications, helped me in brushing up my knowledge on statistics and, as an office room mate, helped to create a futile working atmosphere. Thank you for all that, and also for joining the boycott of the student canteen in favor of the MRI canteen.

A special thank you goes to my work colleagues from the MDSD research group, Jörg Henß, Martin Küster, Erik Burger, Max Kramer, Misha Strittmatter, Michael Langhammer, Georg Hinkel, and Lucia Happe. All of them helped me to forge my ideas. Erik in particular gave me valuable feedback on this whole document at a later stage, without his help this dissertation would be much less readable. I further thank all my colleagues from SDQ, those from the chair, from the Decartes group and from the FZI Software Engineering group, for providing a convenient working environment and giving me honest feedback at several doctoral rounds and research stays.

Many students contributed to the project. I am grateful to Dominik Werle for his intensive endeavor in sharing and forming my ideas of a module concept for model transformations, for providing helpful critics, and last but not least, for skillfully implementing our shared vision of a modular Xtend and QVT-Operational language. Equally, I would like to thank the first of my supervised students, Per Sterner, who started it all with many hours of discussions on semantics of QVT-Relations, for implementing the complete visual analytics framework and his assistance during the empirical experiment. Three students, Dominik Messinger, Joakim von Kistowski and Michael Junker supported my studies as assistant workers, they laid the foundations for my ideas on analysis for clustering by investigating the Bunch tool and creating a working prototype. It is obvious that I couldn't have implemented all the concepts by myself. Finally, I very much appreciated all the students from the practical course on Model-driven Software Development (MDSD) in winter term 2012/2013. They voluntarily served as guinea pigs in my empirical study and helped to bring this part of my project to a success.

I am sincerely lucky for having had the chance to work with extremely skillful researchers from King's College and from Charles University. I am grateful to Steffen Zschaler and Jeffrey Terrell from King's College, London, for introducing me to the Coq proof assistant, and for putting a lot of effort into formalizing the semantics of QVT-Relations. I could not end this list without our collaborators in the Ferdinand project, namely Lubomír Bulej, Andrej Podzimek, Tomás Martinec, Lukás Marek, and Prof. Dr. Petr Tůma. They took well care that we had a wonderful time and stimulating discussions on both of our meetings in Prague. It was also a pleasant coincidence to meet again Andrej and Lubomír at Walter Binder's chair at a conference in Lugano.

Last but definitely not least, I want to heartily thank my girlfriend Katrin, who was very patient and understanding at times when I was more involved with paper and thesis writing than with anything else. Katrin tolerated many days and nights with me working on my laptop, coming home late from office, and traveling. She always made me realize that there is life beyond work, and she gave me good advice on many occasions where I was in doubt. Without her, I would not have had the energy to do all this.

I am grateful to my parents Ingrid and Jürgen, who, from the beginning, supported my efforts as a young computer scientist. Without their support, I would definitively not have had the chance to develop interest in computer science and pursue what started as a kid's passion. I further want to thank my brothers Tobias and Michael, my sister-in-law Sonja, and all of my friends. They gave me mental support particularly during the more stressful periods, and they helped me to maintain a healthy work-life balance.

Thank you all! Without your support, this dissertation would surely not have happened.

Karlsruhe (Germany), February 2015
Andreas Rentschler

Simplicity does not precede complexity, but follows it.

– Alan J. Perlis [Per82]

Contents

1. Introduction

Model-driven software engineering is a technique that was once promised to make software development more efficient. Recently, model-driven software processes have been found to struggle with maintenance problems themselves. Much of the development efforts that arise from manually developed software is shifted away from the source code level to a higher level. At this meta level, model transformations automatically generate large parts of the source code from concise models and thus save much effort. However, both types of first-class artifacts of a model-driven process, the models and the transformations, can get substantially complex and require preventive and reactive measures to be adopted to ensure their maintainability. While a lot of techniques are known from the software engineering discipline that support developers in keeping source code maintainable, they cannot be easily adopted to model transformations. Transformations are designed in special languages with only a minimal amount of programming concepts and tools available. This thesis introduces a module concept, a visualization technique, and a reverse engineering technique for model transformation languages. All three approaches are novel in that they are tailored to the peculiarities of model transformation programs as a specific case of software programs, namely programs designed to manipulate object models in modeling languages akin to the UML.

This introductory chapter motivates the problem of poorly maintainable transformation programs (Sections 1.1–1.3) and determines objectives to alleviate the situation (Section 1.4). It then briefly presents the contributions of this thesis' approaches (Section 1.5), and how they are implemented and validated to meet the goals set (Section 1.6). Section 1.7 concludes this chapter by informing about the remaining parts of this thesis.

1.1. Motivation

In contrast to products from other engineering disciples, software can never wear off. Even so, software requires to be continuously maintained: Requirements constantly change, and previously undetected bugs need to be fixed. Experienced software engineers calculated maintenance costs to contribute to the lifecycle costs of software with an estimated share of 60% average[1], making maintenance a critical cost factor. It is a fact that is known since the seventies [Gla01], and despite emerging software engineering methodologies and techniques, this fact has not substantially changed since then because of the ever growing size and complexity of today's software.

Just as old as the problems that arise from the inherent complexity of software are some of the techniques to improve quality and reduce maintenance costs, ever since Dijkstra considered spaghetti code to hinder comprehension [Dij68]. Around that time, *structured programming* [DDH72] became a well-accepted design technique on the level of subroutines. Not much later, *modular programming* and *object-oriented programming* were widely used, they shifted the abstraction level to the module and class level. These new design structures are situated above the level of subroutines, their main purpose is to hide implementations behind interfaces, encapsulate functionality and data, and separate them by conceptual concerns to gain optimal reuse and understandability.

Soon, standardized modeling languages were discovered as a practical means to capture the design of object-oriented systems for documentation purposes. The Unified Modeling Language (UML) superseded these early notations in the nineties and evolved into a general-purpose modeling language

[1] Robert L. Glass, who coined the *60-60 rule of software*, names a share of 40–80% of the overall costs of a software product that can be attributed to software maintenance [Gla01].

that is modeled by its own means. The UML can be used to describe arbitrary domains and paved the way for model-driven software engineering.

Model-driven Software Engineering (MDSE) is a software engineering methodology that raises the abstraction level another time. Now, instead of the code, metamodels, models and transformations are first-class artifacts. Metamodels, sometimes synonymously called Domain-Specific Languages (DSLs), are used to directly capture the concepts of the target domain, and are much closer to the actual problem than imperative code. Model transformations finally map the models to executable code, so that large amounts of code can be automatically generated.

Early programs that transform models into models were implemented in a third-generation language like Java, but soon software engineers started to apply the MDSE principle to transformation artifacts themselves, crafting languages specific to the domain of modeling and transforming. This led to the emergence of a multitude of transformation languages with varying focus, ranging from purely declarative languages to fully imperative languages with native support for a metamodeling language and a mapping API. On the other hand, transformations that map to textual artifacts are often implemented in template-based languages, where static textual artifacts are furnished with meta expressions filling the dynamic parts.

MDSE has been extensively adopted in industrial software projects, the *Motorola case study* [BLW05] is just one example among others [HWRK11; HRW11; Voe10]. A prominent open-source example that adopts model-driven techniques is the Eclipse GMF Tooling, a set of metamodels and code generators[2]. With Graphical Modeling Framework (GMF) Tooling, sophisticated graphical editors can be generated merely from a description of the elements and their graphical representation. Generated code tends to be less error-prone, and new features must be added only once to be reused for every GMF-based editor.

[2] The Eclipse Graphical Modeling Project; `http://www.eclipse.org/modeling/gmp/`.

Even though generated sources must no longer be maintained, it is obvious that maintainability of the modeling artifacts and transformations as the new principal artifacts remains of equal importance as it used to be for the code. Maintenance effort is shifted away from code artifacts towards metamodels, models, target platform code and model transformations. Particularly transformations are likely to be affected by new requirements as they depend on metamodels and target platform code (co-evolution).

Maintenance issues have been evidenced not only in the context of GMF [HRW09; Fav05], but also in the scope of two studies on long-term experiences from industrial MDSE projects. There, evaluation is based on interviews at 20 companies including Volvo and Ericsson. According to Whittle et al. [WHR+13, p. 9], one of the industrial MDSE practitioners interviews reported that

> the complexity of these little [DSL] languages started to grow and grow and grow... we were trying to share the [code generation] templates across teams and versioning and releasing of these templates was not under any kind of control at all.

Cuadrado et al. [CIM14] gathered similar experiences from transfer of technology projects at two smaller-sized software companies. Despite MDSE's potential to make smaller companies more productive, the companies were severely concerned about the immaturity of the tools as well as the modeling and transformation languages, with good reasons: Since they chose an incremental approach when introducing model-driven techniques, the models and attached transformations had to be constantly updated. This led to high maintenance efforts they had to cope with:

> As the project evolved, the rules and constraints to generate the Java code turned very specific from the company, which caused a great number of modifications in the model-to-text transformation [. . .] , thus hindering its maintenance, readability and evolution. (Cuadrado et al. [CIM14, p. 182])

The application of smaller DSLs is able to reduce complexity – one of MDSE's promises –, but worsens maintainability, because DSLs must be maintained across a whole company or even industry, and with complexity comes maintenance overhead. This coincides with our experiences from the Palladio research project[3], whose software implementation was designed in alignment with MDSE principles and therefore comprises many large and complex model transformations. As it is characteristical for scientific projects in general, new concepts are constantly added, refined, and modified, making metamodels subject to constant evolution; on the other hand, stability of the Palladio tooling is an important goal because it is actively used by several companies.

Since model transformations themselves are usually implemented in domain-specific languages with only few essential language concepts, there is only weak support for high-level concepts that foster maintainability. Although programs in a dedicated transformation language are typically more concise, they can grow large and house complex logic, depending on the size and heterogeneity of metamodels involved. Because transformations are inherently meta programs, they are harder to understand than ordinary programs. Yet they weakly support structuring concepts as they are known from general-purpose languages, concepts which would help to comprehend and maintain them. And even general-purpose object-oriented languages lack concepts to explicitly declare model dependencies at interface level. Next section's example is going to demonstrate that interface concepts of existing transformation languages do not support the maintenance process comprehensively enough.

1.2. Example Scenario

With the aid of a minimalistic transformation program and two realistic maintenance scenarios, we demonstrate the disadvantages of a module sys-

[3] The Palladio approach; `http://www.palladio-simulator.com`.

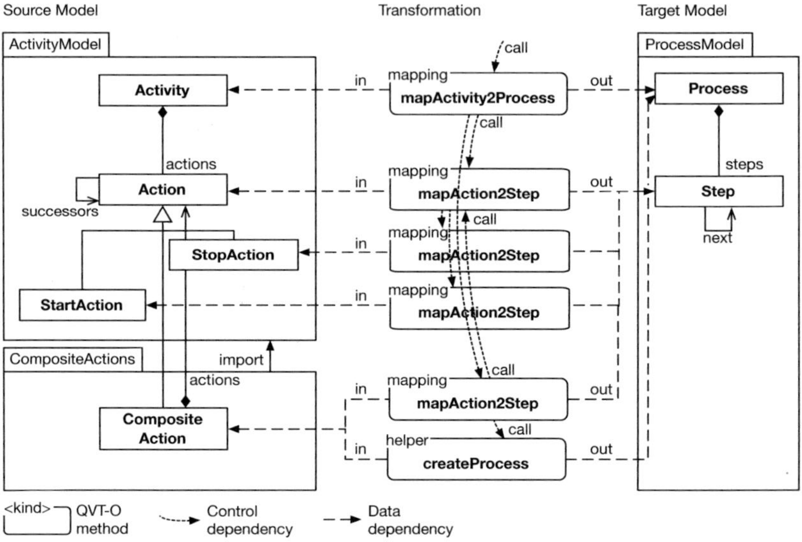

Figure 1.1: Activity2Process transformation in QVTo, method-level dependencies

tem that lacks proper interfaces. The example transformation maps activity diagrams to process diagrams. Activity models are represented by package `ActivityModel`, which contains a root class `Activity` (depicted on the left-hand side of Figure 1.1). Activities are composed of actions, which may refine to either `StartAction`, `StopAction`, or `CompositeAction`. Any action can reference a successor action. A composite action serves as a container for subactions and is placed in a separate package named `CompositeActions`. Process models are represented by package `Process-Model` that contains class `Process` as root (see right-hand side of Figure 1.1). A process is composed of a number of steps of type `Step`. A step can reference one follow-up step and be tagged as a start or stop step by attributes `isStart` or `isStop`.

In most declarative and imperative languages, the previously described transformation is best to be implemented by five mapping rules or methods, one for each class in the source model. One mapping `mapActivity2Pro-`

`cess` creates for an `Activity` object a `Process` object. The remaining mapping methods `mapAction2Step` create for each `Action` object a `Step` object, depending on the concrete subtype. In an imperative language, the latter is typically realized using dynamic dispatching methods, here, dispatching is used to distinguish the specific type of action. Figure 1.1 illustrates data access dependencies for each of the mappings in the imperative language QVT Operational Mappings (QVT-O) [Obj11]: *read* and *write* access is distinguished by annotations *in* and *out*.

For this example, we decided for the imperative transformation language of Query/View/Transformation (QVT), QVT-O, as it features one of the more advanced module systems among prevalent transformation languages. In a procedural language, execution order is predetermined by the containment hierarchy of *composed* references in the source model. Entry point of the transformation is a mapping named `main`, it searches for all instances of class `Activity` (the source model's root class) and calls mapping `Activity2Process` on each element found. Per invocation, mapping `mapActivity2Process` instantiates an object of type `Process` and properly initializes attributes. It further calls one of the mappings `mapAction2Step` for any action contained in an activity, depending on the concrete subtype of action. Call dependencies are depicted as well in Figure 1.1. The main method that forms the entry point (it triggers `mapActivity2Process`) has been omitted for simplicity and is symbolized by an entering call.

Upon creation, the group of overloaded mappings `mapAction2Step` must initialize attributes `isStart` and `isStop` accordingly, and take care that the containment reference `steps` and the reference `next` is correctly set. In a purely imperative language, one cannot generally assume that a successor action is existent when setting the next step. To cope with this problem, imperative transformation languages typically offer some kind of tracing API so transformation developers do not have to be concerned with the order elements are created. Every time a mapping succeeds, a trace record is created. When setting the next step, one can query the trace API for the

Action created for a given action's successor. If it does not exist, setting the next reference is transparently deferred to a later time. In QVT-O, querying trace records is done by a call to function `resolve`. Composite actions are handled in a separate `mapAction2Step` method. Here, a helper method `createProcess` is explicitly called to create a new instance of `Process`, which is then filled with all the steps created from subactions.

Listing 1.1 gives this implementation in QVT-O syntax. Expressions in QVT are pure Object Constraint Language (OCL) expressions augmented with imperative constructs like loops. In the implementation, QVT-O's concept of a mapping operation is used; such methods implicitly create the respective target element and set up a trace record. Because we anticipate that further types of `Action` might be added to the activity model, we put mapping `mapAction2Step` into a separate module `Action2StepModule` (Listing 1.1b) so that changes to actions will not affect parts of the program. We use QVT-O's import concept: the main function and the root mapping are defined in transformation module `Activity2ProcessModule` (Listing 1.1a), whereas mappings `mapAction2Step` are factored out into separate transformation modules `Action2StepModule` and `CompositeAction2StepModule` that are imported by the main module.

```
import Action2StepModule;
import CompositeAction2StepModule;
transformation Activity2ProcessModule(
  in a:ActivityModel, out p:ProcessModel)
  extends Action2StepModule, CompositeAction2StepModule;
main() {
   a.rootObjects()[Activity]->map mapActivity2Process();
}
mapping Activity::mapActivity2Process() : Process {
   result.steps := self.actions->map mapAction2Step();
}
```

(a) First module `Activity2ProcessModule` handles class `Activity`

```
transformation Action2StepModule(
  in a:ActivityModel, out p:ProcessModel);
mapping Action::mapAction2Step() : Step {
   // result.name := self.name;
   result.next := self.successors.late resolveone(Step);
}
mapping StartAction::mapAction2Step() : Step
  inherits Action::mapAction2Step {
  isStart := true
}
mapping StopAction::mapAction2Step() : Step
  inherits Action::mapAction2Step {
  isStop := true
}
```

(b) Second module `Action2StepModule` covers essential subtypes of class `Action`

```
import Action2StepModule;
transformation CompositeAction2StepModule(
  in a:ActivityModel, out p:ProcessModel)
  extends Action2StepModule;
mapping CompositeAction::mapAction2Step() : Step {
  inherits Action::mapAction2Step {
  // map all subactions into a separate process
  createProcess(self);
  // make this step the caller
  name := "Run process " + self.name;
  next := self.successors.late resolveone(Step);
  isStart := false;
  isStop := false;
}
helper createProcess(action : CompositeAction) : Process {
  return object Process {
    name := action.name;
    steps += action.actions->map mapAction2Step();
  };
}
```

(c) Third module `CompositeAction2StepModule` handles class `CompositeAction`

Listing 1.1: Activity2Process example in QVT-O

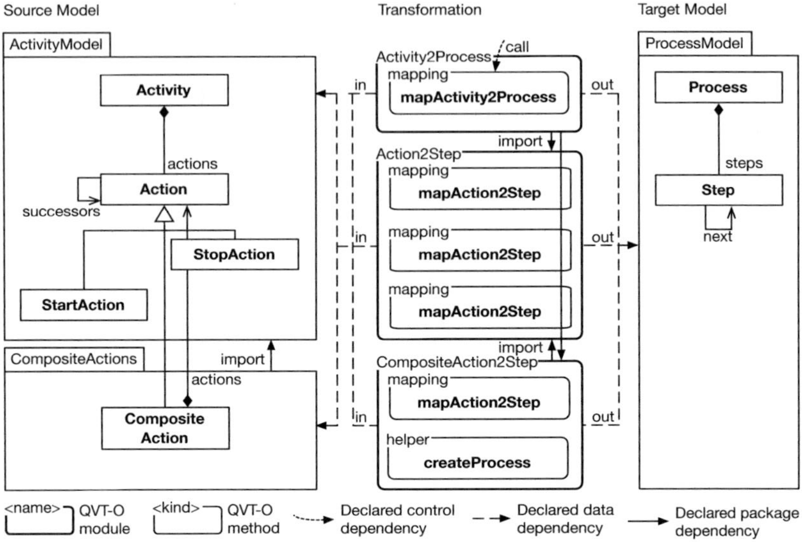

Figure 1.2: Activity2Process transformation, modularized with QVT-O, declared dependencies

Although QVT-O allows for a basic modularization, Figure 1.2 illustrates two significant issues with QVT-O's module concept: From looking at the transformation's signature, one cannot tell (a) which module requires which methods from imported modules, and (b) which of the model elements is processed by which module. Hence, maintainability is hardly improved, which is one of the major reasons for structuring a transformation. We further demonstrate this by three typical change scenarios. In accordance with the IEEE classification of maintenance tasks [IEE06], the first one classifies as a corrective, the second one as an adaptive/corrective, and the third one as a perfective/preventive task. Corrective maintenance is about removing faults, and adaptive maintenance is concerned with adapting code to changing requirements and models. Perfective maintenance aims at an improved performance or maintainability and includes structural refactorings. Preventive maintenance actions are modifications to prevent a problem before it occurs.

Modifying a module's inner logic. Whenever a faulty implementation is reported, we must change a certain mapping's implementation in order to fix it. Suppose that there is a bug in the transformation, resulting in too many `Process` objects created. We suspect the bug to reside in module CompositeAction2Step, in particular an erroneous call to method `createProcess`, but we do not exactly know about which mappings actually call `createProcess`. As the method is part of the inner logic of module `CompositeAction2Step`, calls from other mappings ought not to happen, although we cannot be sure of this with existing concepts. Current module concepts of transformation languages do not specify which of the methods can be accessed from other modules.

Identifying locations of concern. Whenever one of the models evolves, the transformation must be adapted accordingly (co-evolution). Suppose two features already present in the above example had been introduced at a later time, composite actions and the name attribute. Firstly, we would have had to introduce hierarchy by adding a class `CompositeAction` that subclasses `Action`, and secondly, we would have had to introduce a new attribute `name` to classes `Action` and `Step`. In either case we would have had to find out about all the places in the transformation where class `Action` or subclasses thereof are handled. Without an interface concept that describes which of the elements in a model are accessed, we must study any modules' implementations to err on the side of caution. The same pertains for bugs that need to be fixed and that can be traced down to a certain class or attribute.

Refactoring the modular design. If we anticipate regular changes to a certain part of the transformation, it can be worthwhile to factor this part out into a separate module. For instance, in the example above, we decided to factor out logic that handles class `CompositeAction`, since the class already had been factored out into a different package accordingly. When doing so, we must first identify mappings that handle class `CompositeAction` and be aware of all the callers and callees of the affected mappings to be on the safe side. In existing transformation languages, this requires us to study the complete implementation up front.

The example demonstrates that the module concept of QVT-O introduces maintenance issues. While QVT-O has basic support for modularity, the language does not provide concepts to hide complexity behind interfaces. The same is true for many other transformation languages that have been designed in recent years, including ATL [JAB+06], ETL [KPP08], Kermeta [MFV+05], and VIATRA2 [VB07]. Czarnecki observes similar or less powerful modularity features in his classification of transformation languages from 2003 [CH06]. Advanced module concepts were missing in all of the languages, and this has not changed since then. One exception are transformation languages that are embedded into an object-oriented host language, for instance RubyTL [CMT06], SMTL [GWS12] and Xtend. However, class mechanisms of Ruby, Scala and Java do not include metamodel dependencies into their respective interface concept. This thesis introduces a novel module and interface concept to model transformation languages so transformations can be organized in a way that promotes comprehension.

1.3. Problem Statement

Maintainability of model transformations is an important premise for applying MDSE successfully in larger software projects. Transformations are poorly maintainable, because important language concepts to reduce complexity are missing. Early third-generation languages like MODULA-2 and Ada from the 1970s already include module and interface concepts to promote the modular programming style, which can effectively increase maintainability [RC93]. However, in contrast to information hiding as it is supported by general-purpose languages, interfaces must respect dependencies to metamodel elements. Even if we suppose that modular programming will be supported by model transformation languages in the future, two further questions remain to be answered: What makes a good modular design? And how can such a modular structure be automatically re-engineered from legacy code? Due to an often monolithic design and the complexity of dependencies, dependence information is not easy to recover from larger transformation implementations. Maintainability of legacy transformations can be substantially improved if we find a way to automatically extract dependence information. It remains to be studied how developers can make optimal use of this information. One possibility is to explore ways to process such information so it can be optimally used in typical maintenance scenarios. Another possible approach is to use dependence information to re-engineer a suitable modular structure from legacy code.

In summary, the three general research questions managed by this thesis are:

Research Question 1: What modular concept for model transformation languages can improve maintainability?

Research Question 2: When is a transformation program's modular design considered to enhance maintainability?

Research Question 3: Can we make maintenance more efficient for unmodularized legacy transformations?

1.4. Goals and Evaluation Criteria

This thesis' objective is to improve the maintainability of model transformations. There is empirical evidence that maintainability of transformations deteriorates with the size and complexity of metamodels involved [WHR+13]. Maintainability is said to have a major impact on the lifecycle costs of software [Gla01]. In computer science history, the development methodology of modular programming is said to effectively master complexity. Our principal goal is to introduce a rigorous module and interface concept to transformation languages that helps to master complexity. We break this goal down into the following three subgoals:

Goal 1: *Design a new module construct with explicit interface definitions that facilitates separation of concerns and, as a result of this, improves understandability and maintainability.* There already exist language constructs to modularize transformation programs, but they do not make external dependencies explicit. The aim here is to introduce a rigorous interface concept that encourages developers to make these dependencies explicit and reflect on a structured design. On the other hand, the concepts should be concise but clear, and flexible enough to integrate into existing languages. In the end, added concepts should decrease the effort spent to locate concerns in transformation programs. Because there exist transformation languages at various abstraction levels, it must be examined if the approach is applicable to imperative languages on the one side, and declarative languages on the other side of the spectrum.

Goal 2: *Develop an automated approach that supports developers in understanding and maintaining legacy transformation programs.* Legacy transformations are often monolithic or have a deteriorated modular structure. In order to understand or locate concerns, developers must reverse-engineer implicit dependencies. This requires substantial time when carried out manually on large and complex programs. An approach should automatize this by extracting dependence information and present it to developers in a visual form that supports readability.

Goal 3: *Develop a re-engineering method to migrate legacy transformations to the newly developed language extension.* For legacy transformations that are productively used, it pays off in the long run to re-engineer a modular structure which fosters comprehension and maintenance. Determining an adequate structure requires developers to reverse-engineer low-level dependencies and find a suitable modular design, which requires major manual effort. Although there already are clustering approaches that automatize this for imperative languages, they are not tailored to model transformation languages.

Aiming at contributions that are both theoretically sound and applicable in practice, we define a set of evaluation criteria that must be met by the defined goals. Depending on the goal, these are defined as follows:

Soundness. The added module system should abide to the common understanding of modularity. Programs should be considered as well-typed if and only if they adhere to the information hiding principle according to Parnas [Par72].

Genericity. Any of the planned approaches should be applicable to the more prominent kinds of transformation languages. It should be accounted for language aspects of imperative, declarative, and template-based transformation languages, represented by QVT-R, QVT-O, and Xtend, respectively. Further languages to consider are ATL, ETL, Kermeta2 and VIATRA2.

Automation. In practice, real transformations lack structure or their structure has eroded over time. Re-engineering of legacy transformations to a modularized variant should be automated where possible, thus aiming to minimize the effort spent by human developers to reobtain an expedient modular structure.

Efficiency. The module concept and the visualization approach should increase efficiency when carrying out typical maintenance tasks. The re-modularization of legacy transformations should, despite being automated, approximate the quality of an expert developer.

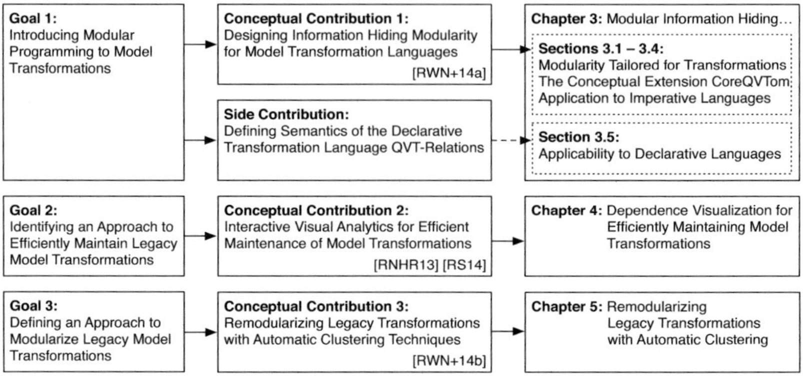

Figure 1.3: Conceptual contributions of this thesis (Arrows depict dependencies)

1.5. Approach and Contributions

Maintenance effort can be high due to the inherent complexity of model transformations. To reduce maintenance effort, this thesis presents a module concept for model transformation languages with information hiding at the interface-level for sound encapsulation and separation of concerns. Moreover, to cope with legacy transformations, this thesis proposes two further approaches. The first approach automatically extracts hidden dependencies and maps them graphically, so the information can be used by developers to locate concerns; the second approach uses the same dependence information to semi-automatically re-engineer an expedient modular structure from legacy code.

In total, this thesis makes three conceptual contributions. Figure 1.3 shows how the individual contributions relate to the research questions posed in context of this thesis.

Contribution 1: *Specification of a module concept and type checking system that introduces interface-based separation of concerns to model transformations.* We build on QVT because of its broad use and standardized definition. Until now, only the typing of OCL has been considered formally [CK01]. Therefore, we first formalize the abstract syntax and type inference rules of a core subset of the QVT-O transformation language. The existing module system is replaced with our own that provides an enhanced interface concept. Available module concepts are neither able to hide implementation details from module users, nor do they establish scoping at the package level of incorporated models. The proposed interface concept facilitates information hiding of methods, as well as model elements via access declarations. Type inference rules are defined that ensure the added module and interface concepts adhere to the information hiding principle. We embed both type inference rules and information hiding principles into Coq's formal language Gallina [The12; BC10] where we then are able to prove that the latter applies to the former. This work has been published at an internal conference with a journal-like reviewing process:

> A. Rentschler *et al.*, "Designing Information Hiding Modularity for Model Transformation Languages," in *Proceedings of the 13th International Conference on Modularity (AOSD '14), Lugano, Switzerland, April 22 - 26, 2014*, Acceptance Rate: 35.0%, New York, NY, USA: ACM, Apr. 2014, pp. 217–228 [RWN+14a]

Although we only apply it to a core of QVT-O, our module concept is generic enough to be applied to declarative languages, as well. As a proof-of-concept, we demonstrate this by example of the declarative language QVT Relations (QVT-R). Because QVT-R still lacks formal semantics, we provide semantics of a relevant subset of the language as a side contribution.

Side Contribution: *Formalization of a declarative transformation specification's core concepts.* Applicability to declarative transformation languages can only be demonstrated with a thorough understanding of declarative concepts. Currently there is an uncertainty regarding semantics of some of the core concepts of the relational transformation language QVT-R. This contribution provides a mapping of a relevant subset of QVT-R to constructive type theory as it is implemented by the Coq proof assistant. The mapping helps to get a thorough formal understanding of the typical language concepts of a declarative transformation language.

Contribution 2: *Definition of a visual analytics methodology to support maintenance of model transformation programs, implemented in widely used domain-specific languages.* Understanding unmodularized transformations and locating concerns during maintenance requires maintainers to spend a substantial amount of time. To alleviate transformation maintainers, we design an interactive visual analytics process to support understanding of model transformations for maintenance. Hidden dependence information is extracted into a generic dependency model for model transformations, a model that unifies control and data flow information in a graph-like structure. The approach comprises a set of task-oriented filter rules to exclude details from the dependency graph that can be considered irrelevant depending on the particular kind of maintenance activity carried out. This work has been presented at an international conference:

> A. Rentschler *et al.*, "Interactive Visual Analytics for Efficient Maintenance of Model Transformations," in *Proceedings of the 6th International Conference on Model Transformation (ICMT '13), Budapest, Hungary*, K. Duddy and G. Kappel, Eds., ser. Lecture Notes in Computer Science, Acceptance Rate (Full Paper): 20.7%, vol. 7909, Berlin–Heidelberg–New York: Springer, Jun. 2013, pp. 141–157 [RNHR13]

Contribution 3: *Development of a re-engineering methodology that automatically decomposes monolithic or badly structured legacy transformations.* We tailor existing clustering techniques to the particular domain of model transformation languages. What differentiates transformation programs from general-purpose programs is that transformations are typically structured in alignment with one of the involved metamodel's package structure, whereas call dependencies are typically considered less important. We design a coherence metric that respects both data and control dependencies. Source or target-driven decompositions are commonly used decomposition techniques in the transformation domain. The approach is applicable to transformations that lack any structure, or transformations that no longer reflect either the logical structure of the implementation or the structure of involved source or target models. This work has been presented to the community in:

> A. Rentschler *et al.*, "Remodularizing Legacy Model Transformations with Automatic Clustering Techniques," in *Proceedings of the 3rd Workshop on the Analysis of Model Transformations co-located with the 17th International Conference on Model Driven Engineering Languages and Systems (AMT@MOD-ELS 2014), Valencia, Spain, September 29, 2014*, B. Baudry *et al.*, Eds., ser. CEUR Workshop Proceedings, vol. 1277, CEUR-WS.org, 2014, pp. 4–13 [RWN+14b]

1.6. Realization and Validation

As a proof-of-concept and as a prerequisite to the validation, all mentioned conceptual approaches have been implemented as software. As target platform we have chosen the Eclipse modeling platform, in particular Eclipse projects *Java development tools (JDT)* and the *Eclipse modeling platform (EMP)*. On the whole, the following three technical realizations have been made.

Technical Realization 1: *Integration of the module concept into two representative transformation languages, QVT-O and Xtend.* QVT-O is an imperative model-to-model transformation language, and Xtend is an extensible domain-specific language with conceptual extensions for writing template-based model-to-text transformations. Both languages are implemented under the Eclipse modeling platform; the Eclipse-based implementation of QVT-O is named *QVTo*. Our language extensions are named QVT Operational Modular Mappings (QVTom) and Xtend Modular Mappings (Xtend2m), respectively. The latter has been published in [RWN+14a].

Technical Realization 2: *Implementation of the visual analytics methodology into a commonly used IDE for transformation development.* We integrated a visual view into the Eclipse IDE. The view displays a dependence graph using the Eclipse Zest API. The graph is automatically laid out according to several styles, is interactive navigable, and the user can choose from several filters. Three transformation languages are currently supported, Eclipse QVTo, Eclipse QVTd and mediniQVT. The latter two are Eclipse implementations of the QVT-R language. Further transformation languages can be easily supported. The tool has been presented at the 2013 MODELS conference's demonstration track:

> A. Rentschler and P. Sterner, "Interactive Dependency Graphs for Model Transformation Analysis," in *Joint Proceedings of MODELS '13 Invited Talks, Demonstration Session, Poster Session, and ACM Student Research Competition co-located with the 16th International Conference on Model Driven Engineering Languages and Systems (MODELS '13), Miami, USA, September 29 - October 4, 2013*, Y. Liu

and S. Zschaler, Eds., ser. CEUR Workshop Proceedings, vol. 1115, CEUR-WS.org, Jan. 2014, pp. 36–40 [RS14]

Technical Realization 3: *Application of the re-engineering method by exploiting available clustering algorithms.* We implemented an extraction mechanism to extract dependence information from QVT-O programs, resembling the extraction mechanism from previous contribution. Call dependencies, model element usage and model package structure dependencies are extracted. To find an optimal clustering regarding our defined metric, we rely on the Bunch clustering system, a received method for automatically re-engineering software systems [MM06]. The Bunch tool uses search heuristics to find a satisfactory solution. Our realization of the approach is described in [RWN+14b].

Based on these implementations, we carried out validations in order to demonstrate that evaluation criteria from Section 1.4 are met, and to further attest to the practical applicability of our approaches.

Validation 1: *Evaluation of the module concept on a real-world transformation in QVTom with realistic maintenance scenarios.* For validation, we examined the effort required to maintain a realistic model transformation. We did so twice, once with and once without using our concept, and compared results. As example scenario, we took a model-to-text transformation from the Palladio research context that had been written in Xtend, re-modularized it using our concept, and studied several maintenance scenarios from past research. The study gives evidence that the actual effort spent to locate concerns when carrying out typical maintenance tasks can be significantly reduced by adequately modularizing a transformation using our modularity concept.

Validation 2: *Evaluation of the visual analytics approach on a real-world transformation in QVTo with realistic maintenance scenarios.* Here again, we analyzed the effort it takes to maintain a real-world model transformation. We conducted an empirical study, comparing a group of tool users against a group of non-tool users. The chosen transformation was a larger transformation from the Palladio research project implemented in the model-to-model transformation language QVT-O. Results show that efficiency is significantly improved for locating concerns relevant to solve realistic maintenance tasks.

Validation 3: *Evaluation of the re-engineering approach on real-world transformations in QVTo and in Xtend.* We compared maintenance efforts of two versions of the same model transformation, one modularized manually, the other modularized using our automatic clustering approach. We decided for two transformations, an in-place model-to-model transformation designed in QVT-O, and a model-to-text transformation implemented in Xtend. The transformations had already been modularized with QVT-O's and Xtend's basic module concept. From the results, we are able to conclude that effort in locating concerns as part of implementing authentic maintenance tasks of the automatically modularized variant is comparable to a manually modularized variant.

In sum, results of all three studies attest to the efficiency, the fourth evaluation criterion stated above, of our approaches in practical scenarios. Therefore, higher efficiency and practicability can be attested for the three contributions that we present in this thesis.

1.7. Outline

The remainder of this thesis is structured as follows. Chapter 2 first provides the scientific background that is needed to understand the subsequent chapters.

Chapter 3 presents the module concept for model transformations, a novel approach for designing model transformations in a more structural manner.

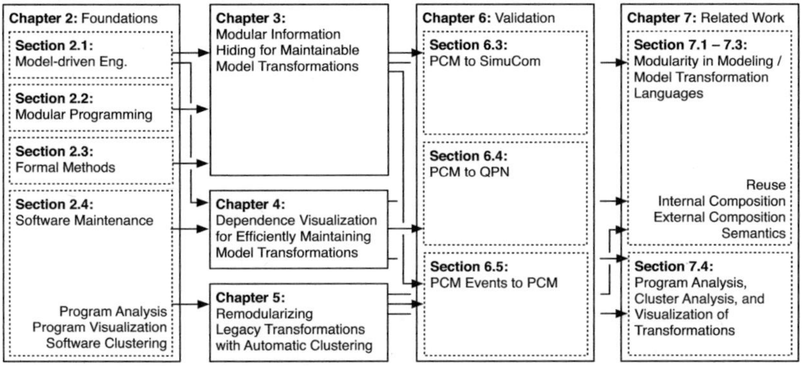

Figure 1.4: Structure of this thesis (Arrows depict dependencies)

The approach is supposed to lead to a better understandability and maintainability of transformation programs. This chapter forms the main contribution and answers research question 1.

Chapter 4 introduces our second contribution that deals with research question 2. We propose a novel approach that applies visual analytics techniques to assist transformation developers who want to understand and maintain a model transformation. Our adapted methodology is explained and a common dependence graph model is defined, together with a set of filter functions.

Chapter 5 describes our solution to research question 3. It presents our third contribution and complements our module concept by automatizing the process of re-engineering a suitable modular structure from legacy transformations. A quality metric for modular transformations is defined, and a clustering algorithm explained that finds optimal clusterings regarding our metric.

Chapter 6 validates the previous three approaches. For each of the approaches, a case study is carried out that examines larger transformations from our research context in realistic maintenance scenarios. Chapter 7 studies relevant work from other researchers and discusses novelty of our contributions. Chapter 8 finally concludes this thesis. It summarizes what has been done, discusses results, lessons learned and limitations, and gives an outlook on what research could be done in this area in the future. A detailed overview of the core chapters and important sections is given in Figure 1.4. It points out reading dependencies for readers who are primarily interested in a particular one of the three contributions.

2. Foundations

In this chapter, general terminology from related research fields is recapitulated to gain a deeper understanding of the contributions presented in the subsequent chapters. There are four general research fields that contributions in this thesis relate to (cf. Figure 2.1). The entire work resides in the field of model-driven software engineering, thus we start with a short introduction to this particular methodology in Section 2.1. The overall objective is to improve maintainability of model-driven software artifacts, therefore we briefly elucidate in Section 2.4 our understanding of software maintenance as well as received standard techniques to optimize maintenance processes. The basic concepts of modular programming are explained in Section 2.2, since, in order to tackle maintenance issues, we later apply this paradigm to model transformation programming. Section 2.3 concludes with an overview on formal methods that had been used to give formal grounds to the module concepts that we will introduce to model transformation languages.

2.1. Model-Driven Engineering

2.1.1. Methodology

Model-driven Software Engineering (MDSE), or synonymously Model-driven Engineering (MDE), is a development methodology that, together with a set of methods, tools and techniques, aims to automatically generate runnable software products from formal models [SV06]. Models are the first-class assets in model-driven approaches, as opposed to model-*based* approaches, where models are mainly for documentation purposes. The idea behind modeling is to understand complex problems through abstraction.

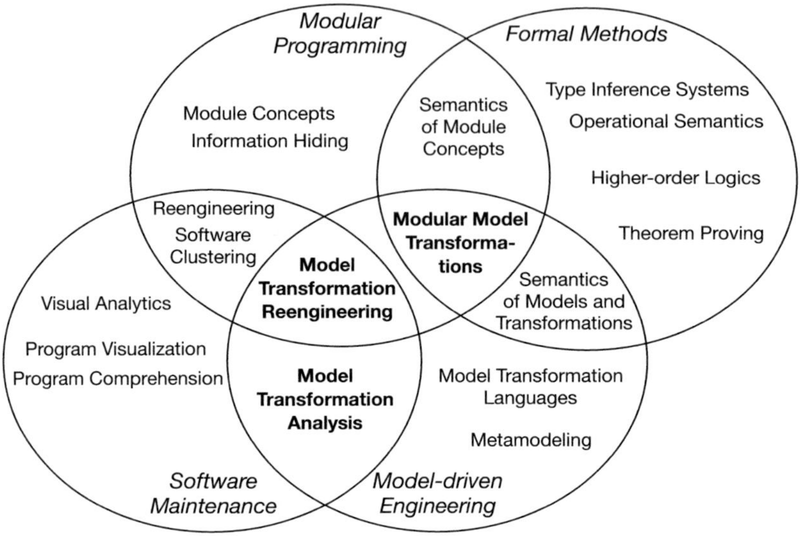

Figure 2.1: Research areas touched by this thesis (including own contributions in bold letters)

Models are abstract and formal at the same time, and processible by computer programs. In a usual software development process, much if not all low-level program code must be developed and maintained manually, which can lead to high development costs. If parts of the code are generated from models, development costs and time are expected to decrease, and software quality is expected to be improved. With the increasing complexity of software, interest in MDE is expected to be growing, too, because of the raised level of abstraction [HWRK11; HRW11].

Together with models, model transformations play a pivotal role, as they describe the logic to translate abstract models to less abstract ones, finally resulting in executable code artifacts. MDE has been standardized by the OMG under the term MDA. Despite being usefulness as a source for definitions, it has been deemed to be too heavy-weight because of its strong focus on the UML. Stahl and Voelter [SV06] proposed the MDSD and its practical

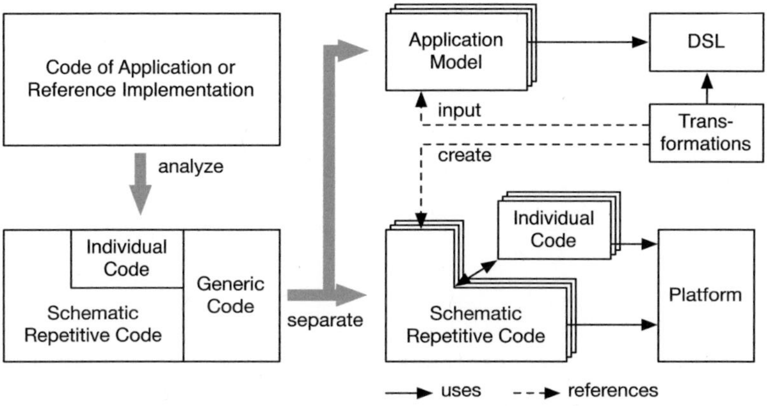

Figure 2.2: Model-driven Software Development (from [SV06, p. 15])

manifestation, the AC-MDSD, as alternative and more practical approaches. Next, we will briefly describe each of the three methodologies and how they relate to each other, before we define the basic terms of MDE.

Model-driven Software Development Model-driven Software Development (MDSD) is a term that generally refers to an approach popularized by Voelter and Stahl [SV06]. Model-driven Software Development (MDSD) pursues a list of practice-oriented goals: it generally seeks to (i) maximize the degree of automation; (ii) enhance software quality through a consequent reuse of domain knowledge and best practices; (iii) improve maintainability by reducing redundancies and concentrating cross-cutting concerns in a single point (namely the transformations); and, finally, (iv) it aims for better portability, interoperability, and manageability of complexity through abstraction and the use of standards. This is achieved through models that are both abstract and formal at the same time, from which as much code as possible is generated.

An MDSD project always starts with a reference implementation (see Figure 2.2). The first step is to analyze the software and extract three classes

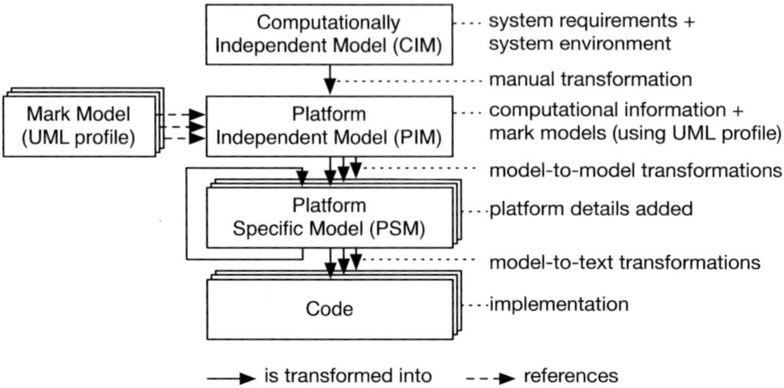

Figure 2.3: Model-driven Architecture

of code. There is (i) code that is generic with respect to the problem domain; (ii) code that is specific to the developed instance but belongs to the targeted domain; and (iii) code that is individual to the customer and that does not exactly belong to the targeted domain. The generic code forms the API and is the cornerstone of the generator framework, hence interfaces must be well-defined and stable. Schematically repetitive code should be entirely generated from an application model, which is a program in a domain-specific language that formally describes the problem domain. The amount of application-specific code that is added manually ought to be small, and proper implementation techniques should be used to separate customized code from the generated code to foster an incremental and iterative development process.

Model-Driven Architecture The Model-Driven Architecture (MDA) is a standardized model-driven software engineering approach [Obj03]. Principal objective of the Model-Driven Architecture (MDA) is to gain an utmost degree of platform independence in order to leverage portability and interoperability. The basic idea is to define multiple models on increasing levels of abstraction. Three types of models exist, the Computationally-

Independent Model (CIM), the Platform-Independent Model (PIM), and the Platform-Specific Model (PSM) (see Figure 2.3).

The CIM is a view on the system that fully remains on the level of the problem domain. It defines functional requirements and the environment of the system (e.g., by means of use cases). It can have the shape of informal text [KWB03], or it might consist of UML models, for instance the Open Distributed Processing (ODP) enterprise and information viewpoints [Obj03; SZ93]. The PIM is derived manually from the former model, and introduces computational and architectural information. The PIM should nevertheless not refer to any platform-specific concepts. The MDA guide recommends to use the UML to semi-formally specify this view. What follows in an MDA process is a group of transformations that introduces platform concepts, before a final transformation maps the PSMs to an execution platform, for instance the Java platform. Each transformation may create a separate PSM instance, or, if the PSMs share a common target platform, it can be more practical to introduce various platform concepts one after the other, resulting in a chain of PSM to PSM transformations. The PIM to PSM transformations typically require further information to decide at which place which platform concepts to add. The guide suggests to use the *UML profile mechanism* to annotate model elements in the PIM/PSM. Annotations can be technically separated in an extra model, so that annotations do not get lost on incremental runs. A profile is constituted of stereotypes to mark classes, tagged values to attach values (which can serve as parameters), and OCL constraints to assert their valid application.

In this approach, despite the notion of a platform being central, it is not clear what a platform actually is. MDA literature gives several platform examples, including middleware platforms like CORBA, JavaEE, and .NET, component models like the EJB, COM or .NET, and programming or specification languages like Java, C++, and XML. These few examples already emphasize that platforms can be on different levels of abstraction. Since one platform can be the platform for another, it is important to be aware that it is a relative concept.

The MDA guide exactly defines how transformations from PIM over PSMs to Code are built, and depends on concrete technologies, such as UML and UML profiles. The MDSD approach, on the other hand, remains technology independent, and describes the transformation from domain concepts to code as a blackbox transition.

Model-driven approaches have been successfully adopted in industrial projects. MDSD success stories are reported for instance by Voelter [Voe10], and also the Object Management Group (OMG) lists many success stories on their site[1]. In a number of surveys, Hutchinson and Whittle interviewed practitioners to identify acceptance and open issues of MDE [HWRK11; HRW11; WHR+13].

Architecture-Centric MDSD This approach is a concrete flavor of MDSD that aims for efficient reuse of domain knowledge across a family of software architectures. Today's business software is complex, and much code is needed to bind domain concepts to the technical infrastructure, for example the JavaEE platform. This code is usually highly redundant and is a good candidate for automation. The architecture of a family of software products plays a central role in this approach, and architectural concepts are typically described as a platform-independent UML model enriched with domain-specific concepts via the UML's profile mechanism. For simplicity, the transformation maps directly to code, sparing the need for mark models. Internally, the transformation can be modularized using intermediate transformations. Round-trip engineering (as favored by the MDA approach) is abandoned in favor of strict forward engineering, together with an appropriate mechanism to separate generated code artifacts from manually encoded custom business logic. An initial reference implementation is considered of extreme importance, it serves as a blueprint for the generative software

[1] MDA success stories, `http://www.omg.org/mda/products_success.htm`

architecture to be developed. Taken together, Architecture-Centric MDSD (AC-MDSD) picks up some of the ideas and concepts of MDA, while it skips others for practicality reasons.

2.1.2. Metamodeling

Models are the first-class assets in model-driven engineering. The idea behind modeling is to understand complex problems through abstraction [Sel03]. With increasing complexity of software, interest in MDE is expected to be growing, too.

The word *model* has a variety of meanings, reaching from copies of physical objects to things mentally conceived of, for instance formal interpretations of theories. There are many definitions, and none seems to be complete. Müller surveys the concept of model [Mül01]. One of the most notable definitions comes from Herbert Stachowiak (1921–2004), he lists three fundamental properties that can be attributed to any model:

- **Mapping Property:** "Models are always models of something: they are mappings from, *representations* of natural or artificial originals that can be models themselves." [Sta73, p. 131]
- **Reduction Property:** "Models in general capture not all attributes of the original represented by them, but rather only those seeming *relevant* to their model creators and/or model users." [Sta73, p. 132]
- **Pragmatism Property:** "Models are not uniquely assigned to their originals per se. They *fulfill* their replacement function (i) for particular – cognitive and/or acting, model using subjects, (ii) within particular time intervals and (iii) restricted to particular mental or actual operations." [Sta73, pp. 131f.]

Stachowiak's description of the concept applies well to our understanding of a formal model. This thesis relies on Anneke Kleppe's formal definitions that are based on graph theory [Kle09, p. 60ff.]. As a prerequisite, we repeat the mathematical definition of a typed graph.

Definition 2.1 (Type Graph): *A type graph G is a combination of a set of vertices V, a set of edges E, a source function $s : E \rightarrow V$ that gives the source node for a particular edge, a target function $t : E \rightarrow V$ that gives the target node for a particular edge, and an inheritance relationship $I \subseteq V \times V$, where I is a reflexive partial ordering.*

With this definition, models can be defined as typed graph structures.

Definition 2.2 (Model): *A model is a combination of a type graph G and a set of constraints C of various types.*

A language specification comprises syntactical and semantic constraints. Syntactical constraints can be classified as abstract syntax and concrete syntax. Constraints regarding the concrete syntax limit the number of possible instances to those which are considered as valid instances.

Definition 2.3 (Model Instance): *An instance m of a model M is a labeled graph that can be typed over the type graph G_M of M and satisfies all the constraints C_M in model M's constraint set.*

Having models and the instance level defined, we can conclude with a definition for models at the meta level.

Definition 2.4 (Metamodel): *A metamodel is a model MM used to specify a language.*

There is an analogy between metamodels and domain-specific languages [Fow10; Kle09; Voe13] which is pointed out by the definition. A language specification consists of a set of four models that specify syntactical and semantic constraints of the language. An *abstract syntax model* defines the set of programs that are considered as valid. A *concrete syntax model* defines the set of programs with a valid concrete representation, be it graphical or textual. A *semantic domain model* defines the valid (static) semantic domain of the language. An example for a language to express abstract syntax is the UML. Concrete textual syntax is usually defined using some form of the EBNF language. Static semantics can be expressed in predicate logic using the OCL. Dynamic semantics are described by mapping the abstract syntax model to another syntax model (abstract or concrete) with well-defined semantics. Plenty of model transformation languages are available that can be used for this purpose.

Seen from a relative point of view, a metamodel can be defined as a model of a model. However, this definition is overly simplified, as it neglects the modeling level on which a model is used. Most metamodeling languages limit the number of meta-levels. The Meta-Object Facilities (MOF) [Obj14] specifies four modeling levels, the level of instances (M0), models (M1), metamodels (M2), and meta metamodels (M3).

M0: Model Instances Models on the lowest level M0 represent real-world object and cannot be instantiated further, they have a direct correspondence to programs in a programming language.

M1: Models Models on the M1 level describe a modeling (or programming) language, usually suited to describe elements of the real world (mapping, isomorphism) from a certain domain (reduction, abstraction) for a certain purpose (pragmatism).

M2: Metamodels Metamodels (M2) form a class of languages used to describe domain-specific languages. The most popular representative for an M2 language is the UML, but also the Extended Backus-Naur Form (EBNF) as a language to specify context-free grammar resides on this level.

M3: Meta Metamodels On the highest level M3 lies the meta metamodel which defines some core concepts, the Essential MOF (EMOF) and the Complete MOF (CMOF). MOF is a closed metamodeling architecture, i.e., it defines its own concepts, thus avoiding the need to define even further levels (M4 and above).

The EMOF language closely corresponds to the facilities found in object-oriented programming languages, and is closed in itself, i.e., it does not depend on CMOF. Because of the EMOF's universality and conciseness, leaner approaches skip the M2 level and use the EMOF itself to specify M1 languages. For instance, the Eclipse Modeling Framework (EMF) [SBPM09] completely relies on Ecore to represent Java code. Ecore is EMF's implementation of the EMOF and is almost fully in alignment with the standards. Note that the OCL, which is used to specify constraints on the models, is itself an instance of M3.

The line between models and programs is blurry; Kleppe even coined the term "mogram", or "prodel", to describe this phenomenon [Kle09]. It is probably due to tradition that models are commonly perceived as descriptive and programs as prescriptive, i.e. models describe an existing system, and programs describe how a system can be automatically constructed [Voe13].

Where models are abstractions of concepts from the real world, metamodels are abstractions from a class of models. The concept of metamodels is closely related to the concept of *ontologies*, as both are used to (semi-)formally represent knowledge within a domain as a set of concepts [OGS09].

2.1.3. Model Transformations

Model transformations are an important facility in the field of MDE, where models are first-class entities. Figure 2.4 illustrates the pivotal role of model transformations in MDE. Text-to-Model (T2M) and Model-to-Text (M2T) transformations are special cases of Model-to-Model (M2M) transformations where concrete textual representations of the input/output models are processed. Transformations can be executed during development, maintenance, or at run-time.

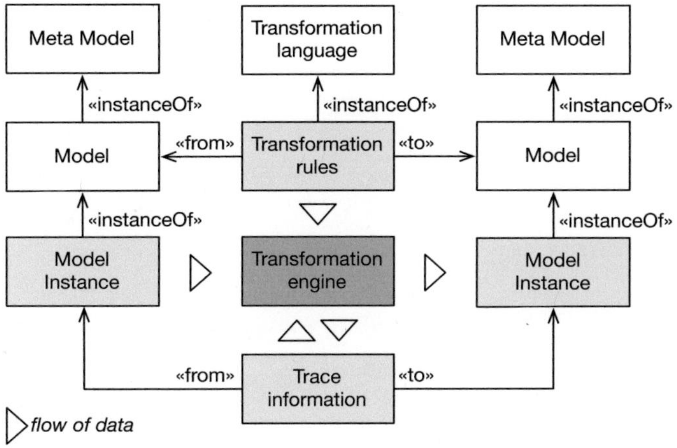

Figure 2.4: The role of transformations in MDE

While it is possible to write any kind of transformation in a general-purpose programming language like Java, there is a wide variety of domain-specific languages available that feature oft-needed transformation concepts to ease development. For example, most (if not all) languages use some kind of model navigation and filtering language akin to the OCL, and have a notion of a relation between model elements. For creating text from a model, a natural language concept to embed model expressions into text templates has become prevalent in most model-to-text transformation languages. The level of abstraction differs heavily, ranging from fully declarative languages to fully imperative languages. Whereas the former have a more formal character (close to graph theory and logic programming), the latter are closer to operational thinking which is typically more accepted by programmers and typically exhibits faster execution times. As a compromise, there are also hybrid languages that combine the benefits from both worlds.

Based on previous definitions, we cite Kleppe's formal definition of a model transformation, slightly modified for the M2T case [Kle09, p. 71].

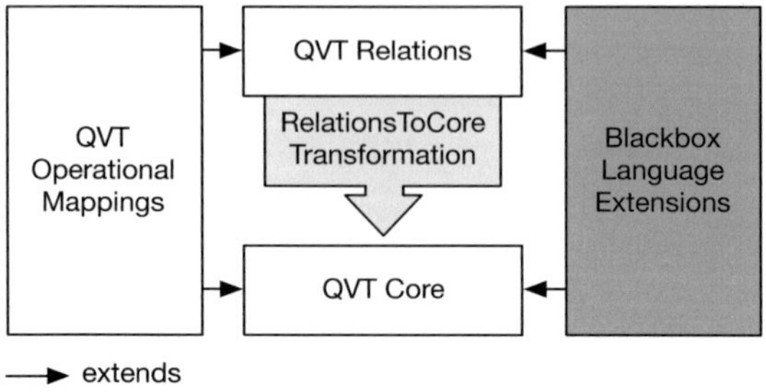

Figure 2.5: The QVT specification – languages and architecture [Obj11]

Definition 2.5 (Model Transformation): *A* model transformation *is a function t that maps from abstract syntax models* $M_1^{in}, \ldots, M_m^{in}$ *to syntax models* $M_1^{out}, \ldots, M_n^{out}$. *If the models in the target domain are abstract syntax models, we speak of a* model-to-model transformation*; if the models in the target domain are concrete syntax models, we speak of a* model-to-text transformation.

QVT is a standard for model transformation defined by the OMG [Obj11] and forms, beneath other standards, an important piece in the MDA puzzle. The QVT standard comprises three languages, QVT-O, QVT-R, and QVT-Core (Figure 2.5). QVT-O is an imperative model-to-model transformation language for writing many-to-many and in-place transformations. QVT-R is a declarative language that supports bidirectional and incremental semantics. Both languages use the OCL language for model querying and filtering. Conceptually, QVT-R translates to a core language with a minimum of relational concepts, QVT-Core. QVT-Core has never been implemented so far, but a modified variant of QVT-Core is currently implemented for the Eclipse platform [WHK13]. *Blackbox language extensions* is a feature that enables to implement some mappings of a QVT-R program in a different language, for instance QVT-O or Java.

State-of-the-art of QVT has been investigated by Kurtev in 2008 [Kur07], and by Helsen in 2006 [Hel06]. Guduric compares QVT-R with QVT-

O [GPT09], and Stevens studies semantics and identifies several flaws in the specification of QVT-R [Ste10].

The Atlas Transformation Language (ATL) is a hybrid transformation language, it also supports imperative constructs to be used whenever declarative constructs turn out to be less appropriate. ATL owes its popularity to the fact that, as a submission for the OMG's request for proposal to the QVT specification, it had much time to mature, while the OMG took years to unify all submitted proposals before it published the QVT standard.

The Epsilon Transformation Language (ETL) [KPP08] is another hybrid, rule-based transformation language that has gained wider acceptance in the community. It is part of a whole stack of languages, including the *Epsilon Generation Language*, the *Epsilon Validation Language*, and the *Epsilon Object Language* on top of which it is built.

Other more formal approaches are based on term/graph rewriting: VIsual Automated model TRAnsformations (VIATRA), for example, is a framework for transformation-based verification and validation environment, based on Graph Transformations (GT) and Abstract State Machines (ASM) to manipulate graph based models. Further graph-based approaches include Graph Rewriting and Transformation (GReAT), Attributed Graph Grammar system (AGG), Fujaba/TGG, and PROGRES. A comparison of the latter three was carried out by Fuss et al. [FMRS07].

Mapping models to textual artifacts, e.g. code, is usually done using dedicated transformation languages based on text templates. Most generated texts are static, with only few parts being dynamically generated from source models. In such cases, using the plain target language and embedding expressions for the dynamic parts within meta tags into the text enhances readability. Alternatively, visitor-based approaches construct textual artifacts by traversing over a source model's elements. If the source model and the text are strongly coherent, for instance when Java syntax is generated from a syntax tree, a visitor approach can be more appropriate. Examples for template-based languages are Xpand (superseded by the latest version of Xtend), VTL, MOFScript, and JET [Ren06].

Transformation languages are still subject to active research, evidenced by the annual Transformation Tool Contest (TTC) that takes place at the International Conference of Model Transformations. At this venue, new languages and language concepts are tested for their practicality. As of today, there is a multitude of languages specific to the domain of model-based transformations. We cannot comprehensively discuss these, yet a lot of literature is available to further enlarge upon this topic. Czarnecki proposes a taxonomy for the classification of model transformation languages [CH03; CH06]. Tamura lists the most important characterization and classification schemes, and analyzes QVT with respect to this set [TC10]. Biehl did a literature study on model transformations [Bie10].

In this thesis, we mainly focus on three languages, QVT Operational Mappings as a representative for imperative transformation languages, QVT Relations as a representative for declarative languages, and Xtend as a representative for a template-based model-to-text transformation languages. The TGG formalism is used in Chapter 4 to formally specify a transformation. These four languages are introduced in the sections that follow.

2.1.4. QVT-Operational

In QVT Operational Mappings (QVT-O), transformations are expressed in an imperative style, where each modification step is made explicit. QVT-O programs are always unidirectional, meaning they have exactly one execution direction. Although a program is able to modify existing models, update semantics must be implemented by hand, because transformation logic is not automatically based on trace information from previous runs. The language is, however, best to be used if source and target models are semantically and structurally less coherent, whereas declarative languages are more concise if there (ideally) is a one-to-one correspondence between classes.

Any QVT-O transformation consists at minimum of a transformation signature. Apart form the transformation's name, the signature indicates the set of model instances that are handled by the transformation. Each of those model parameters must have an access indicator, the variable name of an instance, and the type. There are three different access modes, `in` specifies that an existing model is read but not modified, `out` specifies that a model is freshly created, and `inout` specifies that an existing model is modified. In regards to our introductory Activity2Process example (Listing 1.1a, lines 2-3), transformation `Activity2Process` reads an instance of an `ActivityModel` that is globally accessible by variable `a`, and creates an instance of `ProcessModel`, accessible by variable `p`.

```
transformation Activity2Process(
  in a:ActivityModel, out p:ProcessModel);
```

Models that are involved in a transformation must be introduced with `modeltype` statements prior to the signature. A model type declaration uses a Uniform Resource Identifier (URI) to link a type to a model definition. This is the preferred way, although models can alternatively be resolved by the QVTo IDE that runs under the Eclipse environment. Remember that, when dealing with MOF models, the URI is the unique identifier of a package. For simplicity, we decided for the latter in the example. We could, however, explicitly link the two model types to the URIs of packages `ActivityModel` and `ProcessModel` by prepending these two lines:

```
modeltype ActivityModel uses
    'http://www.kit.edu/Activity/1.0';
modeltype ProcessModel uses 'http://www.kit.edu/Process/1.0';
```

A transformation program consists of method declarations. Besides a mandatory method named `main()` that poses the entry point, methods are of one of three different kinds, mapping operations, helper operations, and query functions. A mapping operation implicitly maps one element to another. The mapping in the example below maps an `Activity` object (the context parameter) to a Process object (the return parameter) in the target domain.It does so by assigning reference steps of the implicitly created Process object a collection of Step objects. The collection is created by calling another mapping, mapAction2Step, on each element that is contained in the source object's actions reference. Note that variable self corresponds to the object in context, and variable result to the object created in the target domain.

```
mapping Activity::mapActivity2Process() : Process {
  result.steps := self.actions->map mapAction2Step();
}
```

QVT-O offers single dynamic dispatching based on a mapping method's context parameter. Having two overloaded mappings StartAction::mapAction2Step() and StopAction::mapAction2Step(), the interpreter decides at call time for the variant with the best matching type. Explicit dispatching is possible via the disjuncts keyword attached to a mapping method, followed by a list of mappings which are invoked in order until one of the called mapping's when guard is satisfied.

What distinguishes QVT-O most from a General-Purpose Language (GPL) is its powerful trace management API. Query operations follow the pattern:

```
[sourceObject. | sourceObjects->][late] [inv]resolve[one][In](
      targetObjectType[,filterExpression][,inMapping])
```

If no source object is provided, the query returns all entries that resolve to type *targetObjectType*. The late option defers resolution and statements that depend on the resulting value to a second pass. This kind of trace resolution is expedient in situations where objects to be queried are created at a later time during execution. Under the hood, the concept of *promised futures* that is known from concurrent programming is applied. The one option queries only one randomly chosen element. When prefix inv is used, elements from the source domain rather than the target domain of involved mappings are queried. Suffix `In` constraints the query to a particular mapping operation *inMapping* which is then to be given as an additional parameter. An optional filter expression *filterExpression* uses OCL to further restrict the elements returned. In the Activity2Process example, we are interested in all `Step` elements that are created for an `Action` object that is referred to via reference `successors`. Late resolution is used, since we cannot be sure that an element's successor has been created at the time the element itself is mapped. Else, we would need to order all elements by their next dependencies manually and make sure that no cycle occurs.

```
next := self.successors.late resolveoneIn(Step,
    mapAction2Step);
```

Only elements that have been implicitly created by a mapping operation are considered by function `resolve`, thus one should always prefer this method type to create elements over explicit instantiations via the `object` or `new` operator. Helper operations follow the same syntax as mapping operations, but do not automatically instantiate an object of the return type. However, although they allow side effects alike, explicit instantiation should only be used to create intermediate elements. The subsequent helper method would replace the original mapping `mapAction2Step` from Listing 1.1b only at a first glance; the `resolve` function inside would yield an empty list.

```
helper Action::mapAction2Step() : Step {
  return new object Step {
    name := self.name;
    // BUG: Step objects are no longer resolvable by QVT-O.
    next := self.successors.late resolveone(Step);
    ⋮
  }
}
```

Whenever a mapping or helper method modifies input parameters, these must be marked with direction mode `inout` in the signature. Query functions, on the other hand, do not allow any side-effect; the body of a query function is a regular OCL expression. A query function must only have one result parameter and a set of input parameters that are automatically tagged with direction mode `in`.

The body of mapping and helper methods is implemented in an extended OCL syntax. Standard OCL is still used to query and filter model elements. Beyond that, QVT-O defines an imperative extension to OCL that allows to define and modify variables (`var` statement), instantiate and modify model elements (`new` and `object` operator), and imperative block statements (`foreach` and `while` loops, `return` and `break` statement). The `map` operator is used to call a mapping on input elements. Remember that the same applies here as for any operator in standard OCL: if a mapping is called on a collection of elements, the arrow operator '`->`' has to follow the collection and precede the `map` statement, whereas the dot operator '`.`' is to be used on single elements.

In the introductory example, we use QVT-O's module concept to decompose the transformation into two separate modules. Transformations can be split across multiple files, given their signature owns exactly the same model parameters. One transformation may use another one by importing it and using the `extends` keyword succeeding the signature (see Listing 1.1a, lines 1–5). Libraries are another concept to structure transformations. As opposed to a transformation signature, the signature of libraries do not have model parameters (i.e., '`library` *libraryName*`();`'). Only helper and query methods can be put into libraries, because they do not rely on model parameters. Transformations gain access to libraries by an '`access` *libraryName*' appended to their signature.

This short introduction does only touch on the syntax of QVT-O and OCL. More details can be found in the QVT and the OCL specifications [Obj11; Obj12]. The Eclipse *QVTo* project[2] is an actively maintained open-source

[2] Eclipse QVTo, `http://www.eclipse.org/mmt/qvto/`

```
transformation Activity2Process(
    activity : ActivityModel, process : ProcessModel) {
  top relation Activity2Process {
    checkonly domain activity a : Activity { };
    enforce domain process p : Process { };
  }
  top relation Action2Step {
    checkonly domain activity a1 : Action {
      activity = a2 : Activity { },
    };
    enforce domain process s : Step {
      process = p : Process { },
    };
    when  { Activity2Process(a2, p); }
    where  {
      StartAction2Step(a1, s);
      StopAction2Step(a1, s);
      CompositeAction2Step(a1, s);
    }
  }
  top relation Successors2Next {
    checkonly domain activity a1 : Action {
      successors = a2 : Action { }
    };
    enforce domain process p1 : Step {
      next = p2 : Step { }
    };
    when { Action2Step(a1, p1); Action2Step(a2, p2); }
  }
  relation StartAction2Step {
    n : String;
    checkonly domain activity a : StartAction { name = n };
    enforce domain process s : Step { name = n; isStart =
        true };
  }
  relation StopAction2Step {
    n : String;
    checkonly domain activity a : StopAction { name = n };
    enforce domain process s : Step { name = n; isStop = true
        };
  }
```

```
40   relation CompositeAction2Step {
41     n : String;
42     checkonly domain activity a1 : CompositeAction {
43       name = n
44     };
45     enforce domain process s : Step {
46       name = 'Run process ' + n
47     };
48   }
49 }
```

Listing 2.1: Activity2Process example in QVT-R

implementation of QVT-O for the Eclipse ecosystem. *SmartQVT*[3] is another EMF-based implementation that is distributed under the Eclipse Public License (EPL), but for which development seems to have come to a halt.

2.1.5. QVT-Relations

In QVT Relations (QVT-R), a transformation is specified declarative rather than by giving step-wise instructions. A transformation defines a set of relations between the elements of at least two model instances. Listing 2.1 shows how the Activity2Process example can be done in QVT-R. This transformation is specified on two domains, where domain variables `a` and `p` represent instances of `ActivityModel` and `ProcessModel`, respectively (lines 1f.).

The top-level construct in the language are relations. A relation definition comprises a set of variable declarations, two or more *domain* sections, plus optional *when* and *where* sections. A domain section specifies an object pattern to be matched on an object rooted in a particular domain (referred to by the domain variable), together with a set of constraints on their attributes and references. A constraint may either introduce another object to be matched within the same domain, or an OCL expression that can reference variables (either object variables or those declared by the relation). The

[3] SmartQVT, `http://sourceforge.net/projects/smartqvt/`

object pattern can be hierarchical, nested up to an arbitrary depth. When and where sections define one or more OCL expressions which may also refer to variables in context of the relation. For a relation to hold, a valid matching of the variables on the source domain must be found, so that the precondition in the when clause evaluates to true, and subsequently a match for the rest of the variables must be found so that the postcondition in the where clause is fulfilled.

QVT-R transformations can be invoked in one of two modes. If invoked in *check-only* mode, the relations are simply checked for consistency to ensure that they hold in one way or another; if no match for all relations can be found, the model instances are considered to be inconsistent. In *enforce* mode, the relations are checked for consistency as well. However, exactly one of the domains is selected as target domain in this mode (it must be a domain that is tagged with keyword `enforce`), and if no valid match is found, elements can be created, deleted, and modified in order to reach a consistent state. Changes should be performed conservatively, i.e., only a minimum of changes should be done (hippocraticness). The behavior is called *check-before-enforce* semantics, and allows for incremental updates in more than one direction. The `key` concept defines a set of key attributes, as in a relational database. These attributes hint QVT-R at deciding if an enforced object can be located among preexisting elements, or if a new object has to be created.

Relations can be tagged as top level (with keyword `top`). A transformation is only then considered to have succeeded if all top level relations hold. However, relations may refer to top and non-top relations in their *when* clauses, and non-top relations in their *when* and *where* clauses. When invoked in such way, root objects of the relation's domains must be assigned a particular value (variables, constants or expressions thereof).

Consider top relation `Action2Step` (lines 7–20). When run in enforce mode, with domain `process` selected as target domain, binding of the relation proceeds as follows. Initially, root variable `a1` is bound to any instance of

Action found in the activity domain. Reference a1.activity is bound to an instance of Activity. On the target domain process, variable p is bound to an instance of Process, so that relation Activity2Process holds on variables a2 and p (line 14). Further on in the process domain, root variable s is bound to an instance of Step. If none exists with a parent activity a1, a new Step is created, and the property is set accordingly. Thereafter, the where clause is enforced: non-top relations StartAction2Step, StopAction2Step and CompositeAction2Step are invoked on parameters a and s. Note that only one can match depending if object a is an instance of StartAction, StopAction, or CompositeAction. Each of the three rules set property 's.name' based on variable n that is retrieved from property 'a.name', and configure properties isStart and isStop accordingly.

Because class CompositeAction inherits both from Action and Activity, any instance of CompositeAction triggers two top-level rules, Action2Step and Activity2Process (Remember that a successful execution of a transformation requires all its top-level relations to hold). Thus the program creates two objects for an instance of CompositeAction, one Step and a separate Process object that is going to serve as container for sub actions.

A substantially more detailed introduction to the various concepts is given in the OMG's QVT specification [Obj11]. There are three implementations of QVT-R. Of these, *ModelMorf*[4] is the one that most faithfully complies to the QVT standard, but like *MediniQVT*[5], it is no longer maintained. *Eclipse QVTd*[6] is a promising implementation for the *Eclipse Modeling Platform* but is still under active development [WHK13].

2.1.6. Xtend

The *Xtend* language is a Java-based general-purpose programming language with two outstanding features,

[4] ModelMorf, http://www.tcs-trddc.com/trddc_website/ModelMorf/ModelMorf.htm
[5] MediniQVT, http://projects.ikv.de/qvt
[6] Eclipse QVTd, http://www.eclipse.org/mmt/?project=qvtd

- providing the *easy extensibility* of the language with domain-specific concepts, feasible through the concept of *extension methods*, and
- offering *concise syntax* with much less clutter than Java, mainly due to lambda expressions and a powerful static type inference system.

Xtend does not deny influences from the object-functional Scala language[7]. Contrary to Scala, which compiles directly to Java byte code, Xtend programs are transpiled into readable Java code thus providing a seamless integration with Java. Furthermore, Xtend offers special constructs for template-based model-to-text transformations, and a simple mapping concept to facilitate model-to-model transformation development. The Xtend language used to be part of the Xpand language, where template expressions had to be written in Xpand, and functional extensions on the model elements in Xtend. From Xtend version 2.x on, Xtend had been completely redesigned and evolved into an extensible language, where template expressions that used to be part of Xpand are only one of the extended concepts of the language. Throughout this dissertation, the name *Xtend* without a version number always refers to the latest version, Xtend2. In sections where we compare the newer Xtend with its predecessor, we explicitly name Xtend *Xtend2*, and the predecessor *Xtend1*.

The rest of this section demonstrates how Xtend can be used to write M2M and M2T transformations in an imperative style. Language concepts are explained alongside that add to model transformation development and give the impression of Xtend being well-suited for this particular domain. First, consider the model-model transformation program from previous sections, this time implemented in Xtend (Listing 2.2).

Conciser syntax The program defines one class and three methods. What is most apparent is that, when compared to Java, a lot of syntactic noise is avoided. Classes and methods are all public per default. Method definitions

[7] Scala, `http://www.scala-lang.org`

```
1  class Activity2Process {
2    var output = new ArrayList<EObject>
3    val factory = ProcessFactory.eINSTANCE
4    def run(List<EObject> input) {
5      output += input.filter(Activity).map[mapActivity2Process]
6      output
7    }
8    def create result:new factory.createProcess
         mapActivity2Process(Activity self) {
9      result.steps += self.actions.map[mapAction2Step]
10   }
11   def dispatch create result:new factory.createStep
         mapAction2Step(Action self) {
12     result.name = self.name
13     result.next = self.successors.mapAction2Step
14     result.isStart = self instanceof StartAction
15     result.isStop = self instanceof StopAction
16   }
17   def dispatch create result:new factory.createStep
         mapAction2Step(CompositeAction self) {
18     result.name = "Run process " + self.name
19     result.next = self.successors.mapAction2Step
20     result.isStart = false
21     result.isStop = false
22     output += self.mapActivity2Process
23   }
24 }
```

Listing 2.2: Activity2Process example in Xtend

are commenced with a `def`, and variable definitions with a `val`, as in Scala. Also, everything is an expression, and a line feed replaces the semicolon character to separate statements. Because the value in line 6 poses the last expression in method `run`, it automatically forms the return value without the need for keyword return. Method `run`'s return type has not been defined explicitly; Xtend's static type inference system is able to automatically derive type `List<EObject>`. The following code snippet shows the Java code that is computed by the Xtend transpiler from lines 4–7:

```
1 public ArrayList<EObject> run(final List<EObject> input) {
2   Iterable<Activity> _filter =
        Iterables.<Activity>filter(input, Activity.class);
3   final Function1<Activity, process.Process> _function = new
        Function1<Activity, process.Process>() {
4     public process.Process apply(final Activity it) { return
          Activity2Process.this.mapActivity2Process(it); }
5   };
6   Iterable<EObject> _map = IterableExtensions.<Activity,
        EObject>map(_filter, _function);
7   Iterables.<EObject>addAll(this.output, _map);
8   return this.output;
9 }
```

It can be easily seen that Xtend's syntax is much more succinct due to a variety of syntactical elements (syntactic sugar) and complementing libraries. We discuss six prominent features of Xtend that are not readily provided by Java, Xtend's collection library, extension methods, closures, create methods, template expressions, and multiple dispatching.

Collection library Xtend is delivered with its own adaptation of the *Google Guava* API for Java (formerly called the *Google Collections Library*), an extension to the Java collections framework. In combination with functional closures, query and filter operations on EMF-based models are syntactically close to OCL expressions. The expression in line 5 first filters all elements of type `Activity` into a list and invokes method `mapActivity2Process` on each element of the list, compiling a new list from the method's return values. The same operation would translate to an OCL expression along the lines of

```
input->select(oclIsTypeOf(Activity))->collect(e |
    e.mapActivity2Process)
```

Extension methods Another distinctive feature of Xtend – the one Xtend actually got its name from – are extension methods. The developer can add additional functionality to classes without the need to modify them. Any method `m` whose first parameter is `T` can be invoked in two ways on an object `t : T`, either the old way, '`m(t)`', or using the new notation '`t.m`' so that the order of appearance mimics the flow of data. This syntactical trick enables to use a more OCL-like syntax (functions from the collection Application Programming Interface (API) can be chained this way, as demonstrated in line 4 by the two collection methods `filter` and `map`), but also a syntax that resembles that of QVT-O's mapping invocations. Line 5 uses the extension method style to call mapping `mapActivity2Process`.

Closures Closures are literal expressions that define anonymous functions. Just like anonymous classes in Java, they capture final variables and parameters in scope, but do not require the artificial overhead of defining an anonymous class to wrap a function. While lambda expressions have been introduced to Java 8, Xtend is still more concise and maintains compatibility with older Java versions. Functions from the OCL library make heavy use of closures, including the select function mentioned above. Like QVT-O, a call to mapping method can be folded over a full collection of that type using `map` from the collection API, else we would need to fall back to iterating over all elements using a `for` loop. Line 9 gives in an example for the abbreviated syntax of a closure function, where '`[mapAction2Step]`' is shorthand for '`[e | e.mapAction2Step]`'.

Create methods In Section 2.1.4 we said that QVT-O's trace API plays an important role to resolve elements from previously invoked mappings. Xtend owns a similar (albeit much less capable) concept, create methods. When a create method is invoked, it first checks if it had been invoked on the same set of parameters prior. If an entry can be found in a dictionary that it keeps, the same entry is returned, else the defined return type is first instantiated,

```
1  class Activity2ActivityXML {
2    // TODO: caller must write return value to an xml file
3    def run(List<EObject> input) {
4      val activity = input.filter(Activity).head
5      mapActivity2ActivityXML(activity)
6    }
7    def mapActivity2ActivityXML(Activity self) '''
8      <activity>
9        «self.actions.map[mapAction2ActivityXML].join»
10     </activity>
11   '''
12   def mapAction2ActivityXML(Action self) '''
13     <action name="«self.name»"
14       isStart="«if (self instanceof StartAction) 'true' else
             'false'»"
15       isStop="«if (self instanceof StopAction) 'true' else
             'false'»"
16       next = "«self.successors.map[name].join(',')»"
17   '''
18 }
```

Listing 2.3: Activity2ActivityXML example in Xtend

then the method is run and finally the return value is stored to the dictionary before it is returned to the caller. Methods can be turned into create methods by prepending the return type with `create result:new`. Mapping methods in Lines 8, 11, and 17 demonstrate the syntax. Only queries on concrete mappings (cf. `resolveIn`, `resolveOneIn`) can be covered by this feature, and resolution cannot be done without creating a new element if no entry is found. In Chapter 3 we use *active annotations* (another Xtend feature) to substitute *create methods* by a much more capable `@Create` annotation and a more powerful trace resolution API.

Template Expressions We already mentioned that Xtend has its roots in Xpand, a domain-specific language for template-based code generation. With Xtend, code generators can be still written using the similar concept of template expressions. A template expression is a multiline string that is delimited by three single quotes, `'''...'''`. What distinguishes these strings from the normal double quotation mark is that Xtend expressions can be embedded into the string surrounded by meta tags, i.e. guillemets, «...». An expression can evaluate to a string value which is directly inserted into the containing string. Inside meta tags, there can also be meta block statements, either conditionals «**IF**...»...«**ENDIF**» or loops «**FOR**...»...«**ENDFOR**». Xtend first introduced smart white-space handling: Indentation inside the expression (relative to the indentation outside the expression) is adopted by the generated string. In combination with a clever highlighting of indentations by the Xtend text editor, creating formatted output without a pretty-printer has become much easier. An example transformation from `ActivityModel` instances to a textual XML representation demonstrates some of Xtend's abilities for code generation (Listing 2.3). Two mappings define template expressions (lines 7ff. and 12ff.). The join operation in line 9 concatenates the strings returned for each `Activity` object.

Multiple Dispatch Methods Not unlike Java, methods are bound based on the static types of the arguments for each call statement. Especially when dealing with models or extension methods, polymorphic behavior can be more adequate. A set of `dispatch` methods shares a single method name, but has distinct parameter types. Depending on the argument type, exactly one method with the closest matching parameter type is invoked. Internally, the transpiler to Java infers `if-instanceof-else` cascades, ordered in a way such that more specific types come first. In the example above, method `mapAction2ActivityXML` (line 12ff.) could be alternatively implemented using two dispatching methods rather than checking the types manually:

```
def dispatch mapAction2ActivityXML(StartAction self) '''
  <action name="«self.name»" isStart="true" isStop="false"
    successors = "«self.successors.map[name].join(',')»">
'''
```

```
def dispatch mapAction2ActivityXML(StopAction self) '''
  <action name="«self.name»" isStart="false" isStop="true"
    next = "«self.successors.map[name].join(',')»">
'''
```

This overview does only scratch the surface. The official *Xtend User Guide* [The13] provides a complete (albeit merely informal) description of the language. The Xtend language[8] is part of the Eclipse stack, and was built with the Eclipse Xtext DSL framework. Historically, the Xtend language even originated from the Xtext project.

2.1.7. Triple Graph Grammar

TGG is a formal approach to model transformation programming that has been developed by Schürr [Sch95] and that has its roots in graph grammars. Early research on graph grammars has been done by Ehrig et al. [EPS73] in the early seventies in order to generalize Chomsky's formal generative grammar theory. A Triple Graph Grammar (TGG) rule consists of a left hand side and a right-hand side object pattern. Informally, each rule defines a single construction step on one model, and how elements on another model must be added to maintain equal semantics on both sides. Rules can specify negative application conditions (NACs), i.e., object patterns that must not occur for the rule to be applied. Further on, rules build a glue (or correspondence) graph that consists of objects that relate semantically equivalent objects on either side. Objects from the glue graph can be referred to from arbitrary rules.

TGGs and QVT-R can be both classified as declarative transformation languages. In fact, both share many concepts, and QVT-R can be (partially) implemented in TGGs [GK10].

In this thesis, we use the compact notation suggested by Kindler [KW07]. The ++ operator annotated on an object or a reference tags those elements

[8] Eclipse Xtend, `https://www.eclipse.org/xtend/`

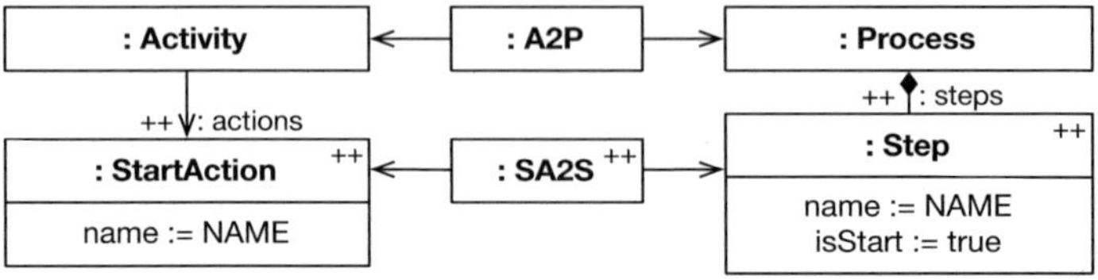

Figure 2.6: Triple graph grammar rule that maps `StartAction` to `Step`

that are to be instantiated or established in one of the three models, model one, model two and a glue graph. Elements that are not tagged as such are to be matched, they constitute the left-hand side of the rule, whereas the right-hand side comprises both matched and created elements.

Figure 2.6 gives a simple example for a such notated rule that equates to QVT-R rules `Action2Step` and `StartAction2Step` from Listing 2.1. When read from left to right, an object of type `Step` is created for any `StartAction`, together with a new gluing object of type `SA2S`. The created `Step` instance is set to be contained by a `Process` object that must have been previously created from object `StartAction`'s container element (and put into relation by an instance of class `A2P`).

2.2. Modular Programming

Modular programming is a software engineering methodology that relies on adequate language concepts to structure large and complex software systems. First, we define important objectives that a modular design technique must support. Then, we provide a list of the key features of modular language concepts, and discern differences between module concepts and class or component concepts.

2.2.1. Software Design Technique

Modular programming is quite an old design method that had been proposed to address maintenance issues of large and complex software systems.

In 1972, Parnas described modularization as "a mechanism for improving the flexibility and comprehensibility of a system while allowing the shortening of its development time" (David L. Parnas [Par72]). In his opinion (one which was shared by others at that time), the chief aim of modular programming methods is to reduce development and maintenance costs that arise from large and inappropriately structured code bases. He recommends to consequently hide design decisions behind interfaces, so that developers responsible for a module can work on its implementation without having others worry that changing decisions might break interfaces to their respective module.

A more exhaustive list of requirements to is given by Bertrand Meyer.

Definition 2.6 (Criteria of a Modular Design Method): *Meyer [Mey97] states five requirements a modular design method must fulfill.*

1. ***Decomposability.*** *"A software construction method satisfies* Modular Decomposability *if it helps in the task of decomposing a software problem into a small number of less complex subproblems, connected by a simple structure, and independent enough to allow further work to proceed separately on each of them."*

2. ***Composability.*** *"A method satisfies* Modular Composability *if it favors the production of software elements which may then be freely combined with each other to produce new systems, possibly in an environment quite different from the one in which they were initially developed."*

3. ***Understandability.*** *"A method favors* Modular Understandability *if it helps produce software in which a human reader can understand each module without having to know the others, or, at worst, by having to examine only a few of the others."*

4. ***Continuity/Maintainability.*** *"A method satisfies* Modular Continuity *if, in the software architectures that it yields, a small change in a*

problem specification will trigger a change of just one module, or a small number of modules."

5. **Protection.** *"A method satisfies* Modular Protection *if it yields architectures in which the effect of an abnormal condition occurring at run time in a module will remain confined to that module, or at worst will only propagate to a few neighboring modules."*

The second criterion, composability, encompasses reusability, the reuse of the same module under a variety of situations. The third criterion, continuity, implies maintainability, i.e., the ease with which a software system can be adapted to changing requirements and bugs can be located and repaired.

The following definition puts the above criteria into a shorter formulation. It adds reduced development time which can be achieved by having multiple modules developed in parallel.

Definition 2.7 (Modular Programming): Modular Programming *is the hierarchical composition of a software system from isolated units with a self-documenting and well-defined interface, yielding a product with a shorter development time that is easier to understand and maintain.*

Bass et al. [BCK03] list two important viewtypes (among others) for module-based architectural structures, the *decomposition structure*, and the *uses structure*. The first is the result of a hierarchical decomposition of a system in a way that likely changes are encapsulated in few isolated modules, with minimal functionality exposed by module interfaces, aiming to minimize future maintenance efforts. The uses structure describes dependencies on the level of procedures exposed by the interfaces, as well as external resources. It serves as an aid in maximizing extensibility and reusability of (subsets of) the system, and supports incremental development.

2.2.2. Module Concepts

In order to design a product in a modular fashion, the programming language used must support modularity. Almost all modern GPLs integrate some concept to structure code, but not all of these concepts offer the same capabilities, and not all are required to structure code on a larger scale. One example is object-orientation, which does not provide means to properly establish information hiding properties [Szy92], and is thus less suitable for structuring software an a coarser grained level. Until today, there is no received definition of what makes a good module concept and what not.

A useful module system facilitates to implement software according to the following five rules.

Definition 2.8 (Rules of Good Modular Design): *According to Bertrand Meyer [Mey97], there are five rules of good modular design.*

1. ***Direct Mapping.*** *"The modular structure devised in the process of building a software system should remain compatible with any modular structure devised in the process of modeling the problem domain."*
2. ***Few Interfaces.*** *"Every module should communicate with as few others as possible."*
3. ***Small Interfaces.*** *"If two modules communicate, they should exchange as little information as possible."*
4. ***Explicit Interfaces.*** *"Whenever two modules A and B communicate, this must be obvious from the text of A or B or both."*
5. ***Information Hiding.*** *"The designer of every module must select a subset of the module's properties as the official information about the module, to be made available to authors of client modules."*

In addition, McConnell emphasizes that a good modular design must maintain a uniform level of abstraction across all modules on the same structural level [McC04, Ch. 5].

From Meyer's rules, and in correlation with Friedmann and Wand [FW08, Ch. 8] we are able to infer informally the key concepts of a module system and requirements therefor. Typically, a module concept enforces logical boundaries between code units by providing *explicit interfaces* that are separate from a module's implementation. The interface exhaustively documents an implementation-independent description of what *functionality* is provided (or `exported`). Additionally, the interface itself – or an implementation, in some cases – specifies external functional dependencies that are needed (or *imported*). Similar to types, interfaces pose a *contract* between the client/user of a module and the implementer of a module. Modules are typically *compile-time* concepts, the linker resolves module dependencies of a program before it is executed. A module system controls the scoping and binding of names and types; implementation-specific details that are not part of the interface are hidden (*information hiding*).

Modules vs. Classes As opposed to the definition of modularity in the traditional sense that we introduced above, object-oriented languages provide a fine-grained notion of modularity, on the basis of Abstract Data Types (ADTs). Classes are run-time concepts, where each class can be instantiated multiple times. Subclassing can be easily used to break interface contracts of a superclass: languages cannot enforce that behavior is maintained by subclasses, due to the halting problem. On a coarser grained level, the notion of classes or Java packages does not establish strong enough boundaries between parts of a system. Object-oriented programming does not substitute the modular programming paradigm, or to put in Szyperski's words, "Import is not Inheritance" [Szy92]. Using class concepts to implement a module structure results in intuitive solutions (Szyperski states the example of inheriting library classes), or just impractical solutions (Szyperski names *spaghetti scoping*, i.e., weakly structured concepts to export methods to friend classes). Module concepts have been added on top of object-oriented languages as a means to package multiple classes behind well-defined interfaces. This is evidenced by the extensive use of OSGi under Java, and the planned integration of an OSGi-compatible module concept, code-named *project JigSaw*, into Java 8.

Modules vs. Components Despite possessing an underlying model for modularity [HC01, Ch. 19], in contrast to modules, components in the common sense are a run-time concept without static dependencies to other components [Szy02, pp. 39ff.]. Components can be dynamically bound and physically distributed (based on a deployment descriptor). Their main objective is to foster large-scale reuse rather than maintainability. An in-depth consideration of the commonalities and differences of abstract data types, modules, classes and objects, and components, is carried out by Reussner [Reu01, Sect. 2.3.1].

According to MacCormack and Parnas, modular programming brings the following benefits (cf. MacCormack [MRB07], Parnas [Par72]):

Encouraging deliberate designs. With languages that support module concepts, implementations are type-checked against their interfaces to ensure contracts are met. This encourages developers to think about a modular design with encapsulated implementation decisions. It also prevents misuse by introducing unintended dependencies from external code.

Fostering team development. Initial development can be carried out more efficiently with a proper interface concept. As soon as a modular design has been created in terms of interfaces, multiple developers may work on implementing different parts of the project in parallel.

Making software easier to understand, use and reuse. Developers generally require less effort to understand software behavior when provided with a view that abstracts from implementation details. Interfaces offer an abstract and often sufficient description of a module's responsibilities and dependencies.

Simplifying modification and repair. If a decision is distributed over multiple modules, ripple-of-change effects occur when that decision is being modified. Localized design decisions help to limit ripple-of-change effect.

Facilitating variability through reconfiguration. Alternative implementations can be easily exchanged for design decisions that are encapsulated behind an interface. This is done by simply exchanging implementations of the same interface.

Reussner names similar benefits for the concept of encapsulation in his dissertation [Reu01, Sect. 2.2.1]: he lists increased understandability, faster development, less redundancy, and higher adaptability. Only few additional benefits [Reu01, Sect. 2.2.2] can be attributed to components but not to modules, due to the added runtime flexibility of components.

2.3. Formal Methods

It is quite common for any engineering discipline to apply mathematical analysis not only to specify and develop an appropriate solution, but also to verify that the solution actually solves a given problem and the absence of design flaws. In computer science, formal methods are mainly a class of techniques that transfer fundamental concepts from theoretical computer science to the field of software and hardware engineering [Hol97]. Depending on the criticality and complexity of a system that is to be development, formal methods have become widely accepted as a means to affirm correctness and safety of a particular software/hardware design. Some of the more famous examples where formal methods could have helped to avoid errors in design or implementation, are the *dangling else* problem in the ALGOL-60 compiler [Kau63], the $370 million Ariane 5 rocket crash [Dow97], and Intel's Pentium II bug in the chip's floating point division unit [Cip95].

2.3.1. Semantics of Programming Languages

A programming language is described by its concrete syntax and its semantics. A program is only then considered a valid program of a language if it conforms to the syntactic rules and *static semantics* of the language. The *dynamic semantics* of a language specifies the meaning of a program in the language.

Most approaches to formally define semantics of a programming language can be associated with one of three major classes [Rey98; FW08]:

Operational Semantics is the most intuitive way to describe the meaning of a program. Each of the constructs in the language is defined by the effects it has on an abstract machine. Structured operational semantics models use rules as part of a deductive system to express executions, where each rule consists of a premise and a conclusion.

Axiomatic Semantics defines the effect of language constructs by logical assertions on the state of the program. Hoare logic is one example, here, each statement is linked to a precondition and a postcondition in predicate logic – the postcondition is established if and only if the precondition is satisfied.

Denotational Semantics defines the meaning of programs in a language by mapping the statements as they appear in the language's abstract syntax onto state-transforming mathematical functions whose behavior is rigorously defined.

Above-mentioned methods (including combinations thereof) are mainly used to specify dynamic semantics, but they can be also employed for defining static semantics: Harper, for example, uses operational semantics to specify a type system based on the abstract syntax [Har92]. Each method brings its advantages and disadvantages. For example, operational semantics can be translated to code with less effort if the abstract machine is close to the real target architecture. A downside is that semantics of the abstract machine need to be understood.

Types The principal reason for typing is (i) to detect errors, (ii) to enforce disciplined programming through "interfaces as types", and (iii) to give programs a self-documenting character. Types can be seen as contracts between users and developers of a program [Hen94]. Depending on the programming language, everything can be typed. Types can represent two complementing aspects of a language, types as a set of values, e.g., primitive types, compound types, and functions, and (ii) types as a means of abstraction, e.g., interfaces of modules and classes.

Type Checking The process of verifying and enforcing the constraints of types is called *type checking*. Type safety may be either verified statically or dynamically, that is, at compile-time based on analysis of a program's text (source code), or at run-time based on run-time type information that is attached to objects in the memory. Dynamic checking can complement static checking, because not all properties can be checked statically, for instance downcasts or meta programming constructs.

Definition 2.9 (Type system [Hen94]): *A* type system, *or type inference system, is a logical system of rules for inferring valid judgements. The ingredients of a type system for programming languages are:*

- *Expressions e: syntactically well-formed program fragments*
- *Types τ: a language of interfaces (properties) we are interested in*
- *Typings (judgments) $e : \tau$ and more generally $A \vdash e : \tau$ mean that "expression e has type τ if assumptions A hold".*
- *Inference rules for deriving valid typings for compound expressions from their constituent expressions.*

Famous instances of type inference systems are the simply typed lambda calculus by Alonzo Church (1940), the Curry-Hindley and the Hindley-Milner type system for the lambda calculus. Type systems are formally studied by type theory.

Type Safety The often-quoted slogan by Robin Milner (1978), "Well-typed programs do not go wrong", summarizes the endeavor that type systems must be sound (or safe[9]), i.e., if a programming language is not able to preserve abstraction at runtime. Milner formulated type safety as two properties, preservation and progress. Progress means to ensure that a well-typed term is not stuck (either it is a value or it can take a step according to the evaluation rules). Preservation assures that, if a well-typed term takes one evaluation step, then the resulting term is again well-typed.

Theorem 2.3.1 (Type Safety [Pie02]). *A type system is safe if, for any pair of expressions e, e', the following two properties are met.*

1. ***Preservation.*** *If e is a well-typed term, that is, $e : \tau$ for some type τ, and $e \rightarrow e'$, then $e' : \tau$.*

2. ***Progress.*** *If e is a well-typed term, $e : \tau$ for some τ, then either e is a value, e val, or there exists e' such that $e \rightarrow e'$.*

Abstraction Safety An additional use of type systems is to enforce data abstraction established by a particular abstraction concept, for example modules, classes and abstract data types. The important role of type systems to build better maintainable systems by enforcing data abstraction has been posited by Reynolds, who points out that "type structure is a syntactic discipline for maintaining levels of abstraction" [Rey83]. There are two properties related to abstraction safety, representation independence and representation invariants.

[9] Luca Cardelli [Car97] distinguishes between soundness and safety: Type soundness is the absence of forbidden errors. Type safety is hurt if a program fragment produces untrapped errors, i.e., errors that go unnoticed, for example an access exceeding an array's bounds.

Representation independence [Mit86] is about giving evidence that a program remains independent of the actual implementation of an abstract type. In other words, two valid manifestations of the same abstract type must be contextually equivalent and can be thus replaced while preserving type safety.

Representation invariants refine the set of valid representations of an abstraction's representation. While one cannot generally decide if two implementations are semantically equivalent, an abstract type declaration can include invariants that must be satisfied by any well-formed implementation of the type. Reasoning about the correctness of an abstraction's representations presumes an *abstraction function* to exist. An abstraction function relates concepts from concrete implementations to concepts of their abstract type.

A substantial body of work deals with protection mechanisms in programming languages, the earliest publications on the topic are arguably those by Morris Jr. [Mor73; Jr73]. The interested reader is referred to Pierce's book "Advanced Topics in Types and Programming Languages" [Pie04], a concise compendium on the topic, with an extensive list of references to original publications.

2.3.2. Program Verification

Program verification is the act of proving (or disproving) if an implementation meets a formal specification of the program. Code can be first implemented and then verified in a separate step, or a proven implementation can be formally derived from the specification (*correct by construction*).

There are two fundamentally different approaches, *model checking*, a systematical and exhaustive exploration of a mathematical model of the given system, and *deductive verification*, where verification is accomplished by providing a formal proof on an abstract mathematical model of the system. Proof assistants like the interactive theorem prover Coq [The12; BC10], Isabelle, or automatic SMT solvers can be used for the latter. In this thesis, we decided to use Coq because of its good reputation for reasoning about type systems including that of Featherweight Java [IPW01].

The Coq Proof Assistant The Coq proof assistant [BC10] is a development environment used to formally prove mathematical assertions. Coq evolves around *Gallina*, a synthesis of a strictly-typed functional programming language, higher-order logics and a potent type system. Gallina's foundation is the Calculus of Inductive Constructions (CIC) [CH88; Pau93], a higher-order typed lambda calculus and an extension of the *Curry-Howard Isomorphism*: Terms in the lambda calculus are associated with natural deduction proofs. A supplemental language of commands, the *Vernacular* [The12], allows users to

- define (co-)inductive types, (well-founded recursive) functions, and logical predicates;
- interactively develop mathematical theorems and prove specifications of programs;
- extract programs in Objective CaML, Haskell and Scheme from proofs of specifications.

Coq's proof system relies on a relatively lean proof checker giving a high confidence on its own correctness. A Coq proof comprises a sequence of *tactics*. Tactics call well-defined proof methods for breaking down an assertion into simpler and simpler parts, until such parts are obtained that can be trivially proven.

In this thesis, Coq is used in two important application areas, the reasoning on type systems, and program certification. We use Coq to verify properties of a type system (namely our module concept for transformations) that is based on inference rules (Appendix A). The second usage of Coq takes place as we verify functional programs to adhere to a transformation specification in the declarative transformation language QVT-R (Appendix B).

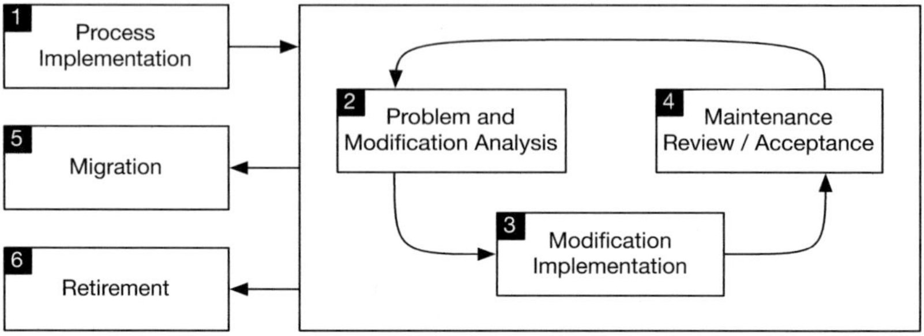

Figure 2.7: IEEE/ISO standardized software maintenance process [IEE06]

2.4. Software Maintenance

In terms of the IEEE Standard Glossary of Software Engineering Terminology [IEE90], software maintenance is defined as "the process of modifying a software system or component after delivery to correct faults, improve performances or other attributes, or adapt to a changed environment." The IEEE Standard 14764 of "Maintenance as a Software Life Cycle Process" [IEE06, p. 4] extends this to "the totality of activities required to provide cost-effective support of software systems. Activities are performed during the pre-delivery stage as well as the post-delivery stage."

Maintainability, according to the ISO 9126 standard, encompasses the quality factors analyzability, changeability, stability and testability. Many sources state maintenance costs of 50 and more percent of the overall software development costs. Though hard to objectively quantify, metrics on architecture- and code-level are expected to be reasonable indicators, like the degree of modularization, the coupling between modules, the degree of documentation, and so forth [HKV07].

2.4.1. Maintenance Process

Maintenance is an enduring activity throughout the life of a software system. The maintenance process by the IEEE Standard 14764 [IEE06] reflects this

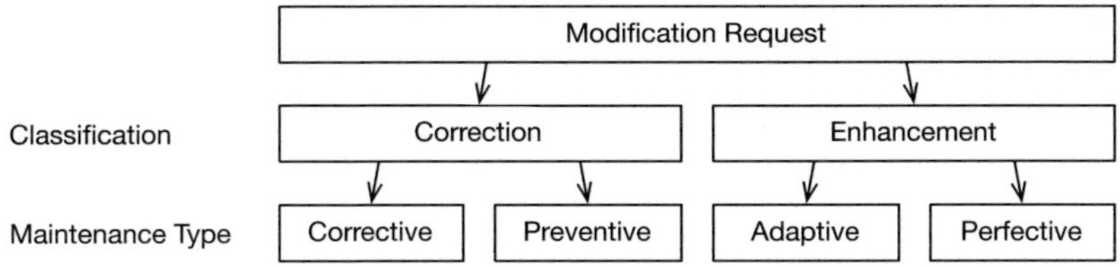

Figure 2.8: IEEE/ISO standardized maintenance types [IEE06]

fact by suggesting an iterative 3-staged cycle (Figure 2.7, thereby incorporating the iterative enhancement model as it is presented by [GT03]):

Step 1: Process Implementation. In response to a modification request or problem report, the maintainer develops plans and procedures that are to be executed.

Step 2: Problem and Modification Analysis. The modification request or problem report is analyzed for its type (cf. classification below), scope (expected costs and time), and criticality. If it is a modification request, development options are identified and approved. If it is a problem report, it is verified and replicated. Analysis results and implementation options of a request or report are to be documented.

Step 3: Modification Implementation. Location of concerns are identified, i.e., software artifacts including affected documentation that have to be modified in order to accomplish the request. Then, the development process is started, complemented by test and evaluation criteria, plus measurements to ensure the completeness, correctness and locality (i.e., original requirements remain unaffected) of the planned modifications. Criteria and test results shall be documented.

Step 4: Maintenance Review / Acceptance. Reviews are to be conducted to determine the integrity of the modifications. Approval is obtained for the satisfactory completion of the modification.

Step 5: Migration. A migration plan is created, which comprises six activities, a requirement/risk analysis, development of migration tools, data and code conversion, the actual migration execution, verification of the migration performed, and providing support for the old environments.

Step 6: Retirement. If pre-defined decisions to retire a software product are met, a retirement plan is created and executed. Decisions are usually economic-based, and may take one or more of the following events into consideration: emerging technologies or those becoming obsolete, degrading maintainability, standardization efforts, and vendor independence.

Throughout the process, the system's documentation is updated accordingly. The IEEE standard defines several types of maintenance activities. An initial modification request can lead to the identification of a problem and a problem report is issued.

Definition 2.10 (Modification requests [IEE06]): *Software maintenance requests (also called change requests) can be classified into four major classes, as shown in Figure 2.8:*

Corrective Maintenance. *Reactive modifications after delivery to correct discovered problems, including unscheduled emergency maintenance activities.*

Preventive Maintenance. *Post-delivery modifications of a product to detect and correct latent faults, before they manifest as operational faults.*

Adaptive Maintenance. *Modifications to adapt a system to changes in the system's environment, e.g., the operating system or a third party framework is updated.*

Perfective Maintenance. *Post-delivery modifications of a product to detect and correct latent faults, before they manifest as a failure. This group includes refactoring and reimplementation activities to improve* *maintainability, optimize the performance and other software quality attributes.*

Model-Driven Software Evolution When model-driven software engineering is practiced, first class artifacts of a product are even more exposed to software evolution. Because of a long-term investment into a framework for a complete family of products, maintainability is even of greater importance than for traditionally developed systems. Van Deursen et al. [vDVW07] identify four dimensions of evolution in MDE:

Regular Evolution. Here, model instances of the domain language are changed to adapt a system to new requirements.

Domain Language Evolution. In this case, the domain model itself is subject to changes, which may require to migrate existing instances to the new model. The enhanced expressiveness must be respected by the modeling infrastructure, which means that transformations and the framework must be extended accordingly.

Platform Evolution. If the target platform is modified, the whole modeling infrastructure including transformations is subject to modifications.

Abstraction Evolution. As further problem domains are sufficiently understood, new modeling languages can be introduced for such domains. The complete model-driven infrastructure must evolve with the gained flexibility, including the target platform, transformations, and existing models.

All dimensions except for the first one may affect model transformation programs and hence lie in the focus of this thesis. Recently, a list of open research challenges has been identified from empirical studies carried out with SAP, Ableton, and Capgemini [HGSS13]. The studies emphasize the aforementioned dimensions as the most important ones. Beyond that, they identify a poor predictability of evolutionary actions during development and maintenance as another critical factor, and conclude that new methods and techniques must be developed that better help to proactively manage evolution in MDE.

2.4.2. Static Program Analysis

Static program analysis is the analysis of program code without executing the program on a machine (which is classified as dynamic program analysis) [NNH05]. If performed by humans without tool support, static program analysis is also called program comprehension. On a higher abstraction level than the level of individual statements but also when working with large code bases, tools can effectively assist humans in automatically analyzing programs for quality and functional issues. These tools range from standard IDE functionality like style checkers and compiler warnings on single statements to more sophisticated techniques which include the complete code, for example the computation of complex software metrics, dead code identification, re-engineering of the modular structure and detection of safety-critical issues. Techniques involve more or less formal methods, for instance control-flow and data-flow analysis, Hoare-style reasoning, model checking techniques, the symbolic execution or the abstract interpretation of code. Type systems that are part of a language compiler can also be counted to the list of static analysis methods.

Static program analysis is used in all three contributions of this thesis; in the first contribution, it is used to establish static typing rules for enforcing modular scoping; in the second contribution, to extract data and control dependence information from programs for the purpose of visualization; and in the third contribution, to extract static dependence information and for automatically reverse engineering a modular structure.

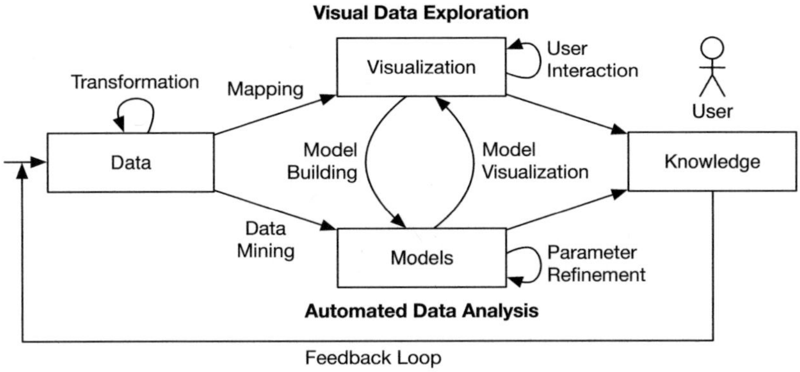

Figure 2.9: The visual analytics methodology [KKEM10]

2.4.3. Program Visualization

As software products tend to become larger and more complex, it can become extremely hard to get the information needed to efficiently perform software maintenance, re-engineering, and reverse engineering. Even though program analysis techniques can be used to extract the required information from the software's artifacts, data can be complex and hard to communicate to a human developer. In such cases, choosing the right form of presentation can be critical for achieving an efficient workflow. Choosing a combination of program analysis and visualization to help software developers comprehend larger systems and to improve their overall productivity when carrying out various development tasks is the principal goal in the research field of software visualization [Die07].

Definition 2.11 (Software Visualization [Ger94; Die07]): *According to Gershon, scientific "visualization is the process of transforming information into a visual form, enabling users to observe the information. The resulting visual display enables the scientist or engineer to perceive visually features which are hidden in the data but nevertheless are needed for data exploration and analysis." [Ger94]. Software visualization methods in particular provide* *graphical representations to "visualize the structure, behavior, and evolution of software." [Die07].*

A notable visualization technique is the visual analytics methodology that has been developed by Keim [KMS+08; KKEM10]. To put it in his words, "visual analytics combines automated analysis techniques with interactive visualizations for an effective understanding, reasoning and decision making on the basis of very large and complex data sets" [KAF+08].

The process is shown in Figure 2.9. The approach includes active user interaction with the view and analysis parameters, hence enabling the exploration of large data spaces by a tight coupling between the user and the extraction and visualization process. The first step is a preprocessing step that integrates multiple and possibly heterogeneous data sources and normalizes the data, summarized by the arrow labeled *Transformation*. In a next step, information can be either visualized directly (*Mapping*), or analyzed automatically using data mining techniques (*Data Mining*). The model that is built can then be evaluated and refined in a human-computer interaction loop. The third step integrates the user, who is able to control the analysis and filtering process by trying out different algorithms and parameters (*Parameter Refinement*). He can further navigate on and zoom in and out of the visualized data (*User Interaction*) to incrementally acquire the knowledge he needs in a specific task context. This last step triggers the first step (*Feedback Loop*) where the model is updated from the available data sources.

Visual analytics has been successfully utilized in software maintenance [TEV10]. In Chapter 4, the visual analytics methodology is exploited to support developers in maintaining model transformation programs.

2.4.4. Software Clustering

Understanding the structure of a software system is vitally important for the process of software maintenance and evolution. Legacy systems often lack architectural descriptions of the design rationale, the documen-

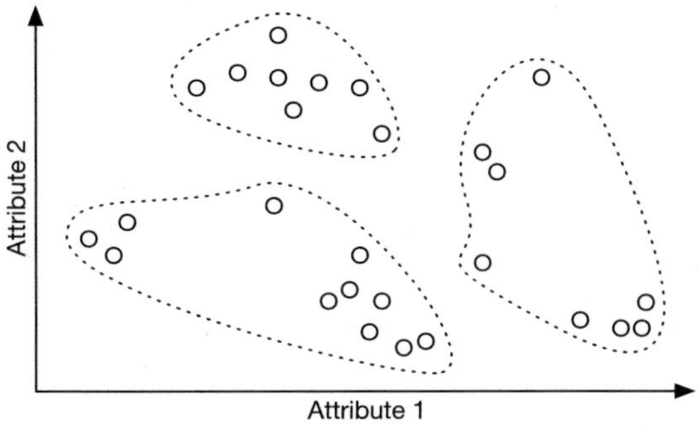

Figure 2.10: Clustering of two-dimensional numerical data, based on the Euclidean distance

tation has become obsolete or the structure has simply eroded over time. In other cases, the system has been implemented in a language that does not even offer information hiding modularity and other concepts required for programming-in-the-large. In any case, restructuring of software is a long-term investment into the quality of software and can be understood as a form of preventative maintenance.

Software clustering is a variety of techniques which group software system entities of a particular granularity level – ranging from variables, procedures, and methods to classes, files and module – into subsystems in a way that helps software engineers in comprehending the high-level structure of large and complex software systems [ST12]. Most techniques work semi if not fully automatically, hence they have the potential to reduce the effort spent for understanding and reverse engineering modular structures significantly. It is a consensus among researchers of the field that automatic clustering approaches are unlikely to be as good as a manual clustering done by experts with a good knowledge of the studied system [Tze01]. However, automatic clusterings can give an initial suggestion of a system that can be manually refined in a subsequent step.

There are four stages of a software clustering process. Firstly, the *clustering objective* is to be set. Depending on the desired level of granularity, the type of system entities is to be selected that is extracted from the system using static or dynamic program analysis techniques. These entities must be equipped with attributes, i.e., the declared name of the entity, and interactions between entities are chosen to be relevant, i.e., *uses*, *creates* and *extends* relationships for classes. Secondly, a *similarity measure* must be chosen that determines the factors that make a pair of entities belong to the same group or cluster (i.e., being similar). Based on the measure, an algorithm attempts to find groups (clusters) with maximal intra-cluster similarity and minimal inter-cluster similarity. In regards to classes, this concept resembles the principle of high cohesion and low coupling. Thirdly and fourthly, a *clustering algorithm* and a *visualization method* has to be selected. Software visualization methods have been already discussed previously in Section 2.4.3. To illustrate this principle, Figure 2.10 depicts a fictitious set of entities, each having two numerical attributes, plotted onto a regular two-dimensional graph. Three groups, drawn in a dashed line, has been identified based on the Euclidean distance measure.

Clustering Algorithms Different kinds of algorithms are applicable to find an optimal clustering based on a similarity measure. Everitt et al. [ELL11] surveys the most common similarity measures. It is important to keep in mind that the choice of a particular algorithm and similarity measure may impose some possibly unreasonable structure rather than it may discover an existing but hidden structure. Obviously, there are careful considerations among several factors taken by experts which a sufficiently simple measure can hardly take into account.

According to Wiggerts' characterization [Wig97], we distinguish between four classes of algorithms each having their own notion of a cluster: graph-theoretical algorithms, construction algorithms, optimization algorithms and hierarchical algorithms. *Graph algorithms* aim to find cliques (a subgraph with any pair of vertices connected by an edge) or quasi-cliques in a graph representation of the entities and their relations. *Construction algorithms* assign entities to clusters in a single pass. Optimization algorithms search for a solution that maximizes (or minimizes) the computed values of an objective function. The hill-climbing algorithm is an example of a heuristic that searches iteratively for a local optimum. It does so by tentatively reassigning random entities to neighbored clusters and reverts if the objective function's value is not improved. Hierarchical algorithms look for a hierarchy of partitions based on distance connectivity, and can create an agglomerative clustering (if partitions are successively composed bottom-up), or divisive clustering (if partitions are repeatedly split). Many clustering algorithms are integrated into prevalent mathematical frameworks (R Project, Mathematica, SPSS, Maple, and the kind).

The Bunch Tool *Bunch* [MMCG99; MM06] is a clustering tool for the software engineering domain. The tool was developed at Drexel University, the first publication dates back to 1998. Bunch can use one of three optimization algorithms, exhaustive search, the hill-climbing, and a genetic algorithm. The tool offers both a purely automatic and a semiautomatic mode, in which developers can, for instance, manually declare a set of entities to belong to a predefined cluster. This can come in handy to keep cross-cutting platform API methods from interfering with the software system's methods.

Bunch uses a so-called *Module Dependency Graph (MDG)* to represent the system entities and references. The MDG is a weighted directed graph $G = (V, E)$, where vertices V represent the set of entities, and edges E correspond to the set of dependencies between entities: $(u, v) \in E$ iff entity u depends on entity v. Despite the naming, entities must not be modules, but can stand for other types of entities. The task to extract a graph from a given system is left to the user; thus, the user can differentiate between different types of references by assigning different weights to the edges in the graph, $w : E \rightarrow \mathbb{R}$. As input file format, the Bunch tool uses a simple text-based graph definition: A line in the file consists of the starting and ending entities' unique name followed by an optional weighting number, each of the three separated by spaces. Third party source code analysis tools can be used, for instance Acacia, when chained with a custom generator that translates into the MDG file format.

A partition (or clustering) of G into n clusters (n-partition) is then formally defined as $\Pi_G = \bigcup_{i=1}^{n} G_i$ with $G_i = (V_i, E_i)$, and $\forall v \in V \; \exists_1 k \in [1,n], v \in V_k$. Edges E_i are edges that leave or remain inside the partition, $E_i = \{\langle v_1, v_2 \rangle \in E : v_1 \in V_i \wedge v_2 \in V\}$.

The similarity measure employed by the Bunch approach is the *Modularization Quality (MQ)* index [MM06][10]. Through this metric, a high cohesion within the clusters and a low coupling between the clusters is rewarded with a higher score. The score for a single cluster is a fraction with the doubled weight of intra-edges μ_i as the numerator, and the doubled weight of intra-edges μ_i plus the weight of inter-edges ε_i as the denominator. The scores of all k clusters is added up to form the final MQ value,

$$MQ = \sum_{i=1}^{k} \frac{2\mu_i}{2\mu_i + \varepsilon_i}, \quad \text{with intra edges} \quad \mu_i = \sum_{\substack{e=(u,v)\in E \\ u,v \in C_i}} w(e)$$

$$\text{and inter edges} \quad \varepsilon_i = \sum_{\substack{e_{\rightarrow}=(u,v)\in E \\ u\in C_i, v\notin C_i}} w(e_{\rightarrow}) + \sum_{\substack{e_{\leftarrow}=(u,v)\in E \\ u\notin C_i, v\in C_i}} w(e_{\leftarrow})$$

Bunch does not differentiate between types of nodes, although edges can be given different weights. Other software clustering approaches exist, a survey by Maqbool et al. [MB07] lists ARCH, ACDC [Tze01], LIMBO, and others. ARCH is an earlier approach specifically designed to group procedures. ACDC is a divisive/agglomerative algorithm for comprehension-driven clustering. The input graph is decomposed based on seven sub-system patterns, and in this process, isolated nodes are assigned to already created clus-

[10] Note that we refer to the latest definition from 2006 [MM06], not the original one from 1999 [MMCG99].

ters (orphan adoption algorithm). LIMBO is an agglomerative hierarchical algorithm and employs an information loss measure to judge alternatives.

An in-depth discussion of the various kinds of software clustering algorithms in general and those provided by the Bunch tool has been carried out by Dominik Messinger in his seminar paper [Mes14]. The third contribution in this thesis (Chapter 5) applies software clustering techniques implemented by Bunch to re-engineer modular structures from model transformation programs.

3. Modular Information Hiding for Maintainable Model Transformations

Chapter 1 pointed out that maintenance issues of larger and more complex model transformation programs are essentially caused by a lack of suitable concepts for organizing programs in a structured way. In this chapter, we develop a module concept that is much better tailored to the domain-specific nature of model transformation engineering than existing concepts. The aim of our approach is to gain the same advantages for model transformations as they have been promised for real information hiding modularity, namely improved understandability, maintainability and adaptability [SGCH01].

We formalize our concept by developing syntax and a type system for *Core QVT-OM*, a compact subset of the transformation language QVT-O that is enriched with our module concept. To meet the special demands of transformations, module interfaces give control over both model and code accessibility.

We discuss applicability to various transformation languages, including those that follow the imperative language paradigm (QVT-O), the declarative language paradigm (e.g., QVT-R), or those that natively support code generation (e.g., Xtend).

To give a proof-of-concept and to demonstrate applicability, we integrate our modular concept into the languages QVT-O and Xtend. The integration into Eclipse QVTo turned out to be straight-forward due to our conceptual definition in QVT-O and QVTo being to the widest extent compliant with the QVT-O standard. We further chose Xtend because Xtend comprises a few transformation concepts that it inherited from Xpand, a template-based model-to-text transformation language. Xtend is a GPL designed with extensibility in mind, in the spirit of Fowler's definition of an internal DSL [Fow10]. Finally, we can exploit interface and class concepts provided by Xtend's host language, Java, and adapt them to our needs using Java annotations.

To a large extent, this chapter's content is based on text that has been presented at the International Conference on Modularity in 2014, previously known as the Conference on Aspect-Oriented Software Development. From feedback gained at the conference, we improved grammar and type inference rules. Further on, a discussion of the applicability to other transformation languages has been added a posteriori. The prototypical implementation for Xtend originates from Dominik Werle's bachelor thesis, supervised by the author of this thesis. The embedding of the QVT-R language into higher-order logics (HOL) stems from a collaboration with Jeffrey Terrell and Steffen Zschaler from King's College, London.

Presentation of this work is organized as follows. In Section 3.1, we motivate on the need for information hiding properties by the introductory example. Section 3.2 uses the same example to show how information hiding modularity can be integrated into QVT-O. Section 3.3 presents the syntax and a type system for checking information hiding properties. Sections 3.4 and 3.5 study applicability to prevalent transformation languages of imperative and declarative nature, respectively. Conclusive words in Section 3.6 end the chapter.

3.1. Modularity Tailored for Transformations

In Section 1.2 in the introductory chapter, we have worked out deficiencies of the structuring concepts provided by QVT-O and other prevalent transformation languages. By the Activity2Process scenario, we have studied three types of maintenance requests that typically occur during transformation development: (i) a corrective maintenance request, "Modifying a module's inner logic", (ii) a corrective/adaptive maintenance request, "Identifying locations of concern", and (iii) a perfective/preventive maintenance request, "Refactoring the modular design".

We had to notice that existing structuring concepts are overly simple to offer adequate assistance in any of the three scenarios. The gravest problem is that transformation languages do not offer suitable methods by which information can be hidden within privileged scopes. Without such a language concept, however, it is impossible to improve program designs by hiding away the complexity behind the public interfaces.

To solve mentioned issues, our idea is to introduce a proper linguistic concept that facilitates information hiding. Protecting the internal details of a piece of software from any other piece and encapsulating design decisions that are likely to change bring several benefits, including better modular designs, the chance to develop in teams, a better understandability and maintainability of the code, and better support for reuse through reconfigurations (For a detailed list of the benefits of modular programming, the reader is referred to Section 2.2).

So that developers can exploit these benefits to the fullest, we expect a model transformation language to integrate a module concept that abides to the information hiding principle. Our understanding of the principle is described by two rules:

R1: Separation of interfaces from their implementations. Implementation details are hidden behind interfaces. This means that a program compiles independently from the implementation chosen for a particular interface, as long as the implementations conform to the interface and behave semantically identical. In the case of model transformations, typical candidates to remain private are query functions, helper methods, and the internal state. Per required interface, a unique implementation exists. In literature[Pie04], this property is called *representation independence*. It is the irrefutable property of any abstraction mechanism, as it ensures that client behavior does not depend on the details of an abstraction.

R2: Conformance of interface and implementation. Rule R1 uses a conformance relation between an implementation and an interface. This relation must possess three properties:

R2a: Method provisioning. There must exist exactly one one-to-one relation between exported and implemented methods to avoid both underspecification and ambiguity. Implemented methods must conform to exported method signatures. This means that method name and the number of arguments have to be equal, and types must be substitutable according to Liskov (contravariance of argument types, covariance of return types).

R2b: Method access control. From a module implementation's perspective, only methods that are either defined locally or by an imported interface are visible. Any other method is not visible and can therefore not be accessed. This covers any kind of reference, including call and trace resolution statements.

R2c: Model access control. Regarding this rule, our domain-specific module concept differs from module concepts for general-purpose programming languages. In order to provide an implementation for a module interface, only a small subset of the models involved must be actually accessed. Larger models are usually structured into packages, where one describes a particular viewpoint of the modeled domain. When declaring interfaces for a transformation's modular decomposition, the transformation designer can, more often than not, restrict the visible parts of the models to the viewpoints required for fulfillment. Interface declarations allow to make the scope of referencable and/or instantiable model elements explicit. Any implementation can access only model elements that are defined by exported interfaces. For greater flexibility, access restrictions on models should be definable not only at class-level but also at package-level. The latter is equivalent to explicitly stating any of the directly nested classes, comparable to Java's star import statement.

Generally, an abstract interface declares a set of assumptions that developers of one module can make about another they intend to use. The idea is to allow developers to program against modules without knowledge about their implementation-specific internals, which even do not need to exist. For this to work, an implementation must be providable in separation from its interface declaration (Rule R1). Since the interface constitutes the contract an implementor of the interface must fulfill, it is vital to check implementations against their interface (Rule R2a).

Usually, functionality provided by a module is published in terms of a method signature that states the method's name as well as input and output parameters of the method. Depending on the language for which the concept is designed, the kind of top-level constructs offered by an interface vary. Whereas interfaces in Java allow to declare method signatures, an imperative transformation language like QVT-O typically includes ordinary methods, mapping methods, and query functions as top-level constructs; a declarative transformation language like QVT-R, on the other hand, provides relations or a similar notion of a rule declaration, and query functions. These domain-specific concepts must be taken into account by our module concept (Rule R2b).

Moreover, transformation constructs can be referred to in different ways: a QVT-O mapping method, for instance, can be either called directly or queried indirectly from a trace resolution statement. When designing a module concept for a transformation languages, it must be considered which of the top-level constructs to include in an interface description, and what types of invocations to allow (Rule R2b).

Rules R1, R2a, and R2c apply to any programming language irrespective of the supported paradigm and domain specifity of the concepts. What sets transformation languages apart from general-purpose languages, is that their main purpose is to operate on richly structured and often large

```
transformation interface IMain(
    in a : ActivityModel, out p : ProcessModel) {
  scope in ActivityModel[Activity];
  scope out ProcessModel[Process];
  mapping Activity::mapActivity2Process() : Process;
}
transformation module Activity2Process
    export IMain,
    import IAction2Step, ICompositeAction2Step {
  mapping Activity::mapActivity2Process() : Process {
      result.steps := self.actions->map mapAction2Step();
  }
}
```

(a) First module

```
transformation interface IAction2Step(
    in a : ActivityModel, out p : ProcessModel) {
  scope in ActivityModel[StartAction, StopAction];
  scope out ProcessModel[Step];
  mapping Action::mapAction2Step() : Step;
  mapping StartAction::mapAction2Step() : Step;
  mapping StopAction::mapAction2Step() : Step;
}
transformation module Action2Step
    export IAction2Step {
  mapping Action::mapAction2Step() : Step {
    result.name := self.name;
    result.next := self.successors.late resolveone(Step);
  }
  mapping StartAction::mapAction2Step() : Step {
    result.name := self.name;
    result.next := self.successors.late resolveone(Step);
    result.isStart := true
  }
  mapping StopAction::mapAction2Step() : Step {
    result.name := self.name;
    result.next := self.successors.late resolveone(Step);
    result.isStop := true
  }
}
```

(b) Second module

```
transformation interface ICompositeAction2Step(
    in a : ActivityModel, out p : ProcessModel) {
  scope in ActivityModel[CompositeAction];
  scope out ProcessModel[Process, Step];
  mapping CompositeAction::mapAction2Step() : Step;
}
transformation module CompositeAction2Step
    import IAction2Step,
    export ICompositeAction2Step {
  mapping CompositeAction::mapAction2Step() : Step {
    createProcess(self);
    result.name := "Run process " + self.name;
    result.successor := self.next.late resolveone(Step);
  }
  helper createProcess(ca : CompositeAction) : Process {
    return object Process {
      name := ca.name;
      steps += ca.actions->map Action2Step();
    };
  }
}
```

(c) Third module

Listing 3.1: Activity2Process example in QVT-OM

data models. Models are specified independently from transformations in a separate object-oriented modeling language. Modeling languages that are based on the MOF have their own notion of modularity, a package mechanism that allows to group model elements by packages, which can be split physically across multiple files. With the ability to modularize models into packages, a module concept for model transformations must pick up on this and provide a mechanism that supports to import specific packages of a model rather than complete models. Per model import, it should be even possible to declare the type of access at the interface level (Rule R2c).

With the two rules mentioned, interfaces are able to exactly declare which functionality implementations must provide and which functionality and model context they minimally require. This eases exchangeability and testability of implementations.

Violation of interface contracts should be detected at design-time employing static type checking. A compile-time error should be issued if methods that are hidden are accessed, if model elements are referenced that are not declared as modifiable or readable, or if methods that are declared in an interface remain unimplemented or with incompatible signatures.

3.2. Augmenting QVT-Operational with Information-Hiding Modularity

We propose a derivative of QVT-O, we name it QVT Operational Modular Mappings (QVT-OM), that replaces the existing module concept with a more elaborate one. To give an idea of the notation, we rewrite the previous example in QVT Operational Modular Mappings (QVT-OM)'s modified syntax (cf. Listing 3.1). A module (keyword `transformation module`) must implement at least one interface and can depend on an arbitrary number of interfaces, stated by keywords `export` and `import`, respectively. An interface (keyword `transformation interface`) must be exported by exactly one module implementation. An interface declares a transformation signature, which is a list of typed model parameters. Signatures of an implementation's exported interfaces must be identical, except for access restrictions. Access restriction definitions commence with keyword `scope`, followed by one of the directives `in`, `out` or `inout`, which indicate the direction, and a model's type name. Access is restricted per model type to the classes and packages listed in trailing square brackets `[]`. A package name is a shortcut for any directly contained classes in the package. Modules must define at least the methods declared in an exported interface with compatible signature.

There has to be one dedicated interface `IMain` with exactly one mapping that forms the entry point of a transformation. This approach is borrowed from the MODULA-3 language. In our example, module `Activity2Pro-`

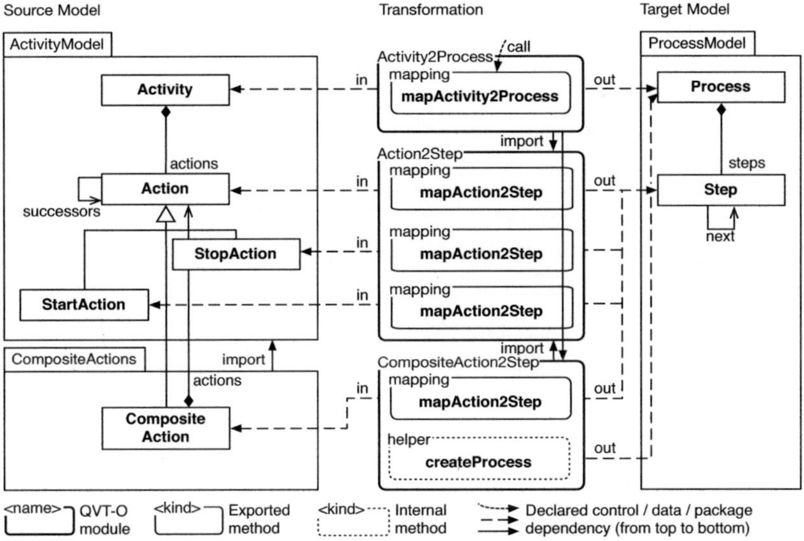

Figure 3.1: Activity2Process transformation in QVT-OM, declared dependencies

`cess` exports `IMain` (Listing 3.1a), so that mapping `mapActivity2Process` forms the entry point.This mapping calls another set of mappings provided by interfaces `IAction2Step` and `ICompositeAction2Step`, which are implemented by modules `Action2Step` and `CompositeAction2Step`, respectively (Listings 3.1b and 3.1c). Because all four mappings have identical names, parameter types and return type, dispatching occurs. Module `CompositeAction2Step` internally declares a helper method `createProcess` for internal use, which again calls all the four mappings on type Action and subtypes.

Figure 3.1 graphically illustrates the modular decomposition of this revised variant of the Activity2Process implementation. Note, that cyclic dependencies are allowed, whereas QVTo's original concept forbade them. Module `CompositeAction2Step` remains independent from the core transformation, except for the import dependence from module `Activity2Process`. Furthermore, model scope is defined on a class-level. This eases testability, but for less fine-grained decompositions, package-level scoping may seem more appropriate.

Implementations of each interface are granted restricted read or read/write access to distinct subsets of the models, with access to a class automatically implicating access to the class's features. In the example, implementations of `IMain` can only access instances of `Activity`, and create or modify instances of `Process`. On the other hand, implementations of `IAction2-Step` can only refer to instances of `StartAction` and `StopAction`, and create or modify objects of class `Step`. If the latter module implementation would define further queries or mappings, these would not be visible to the former module's implementation.

The purpose of a module system is namespace control and data abstraction. There are no extra semantics added besides definition and resolution of namespaces, access control on top of namespaces, and an aligned mechanism for entry point definition. Thus, QVT-OM programs can always be transformed into non-modular QVT-OM or QVT-O programs by giving unique names to entities.

Revisiting both example scenarios from Section 1.2, we can easily see that the proposed module system brings certain benefits. Refactoring the modular structure requires less effort, as all of the information required for reasoning can be deducted from the interface definitions alone. When it comes to adapting the example to an evolving model, we can locate the affected module much quicker from reading the interface descriptions as well: only one of the two modules has access to subclasses of `Action`.

3.3. The Conceptual Extension Core QVT-OM

In the style of Featherweight Java (FJ) [IPW01] we formalize a minimal subset of QVT-OM that we call *Core QVT-OM*. Main purpose of Core QVT-OM is to demonstrate the added modular system. While retaining core features of transformation languages, we skip several of QVT-O's features that do not add to the general idea and should be integrable straightforwardly. In this section, based on the syntax, we present a calculus for type inference and prove its soundness. We guarantee that a well-typed program enforces information hiding postulated by the two rules from the previous section.

Core QVT-OM skips several metamodeling concepts (e.g., abstract classes, primitive types, multiplicities), many of QVT-O's concepts (e.g., helpers, queries, constructors, variables and globals, superimposition, disjunct calls, guards and sections), and most concepts of the underlying OCL (conditional operator `if`, assigment operator `let`, collection operations, and functions from the standard library `stdlib`). QVT's existing module concept, including superimpositioning semantics, have been completely removed to be replaced by our concepts, e.g., `import`, `access`, `extend`, `transform`, and `main`.

We realize modularity as a second-class module system. This means that the module system is separated from the core language's system. Modular definitions are evaluated statically at compile-time, hence at runtime, expressions cannot reflect on modules nor can they manipulate them. If a program is well-typed it conforms to the information hiding rules. Later at runtime, the module structure can be ignored as it is no longer needed. Of course, one can defer static evaluation of information hiding to runtime – this is not pursued any further, because static type checking can be considered superior.

3.3.1. Syntax

Syntax The syntax is minimal, though expressive enough to demonstrate relevant features and interaction of the added features together with core features of QVT-O. The abstract syntax is presented in Figure 3.2 using a variant of the Backus-Naur form. A transformation T comprises three parts, metamodel definitions, interface definitions, and module implementations, the latter defining mapping implementations with a minimal QVT-O syntax.

Metavariables p, c, f, i, t, s, x range over unique names of packages, classes, fields, interfaces, domains, mappings, and both arguments and vari-

Syntax:

T	$::=$	$\overline{P}\,\overline{I}\,\overline{M}$	Transformation program
P	$::=$	$\texttt{package}\ p\ \{\ \overline{P}\,\overline{C}\ \}$	Metamodel specification
C	$::=$	$\texttt{class}\ c\ (\texttt{extends}\ c')^?\ \{\ \overline{F}\ \}$	Class declaration
F	$::=$	$(\texttt{composes} \mid \texttt{references})\ f\ :\ c\ (\texttt{[1]} \mid \texttt{[*]})\texttt{;}$	Feature declaration
I	$::=$	$\texttt{transformation}\,\texttt{interface}\ i$ $(\overline{(\texttt{in} \mid \texttt{out})\ t : p})\ \{\ \overline{V}\,\overline{S}\ \}$	Module interface declaration
V	$::=$	$\texttt{scope}\ (\texttt{in} \mid \texttt{out})\ p\texttt{[}\overline{p'}\,\overline{c}\texttt{];}$	Model scope declaration
S	$::=$	$\texttt{mapping}\ c\ \texttt{::}\ s\texttt{(}\overline{\texttt{in}\ c'}\texttt{)} : c''\texttt{;}$	Method signature declaration
M	$::=$	$\texttt{transformation}\,\texttt{module}\ m$ $\texttt{export}\ i\ (\texttt{import}\ \overline{j})^?\ \{\ \overline{O}\ \}$	Module implementation def.
O	$::=$	$\texttt{mapping}\ c\ \texttt{::}\ s\texttt{(}\overline{\texttt{in}\ x : c'}\texttt{)} : c''$ $(\texttt{inherits}\ \overline{s'})^?\ \{\ \overline{B}\ \}$	Method implementation def.
B	$::=$	$\texttt{result.}f\ \texttt{:=}\ E\texttt{;}$	Assignment
E	$::=$	$E\texttt{.late}\,\texttt{resolveone(}c\texttt{)}$	Trace resolution call
	$\mid$	$E\ \texttt{->map}\ s\ \texttt{(}\overline{x}\texttt{)}$	Mapping invocation
	$\mid$	$E\texttt{.oclIsTypeOf(}c\texttt{)}$	Type checking
	$\mid$	$E\texttt{.}f$	Feature access
	$\mid$	$\texttt{new}\ c(\overline{E})$	Class instantiation
	$\mid$	$\texttt{self}$	Context access
	$\mid$	x	Variable access

Figure 3.2: Core QVT-OM's syntax.

ables, respectively. Typing judgments on sequences are abbreviated, $\overline{P}$ is shorthand for whitespace or comma separated lists $P_1 \ldots P_n$ with zero or a finite number of elements, analogous for $\overline{C}$, $\overline{F}$, $\overline{V}$, $\overline{S}$, $\overline{O}$, $\overline{B}$. The ? operator marks grammatical expressions as optional, the | operator separates alternative choices.

Metamodels are formulated with the same notation as described in the QVT specification, with one extension: Packages p not only define classes, they define subpackages as well. A class c can inherit from another class c', and define contained or referenced elements. A field f is typed with a class c and can have multiplicities 1 or $0..*$.

As an example, Listing 3.2 defines both example models, Activity and Process, in a simple textual syntax that is described in the QVT specifi-

Metamodel primitives:

$$\texttt{package}\ \mathcal{G}\ \texttt{\{ class Object \{\}; class Boolean \{\}; class String \{\}; \}}$$

Metamodel subtyping:

$$c <: c \qquad \frac{c <: c' \quad c' <: c''}{c <: c''} \qquad \frac{\texttt{class}\ c\ \texttt{extends}\ c'\ \texttt{\{ ... \}}}{c <: c' \quad c <: \texttt{Object}} \qquad \frac{\texttt{class}\ c\ \texttt{\{ ... \}}}{c <: \texttt{Object}}$$

Lookup of metamodel packages, classes and features:

$$\frac{\texttt{class}\ c\ (\texttt{extends}\ c')^?\ \texttt{\{...\}}}{classes_C(c) = c, classes_C\big((c')^?\big)}$$

$$\frac{\begin{array}{c}\texttt{package}\ p\ \texttt{\{}\ \overline{P}\,\overline{C}\ \texttt{\}} \\ \overline{P} = \overline{\texttt{package}\ p'\ \texttt{\{...\}}} \qquad \overline{C} = \overline{\texttt{class}\ c\ (\texttt{extends}\ c')^?\ \texttt{\{...\}}}\end{array}}{packages_P(p) = \overline{p'} \qquad classes_P(p) = \overline{c}, \left[_k\ classes_C\big((c'_k)^?\big)\ \right]}$$

$$\frac{\texttt{class}\ c\ (\texttt{extends}\ c')^?\ \texttt{\{}\ \overline{(\texttt{composes} \mid \texttt{references})\ f\ :\ c\ (\texttt{[1]} \mid \texttt{[*]})\texttt{;}}\ \texttt{\}}}{features_C(c) = features_C\big((c')^?\big), \overline{f} : \overline{c}}$$

Lookup of declared and implemented mapping types:

$$\frac{\begin{array}{c}\texttt{transformation interface}\ i\ \ldots\ \texttt{\{}\ \overline{V}\,\overline{S}\ \texttt{\}} \\ S = \texttt{mapping}\ c\ \texttt{::}\ s\texttt{(}\overline{\texttt{in}\ c'}\texttt{)}\ \texttt{:}\ c''\end{array}}{mappings_I(i) = \bigcup_{S \in \overline{S}} \Big\{(i, c, s, \overline{c'}, c'')\Big\}}$$

$$\frac{\begin{array}{c}\texttt{transformation module}\ m\ \ldots\ \texttt{\{}\ \overline{O}\ \texttt{\}} \\ O = \texttt{mapping}\ c\ \texttt{::}\ s\texttt{(}\overline{\texttt{in}\ x : c'}\texttt{)}\ \texttt{:}\ c''\ \ldots\ \texttt{\{...\}}\end{array}}{mappings_M(m) = \bigcup_{O \in \overline{O}} \Big\{(\texttt{this}, c, s, \overline{c'}, c'')\Big\}}$$

Lookup of declared model scope:

$$\frac{\begin{array}{c}\texttt{transformation interface}\ i\ \ldots\ \texttt{\{}\ \overline{V}\,\overline{S}\ \texttt{\}} \\ S = \texttt{mapping}\ c\ \texttt{::}\ s\texttt{(}\overline{\texttt{in}\ c'}\texttt{)}\ \texttt{:}\ c''\end{array}}{scope_M(i) = \bigcup_{S \in \overline{S}} \Big(\{c, c''\} \cup \bigcup_k c'_k\Big) \times \{\texttt{in}\}}$$

$$\frac{\begin{array}{c}\texttt{transformation interface}\ i\ \ldots\ \texttt{\{}\ \overline{V}\,\overline{S}\ \texttt{\}} \\ V = \texttt{scope}\ (a = \texttt{in} \mid \texttt{out})\ p\texttt{[}\overline{p'}\ \overline{c}\texttt{]} \\ \texttt{transformation module}\ m\ \texttt{export}\overline{i}\ (\texttt{import}\overline{j})^?\ \texttt{\{ ... \}}\end{array}}{\begin{array}{c} scope_I(i) = \bigcup_{V \in \overline{V}} \Big(\bigcup_k \big(classes_P(\overline{p'}_k) \cup classes_C(c_k)\big) \times \{a_k\}\Big) \\ \cup \bigcup_k scope_M(j_k) \cup \big(classes_P(\mathcal{G}) \times \{\texttt{out}\}\big)\end{array}}$$

Figure 3.3: Core-QVT-OM's primitives, subtyping rules, and auxiliary functions.

cation [Obj11]. Package `CompositeActions` that imports root package `ActivityModel` for extension is omitted. The namespace concept known from the UML's Meta-Object Facilities (MOF) superstructure is used to group classes and subpackages. In this case, root packages `ActivityModel` and `ProcessModel` represent the metamodels.

Module structure is well-formed:

$$\frac{\vdash \overline{I}\ \mathtt{WF} \qquad \vdash \overline{M}\ \mathtt{WF}}{\vdash T\ \mathtt{WF}} \tag{WF-Program}$$

$$\frac{\begin{array}{l} \forall V \in \overline{V},\ V = \mathtt{scope}\ (b = \mathtt{in} \mid \mathtt{out})\ p'\ \mathtt{[}\overline{p''}\ \overline{c}\mathtt{]} : \\ \overline{p''}_k \subset \mathit{packages_P}^{+}(p'_k) \wedge \mathit{classes_C}^{*}(\overline{c}_k) \subset \mathit{classes_P}^{*}\left(\mathit{packages_P}^{+}(p_k)\right) \wedge \exists\, l : p' = \overline{p}_l \\ \qquad\qquad \Delta\left[\ \mathit{scope_I}(i)\ \right] \vdash \overline{S}\ \mathtt{WF} \end{array}}{\vdash \mathtt{transformation\,interface}\ i\ \mathtt{(}\overline{(a = \mathtt{in} \mid \mathtt{out})\ t : p}\mathtt{)}\ \mathtt{\{}\ \overline{V}\ \overline{S}\ \mathtt{\}}\ \mathtt{WF}} \tag{WF-Interface}$$

$$\frac{\begin{array}{c} \mathtt{transformation\,module}\ m\ \mathtt{export}\ i\ \ldots\ \mathtt{\{\ldots\}} \\ \mathit{mappings_M}(m) \ni (\mathtt{this}, c_0, s, \overline{c'_0}, c''_0) \\ \Delta \ni (c,\cdot), (\overline{c'},\cdot), (c'',\mathtt{out}) \\ c_0 <: c \qquad \overline{c'} <: \overline{c'_0} \qquad c'' <: c''_0 \end{array}}{\vdash \mathtt{mapping}\ c\ \mathtt{::}\ s\mathtt{(}\overline{\mathtt{in}\ c'}\mathtt{)}\ \mathtt{:}\ c''\ \mathtt{WF}} \tag{WF-MappingDecl}$$

$$\frac{\begin{array}{l} \quad \mathtt{transformation\,module}\ m'\ \mathtt{export}\ i\ \ldots\ \mathtt{\{\ldots\}} \Rightarrow m' = m \\ \quad \mathtt{transformation\,interface}\ i\ \mathtt{(}\overline{a = (\mathtt{in} \mid \mathtt{out})\ t : p}\mathtt{)}\ \mathtt{\{\ldots\}} \\ \forall\, k,n : \mathtt{transformation\,interface}\ \overline{j}_k\ \mathtt{(}\overline{(c = \mathtt{in} \mid \mathtt{out})\ t' : p'''}\mathtt{)}\ \mathtt{\{\ldots\}} \Rightarrow \\ \quad \overline{a}_n = \overline{c}_n \wedge \overline{t}_n = \overline{t'}_n \wedge \overline{p}_n = \overline{p'''}_n \\ \Delta\left[\ \mathit{scope_I}(i)\ \right], \Omega\left[\ (\cup_k \mathit{mappings_I}(\overline{j}_k)) \cup \mathit{mappings_M}(m)\ \right] \vdash \overline{O}\ \mathtt{WF} \end{array}}{\vdash \mathtt{transformation\,module}\ m\ \mathtt{export}\ i\ \mathtt{(import}\ \overline{j}\mathtt{)}^{?}\ \mathtt{\{}\ \overline{O}\ \mathtt{\}}\ \mathtt{WF}} \tag{WF-Module}$$

$$\frac{\begin{array}{c} \Delta \ni (c,\cdot), (\overline{c'},\cdot), (c'',\mathtt{out}) \\ \Gamma[\mathtt{self} \mapsto c, \overline{x} \mapsto \overline{c'}, \mathtt{result} \mapsto c''], \Delta, \Omega \vdash \overline{B}\ \mathtt{WF} \end{array}}{\Delta, \Omega \vdash \mathtt{mapping}\ c\ \mathtt{::}\ s\mathtt{(}\overline{\mathtt{in}\ x : c'}\mathtt{)}\ \mathtt{:}\ c''\ \mathtt{\{}\ \overline{B}\ \mathtt{\}}\ \mathtt{WF}} \tag{WF-MappingImpl}$$

$$\frac{\begin{array}{c} \Gamma(\mathtt{result}) = c \qquad c_0 <: c' \qquad \Delta \ni (c,\mathtt{out}), (c_0,\cdot) \\ \mathit{features_C}(c) \ni f : c' \qquad \Gamma, \Delta, \Omega \vdash e_0 : c_0 \end{array}}{\Gamma, \Delta, \Omega \vdash \mathtt{result}.f\ \mathtt{:=}\ e_0\mathtt{;}\ \mathtt{WF}} \tag{WF-Assignment}$$

(a) Well-formedness rules

Expression typing and conformance checks:

$$\frac{\Gamma,\Delta,\Omega \vdash e_0 : c_0 \qquad \Delta \ni (c_0,\cdot) \qquad \Delta \ni (c,\cdot)}{\Gamma,\Delta,\Omega \vdash e_0\texttt{.late resolveone(}c\texttt{)} : c} \quad \text{(T-TRACERES)}$$

$$\frac{\begin{array}{c} c_0 <: c \qquad \overline{c} <: \overline{c'} \qquad \Delta \ni (c_0,\cdot),(c'',\cdot),(\overline{c},\cdot) \\ \Omega \ni (i,c,s,\overline{c'},c'') \qquad (\cdot,\hat{c},s,\overline{c'},c'') \in \Omega \Rightarrow c <: \hat{c} \\ \Gamma,\Delta,\Omega \vdash e_0 : c_0 \qquad \Gamma,\Delta,\Omega \vdash \overline{e} : \overline{c} \end{array}}{\Gamma,\Delta,\Omega \vdash e_0\texttt{->map}\ s\ \texttt{(}\overline{e}\texttt{)} : c''} \quad \text{(T-MAPPINGINV)}$$

$$\frac{\Gamma,\Delta,\Omega \vdash e_0 : c_0 \qquad \Delta \ni (c,\cdot)}{\Gamma,\Delta,\Omega \vdash e_0\texttt{.oclIsTypeOf(}c\texttt{)} : \texttt{Boolean}} \quad \text{(T-TYPECHECK)}$$

$$\frac{\begin{array}{c} \mathit{features}_C(c_0) = \overline{f} : \overline{c} \\ \Gamma,\Delta,\Omega \vdash e_0 : c_0 \qquad \Delta \ni (c_0,\cdot),(c_i,\texttt{out}) \end{array}}{\Gamma,\Delta,\Omega \vdash e_0\texttt{.}f_i : c_i} \quad \text{(T-FEATURE)}$$

$$\frac{\Gamma,\Delta,\Omega \vdash \overline{e} : \overline{c'} \qquad \Delta \ni (c,\texttt{out}),(\overline{c'},\cdot)}{\Gamma,\Delta,\Omega \vdash \texttt{new}\ c(\overline{e}) : c} \quad \text{(T-CLASSINST)}$$

$$\frac{\Gamma(\texttt{self}) = c \qquad \Delta \ni (c,\cdot)}{\Gamma,\Delta \vdash \texttt{self} : c} \quad \text{(T-CONTEXT)}$$

$$\frac{\Gamma(x) = c \qquad \Delta \ni (c,\cdot)}{\Gamma,\Delta \vdash x : \Gamma(x)} \quad \text{(T-VARIABLE)}$$

(b) Expression typing rules

Figure 3.4: Core-QVT-OM's typing rules.

A module interface i specifies a list of model domains $\overline{t : p}$ the transformation unit is operating on, where a domain either acts as input or output (`in` or `out`). A domain owns a unique model domain identifier t that is part of any model element reference, and that is typed by a root package p. Interface declarations comprise declarations of model scope $\overline{V}$ and method signatures $\overline{S}$. A model scope declarations commences with an access modifier and a root package p, followed by the exact elements contained in the root package that are accessible by implementations must be declared in trailing square brackets. This can be a list of classes $\overline{c'}$ and packages $\overline{p'}$. Naming a package equals to naming all directly contained classes in the package. Method signatures of mappings are identical to QVT-O's syntax. Each metamodel

```
package ActivityModel {
  class Activity { composes actions : Action [*]; }
  class Action { references successor : Action [0..1]; }
  class StartAction extends Action { }
  class StopAction extends Action { }
}
package ProcessModel {
  class Process { composes steps : Step [*]; }
  class Step {
    references next : Step [0..1];
    composes isStart : Boolean [1];
    composes isStop : Boolean [1];
  }
}
```

Listing 3.2: Activity2Process example – Source and target models

element, the calling context c, parameters $\overline{c'}$ and the target element c'', is prefixed by the respective domain that marks the context, t, $\overline{t'}$, and t''.

A module m implements exactly one interface i. To do so, it can rely on one or more interfaces $\overline{j}$. This time, mapping signatures are supplemented by a list of statements. Again, this syntax is limited for the sake of simplicity – we imagine a full QVT-OM where module implementation definitions can implement multiple interfaces, and where syntax spans the full range of statements available in QVT-O. Assignment expressions can be used to setup fields of target model elements built from QVT-O expressions. We have seven types of expressions in Core QVT-OM: Querying a target object created from a source object, invoking a mapping s defined by an exported or imported interface j, checking the type of an expression, accessing a field f, instantiating a class c in domain t with constructor parameters $\overline{e}$, accessing the surrounding mapping's source context, and accessing an argument or variable x. This is a valid subset of QVT-O's rich syntax. We now aim at showing how information hiding is enforced on this variety of concepts.

Metamodel primitives and subtyping To any metamodel defined, a global package $\mathcal{G}$ introduces the primitive data types `Object`, `Boolean`, and `String`, see the upper section in Figure 3.3. Respective fields have been omitted for simplicity.

Like in FJ, a subtyping relationship between classes is established by an operator <: that is based on the `extends` keyword. Subtyping is reflexive, transitive, but also antisymmetric, i.e. no cycles are permitted. For convenience, any class except `Object` inherits from `Object` by default. The middle section in Figure 3.3 lists the subtyping rules for our language.

Auxiliary methods We introduce auxiliary methods for metamodel and mapping lookup. These methods are utilized by the typing rules hereinafter, they are defined in Figure 3.3 in the lower section. Function $classes_C : C \rightarrow \mathcal{P}(\mathbb{N} \times C)$ maps a class to a list of inherited classes including itself. In case that $(\texttt{extends } c')^?$ is omitted, c' evaluates to `Object`, and $classes_C(\texttt{Object}) = \varepsilon$. For a given package, functions $packages_P : P \rightarrow \mathcal{P}(\mathbb{N} \times P)$ and $classes_P : P \rightarrow \mathcal{P}(\mathbb{N} \times C)$ compute all packages and classes directly contained in the package, respectively. And finally, for a given class, function $features_C : C \rightarrow \mathcal{P}(\mathbb{N} \times F)$ retrieves directly contained features. Note that here – and similarly, in the rest of this section –, for brevity, we abbreviate typing judgments on sequences, writing $\overline{f} : \overline{k}$ as shorthand for $f_1 : k_1, \ \ldots, \ f_n : k_n$ (cf. [IPW01]).

Function $mappings_I : I \rightarrow \big((I \times S) \rightarrow ((C \times \mathcal{P}(\mathbb{N} \times C)) \times C)\big)$ creates for a given interface identifier a function that relates pairs of interface and mapping identifiers to the mapping's signature type. Analogously, $mappings_M : M \rightarrow \big((I \times S) \rightarrow ((C \times \mathcal{P}(\mathbb{N} \times C)) \times C)\big)$ creates such a function for any mapping defined in a module implementation – here, we use `this` for identifying the interface whose implementation is currently being defined.

The scope of model elements that are accessible for implementations of an interface i is computed by functions $scope_M, scope_I : I \rightarrow \mathcal{P}(\mathbb{N} \times \{\texttt{in}, \texttt{out}\})$, where $scope_M$ evaluates explicit scope definitions and joins types that are implicitly accessible. The latter are accumulated by $scope_I$ and comprise context, parameter and return types of imported methods; these types must be read-accessible by implementations to execute a delegating call and further process the returned value. In addition, primitive types are globally defined.

For any of these functions being special kinds of binary relations, the $+$ operator denotes their transitive closure. The $*$ operator is short for a functional closure on sets, for instance, $classes_P{}^*(P) := \bigcup_{p \in P} classes_P(p)$.

3.3.2. Typing

We build a type system in the style of the classical Hindley-Milner type system. Several ideas and many notational elements are borrowed from FJ [IPW01]. Primary judgment of our type system is that of type well-formedness with respect to the modular structure, $\vdash T$ WF. To attain this goal, we must judge about the typing of expressions to determine any explicit and implicit type references. We use a type system where typing relations take the form $\Gamma, \Delta, \Omega \vdash e : t$. This reads: "In a scoped type environment Γ, Ω, Δ of variables, methods, and model elements, the term e has type t".

We capture scoping information in a type environment that consists of three parts: a variable environment Γ, a method environment Ω, and a model element environment Δ. The variable environment is a function mapping identifiers in scope to types, $\Gamma ::= \emptyset \mid \Gamma, [^n_{k=0}\; v_k \mapsto c_k]$. The method environment stores quintuples that consist of interface identifier, context type, mapping identifier, parameter types, and return type, $\Omega ::= \emptyset \mid \Omega, [^n_{k=0}\; (i, c_k, s_k, \overline{c'}_k, c''_k)]$. Similarly, the model element environment captures accessible model elements, $\Delta ::= \emptyset \mid \Delta, [^n_{k=0}\; (c_k, a_k)]$, where c_k is the class identifier and a_k is the access type, in or out, the pair of both defining accessibility for a single class.

Notation $\Gamma[x_0 \mapsto c_0,\ \ldots,\ x_n \mapsto c_n]$ is the type environment Γ updated at $x_k, k = 0..n$ to map x_k to c_k. For an overlined syntax expression $\overline{x : c}$, type variables are represented as sequences $(x_k)^n_{k=0}$, $(t_k)^n_{k=0}$, and $(c_k)^n_{k=0}$. Then,

$\Gamma[\overline{x} : \overline{c}]$, $\Gamma[_k\ x_k \mapsto c_k]$, and $\Gamma[\{x_0 \mapsto c_0,\ \ldots,\ x_n \mapsto c_n\}]$ are short forms for the notation mentioned above.

Type inference rules are displayed in Figure 3.4. They are completely syntax directed, thus defining small-step semantics. As we already mentioned, our type system is designed to prove that a modular transformation program in Core QVT-OM is well-formed regarding the information hiding principle. In accordance with Rule WF-PROGRAM (Figure 3.4a), A transformation program T is only then well-formed, if its interface definitions and module implementations are well-formed.

An interface signature defines a sequence of modeling domains on packages $\overline{p}$, and model scope statements declare for each domain a list of packages $\overline{p'}$ and classes $\overline{c}$ on which access is opened up. These elements must be (directly or transitively) contained in the respective domain's root package p (Rule WF-INTERFACE). It is also ensured that scope information is only given for packages that are part of the transformation signature.With the auxiliary function $scope_I$, an environment Δ is built that contains the list of accessible classes.

Now, mapping signatures declared inside the interface definition are tested to be wellformed. Any of these declared signatures must be implemented by a module m with compatible types, and any type used must be accessible (Rule WF-MAPPINGDECL). Type conformance is checked according to the Liskov principle, and accessibility is checked based on the Δ environment. Remember that $\Delta \ni (\overline{c'}, \cdot)$ is shorthand syntax for $\Delta \ni (c'_0, \texttt{in}) \vee \Delta \ni (c'_0, \texttt{out}), \Delta \ni (c'_1, \texttt{in}) \vee \Delta \ni (c'_1, \texttt{out}), \ldots, \Delta \ni (c'_n, \texttt{in}) \vee \Delta \ni (c'_n, \texttt{out})$ with n representing the length of list $\overline{c'}$, $n := \#\overline{c'} - 1$. The dot operator $\cdot$ is a placeholder for arbitrary values in a tuple ("don't care" semantics), and is used whenever a type is tested for read access, because a declared write access encompasses read accessibility.

Rule WF-MODULE makes sure that there is exactly one implementation per interface defined. The transformation signature of the implemented interface and imported interfaces must be identical. A module inherits model visibilities from the interface it implements, so Δ is configured in the same way as in Rule WF-INTERFACE. The Ω environment is filled with methods provided by imported interfaces plus those defined locally.

According to Rule WF-MAPPINGIMPL, a mapping implementation must have any of its signature's type accessible. Two variables plus their respective types are added to its scope, `self` and `result`. In the body of a mapping, the target object's features can be initialized. Rule WF-ASSIGNMENT states that the target object's features used here must be a valid feature of the object's type, both sides of the assignment must have matching types, and the result's type must be write accessible. Please note that only the feature's parent object is modified, hence only the feature's parent type must be permitted write access on the left-hand side of an expression.

Expression typing presented in Figure 3.4b is obvious, insofar that we infer for each syntactical element related types, and check that the element is visible and excels a valid accessibility mode. Rule T-TRACERES tests the context and return type for accessibility. Rule T-MAPPINGINV checks read-access rights that arise from mapping invocations; these are implicitly permitted as long as the called mapping has been imported correctly (see our explanations on Rule WF-MODULE). The rule also ensures that parameter types are compatible, and ensures that the mapping with the closest context type is chosen if overloaded methods exist. Checks on a specific type require the context type and the type checked against to be accessible (Rule T-TYPECHECK). Access to a feature demands read access to the parent type and the feature type, which must be a valid feature of the given class (Rule T-FEATURE). If an object is created, we check if its type is write accessible, and if parameter types of the constructor are read accessible (Rule T-CLASSINST). Context and variables are checked if they are in scope and their type is at least read accessible (Rules T-CONTEXT, T-VARIABLE).

$$
\begin{array}{l}
\Gamma(\texttt{self}) = \texttt{Activity}\\
\Delta \ni (\texttt{Activity},\cdot) \quad (\text{T-CONTEXT})\\
\hline
\mathit{features}_C(\texttt{Activity}) \ni \texttt{actions} : \texttt{Action[}*\texttt{]}\\
\Gamma,\Delta,\Omega \vdash \texttt{\textbf{self}} : \texttt{Activity}\\
\Delta \ni (\texttt{Activity},\cdot),(\texttt{Action},\texttt{\textbf{out}}) \qquad (\text{T-FEATURE})\\
\hline
\texttt{Action} <: \texttt{Action} \qquad \overline{c} = \emptyset\\
\Omega \ni (\texttt{IAction2Step},\texttt{Action},\texttt{mapAction2Step},\emptyset,\texttt{Step})\\
\Gamma,\Delta,\Omega \vdash \texttt{\textbf{self}}\texttt{.actions} : \texttt{Action} : \texttt{Action[}*\texttt{]} \qquad (\text{T-MAPPINGINV})\\
\hline
\Gamma(\texttt{\textbf{result}}) = \texttt{Process} \qquad \texttt{Step[}*\texttt{]} <: \texttt{Step[}*\texttt{]}\\
\Delta \ni (\texttt{Process},\texttt{\textbf{out}}),(\texttt{Step},\cdot) \qquad \mathit{features}_C(\texttt{Process}) \ni \texttt{steps} : \texttt{Step[}*\texttt{]}\\
\Gamma,\Delta,\Omega \vdash \texttt{\textbf{self}}\texttt{.actions->}\\
\qquad \texttt{\textbf{map}}\ \texttt{mapAction2Step()} : \texttt{Step[}*\texttt{]} \qquad (\text{WF-ASSIGNMENT})\\
\hline
\Delta \ni (\texttt{Activity},\cdot),(\texttt{Process},\texttt{\textbf{out}})\\
\Gamma = \{\ \texttt{\textbf{self}} \mapsto \texttt{Activity}, \texttt{\textbf{result}} \mapsto \texttt{Process}\ \},\Delta,\Omega\\
\quad \vdash \overline{B} = \texttt{\textbf{result}}\texttt{.steps := }\texttt{\textbf{self}}\texttt{.actions->}\\
\qquad \texttt{\textbf{map}}\ \texttt{mapAction2Step();}\ \texttt{\textbf{WF}} \quad (\text{WF-MAPPINGIMPL})\\
\hline
\texttt{\textbf{transformation module}}\ m'\ \texttt{\textbf{export}}\texttt{IMain}\ \{\ldots\}\\
\quad \Rightarrow m' = \texttt{Activity2Process}\\
\Delta = \{\ (\texttt{Activity},\texttt{\textbf{in}}),(\texttt{Process},\texttt{\textbf{out}})\ \} \cup\\
\quad \{\ (\texttt{Action},\texttt{\textbf{in}}),(\texttt{StartAction},\texttt{\textbf{in}}),(\texttt{StopAction},\texttt{\textbf{in}}),(\texttt{Step},\texttt{\textbf{out}})\ \} \cup\\
\quad \{\ (\texttt{Object},\texttt{\textbf{out}}),(\texttt{Boolean},\texttt{\textbf{out}}),(\texttt{String},\texttt{\textbf{out}})\ \}\\
\Omega = \{\ (\texttt{IMain},\texttt{Activity},\texttt{mapActivity2Process},\emptyset,\texttt{Process}),\\
\quad (\texttt{IAction2Step},\texttt{Action},\texttt{mapAction2Step},\emptyset,\texttt{Step}),\\
\quad (\texttt{IAction2Step},\texttt{StartAction},\texttt{mapAction2Step},\emptyset,\texttt{Step}),\\
\quad (\texttt{IAction2Step},\texttt{StopAction},\texttt{mapAction2Step},\emptyset,\texttt{Step})\ \}\\
\quad \vdash \overline{O} = \texttt{\textbf{mapping}}\ \texttt{Activity::mapActivity2Process()}\\
\qquad : \texttt{Process}\ \{\ \overline{B}\ \}\ \texttt{\textbf{WF}} \qquad (\text{WF-MODULE})\\
\hline
\vdash \texttt{\textbf{transformation module}}\ \texttt{Activity2Process}\\
\quad \texttt{\textbf{export}}\ \texttt{IMain}\ \{\ \overline{O}\ \}\ \texttt{\textbf{WF}}
\end{array}
$$

Figure 3.5: Example inference rules – Interface-compliant implementation of module Activity2Process.

3.3.3. Example Derivation

For a better understanding of the typing rules, we give an example derivation on a subset of the Activity2Process example. We exclude the third module `CompositeAction2Step`, as it uses syntactical elements not covered by our core calculus. For this, we have to remove the import statement in line 4 of Listing 3.1a.

We start right after Rule WF-PROGRAM, has been applied, demanding to show well-formedness for interface declarations and implementation definitions of both modules.

The derivation given in Figure 3.5 aims to show that the implementation of the main module, module `Activity2Process`, is wellformed according to our rewriting system. Six rules are applied, Rules WF-MODULE, WF-MAPPINGIMPL, WF-ASSIGNMENT, T-MAPPINGINV, T-FEATURE, and T-CONTEXT, one for each structural element of our syntax.

Rule WF-MODULE verifies that there is not a second implementation of the same interface, and builds two environments, the Δ and the Ω environment. The Δ environment captures all the model elements that are in scope, and the Ω environment captures all mappings that are in scope, these are mappings from imported interfaces, and local mappings.

Then, Rule WF-MAPPINGIMPL is applied to each of the module's mappings. There is only one mapping defined, method `mapActivity2-Process`. There are two premises, one queries the Δ environment, if all parameters are correctly accessible. The other updates the Γ environment by adding variables `self` and `result` that represent the context and return value, variables for each input parameter. To each of the variables the declared type is assigned.

The rule asks to give evidence that the methods body is wellformed, which consists of a single assignment statement, on which we can apply Rule T-ASSIGNMENT. This boils down to several premises that query the feature type to test accessibility and type compatibility of the left and right hand side expressions.

The remaining expression is call statement, so we can apply Rule T-MappingInv. There are three methods in scope whose context, parameter and return type would match, though we must only provide one of them. Later at runtime, dynamic dispatching comes into play. Type conformance according to Liskov's substitution principle is approved on context and input parameters. In our example, we only need to check the context parameter.

The next rule, Rule T-Feature, ascertains that class Activity actually possesses a feature `actions` that is accessed here, and that the feature's type is read accessible. T-Context is the last rule which applies. Finally, Rule T-Context retrieves the type of variable `self`, and ascertains that it is in scope.

3.3.4. Properties

Now that syntax and typing rules are defined, we must give evidence that hiding actually works, i.e., a program is well-typed if and only if it is abstraction safe.

Type systems generally help to detect the presence of a class of type-related runtime errors, called syntactic *type safety*. Soundness of the semantics with respect to a type system generally means that "well-typed programs cannot go wrong", and can be justified on the basis of two properties, progress and preservation. Since we mainly reuse typing rules from the OCL and QVT, we assume our type system to be type safe. We can do so, since modularity here is not first-class, i.e., a module itself cannot be reasoned about in the program. Thus, typing of our abstraction mechanism is distinct from expression typing, although conformance of module implementations to their interfaces rest upon subtyping rules.

However, added syntactical elements and the type system have been particularly designed for the purpose of enforcing *abstraction safety*. Abstraction safety ascertains that well-typed programs at runtime abide to the information hiding principle. Assuming syntactic type safety, what remains to be shown is that the type system establishes representation independence and representation invariants (cf. Section 2.3). Both of these properties are captured by rules R1 and R2 postulated in Section 3.1 at the beginning of this chapter. In the following, we formalize our rules, and provide proof sketches for each of them.

R1: Separation of interfaces from their implementations This property relates to representation independence. According to Pierce's definition [Pie02], separation is possible exactly when modules that implement the same interface can be exchanged while maintaining type conformance.

Theorem 3.3.1. *For any pair of transformations T and T', where*

$$\begin{aligned} T &= \overline{P}\,\overline{I}\,M_0 \ldots M_k \ldots M_n \\ T' &= \overline{P}\,\overline{I}\,M_0 \ldots M'_k \ldots M_n\,, \end{aligned}$$

with module implementations M_k, M'_k of the same name $m_k = m'_k$, both exporting the same interface $i_k = i'_k$, and both being well-formed, i.e., $\vdash M\ \mathtt{WF}$ and $\vdash M'\ \mathtt{WF}$, we can say that $\vdash T\ \mathtt{WF} \Leftrightarrow \vdash T'\ \mathtt{WF}$.

Proof. In the type system, wellformedness is checked independently for each module implementation: a transformation T is wellformed iff interfaces and implementations are wellformed (WF-PROGRAM). A module implementation may only reference methods declared in one of its imported interfaces. Method signatures are bound to exactly one method implementation of exactly one implementation of that module, secured by WF-MAPPINGDECL. Required and provided method signatures must be compatible in terms of Liskov's substitution principle, as encoded by rules WF-MAPPINGDECL for module implementations and T-MAPPINGINV for method invocations. Therefore, any module implementation remains independent of any other module implementations. □

R2: Conformance of interface and implementation This rule corresponds to representation invariants of our module system. There are certain invariants enforced upon a module implementation by the interface that it implements: Firstly, all of the method signatures declared in the interface must be implemented. Secondly, implemented code must obey access restrictions on externally defined methods, and thirdly, it must only access model elements declared to be in scope. We go through each class of invariant by providing a formal definition and a proof sketch.

R2a: Method provisioning A program is only then well-formed if there exists exactly one implementation per interface. If an interface misses an implementation potential method calls cannot be resolved. If an interface is implemented multiple times it is not clearly expressed which implementation to choose, resulting in nondeterministic behavior.

Theorem 3.3.2. *For any interface $i \in I$, there exists exactly one implementation $m \in M$ for i. For this implementation we can find exactly one bijective mapping between implementation and interface methods $f_{m,i} : O|_m \to S|_i$, so that each method $o \in O|_m$ maps to a method $s \in S|_i$ with equal name and an equal number of arguments, $o = s$ and $|\overline{c'_o}| = |\overline{c'_s}|$, and signature types are pairwise compatible according to Liskov (contravariant argument types, covariant return types).*

Proof. Suppose for an implementation $m \in M$ of interface $i \in I$ exists another implementation $m' \in M$ of that same interface. Then, implementations m, m' must be identical, as guaranteed by rule WF-MODULE: $m = m'$. In addition, WF-MAPPINGDECL guarantees that for any method implementation (which there must be exactly one, as we have just shown), type conformance constraints according to Liskov are met. □

R2b: Method access control In an implementation, only model types or mappings are referenced that are imported by the prefixed interface, and the interface is imported by the implemented interface.

Theorem 3.3.3. *For any implementation of a module m,*

$$\texttt{transformationmodule}\ m\ \texttt{export}\ i\ (\texttt{import}\ \overline{j})^?\ ,$$

if a method implementation $o \in O|_m$ references a method o that is not locally defined, then it must be defined in at least one of the imported interfaces, $j' \in \overline{j}$, and the signature of o is compatible (regarding to Liskov's substitution principle) to the signature of o specified in the interface j'.

Proof. Only mapping invocation expressions may refer to methods by the method's name o and a list of variables. There are two cases, either a called mapping o is defined locally with matching parameter types, or the mapping is dereferenced by imported interfaces. By inquiring the Ω environment, rule T-MappingInv ascertains that only methods in scope (i.e., local or imported ones) are referenced. The same rule tests for type conformance, as well. □

R2c: Model access control In an implementation, only those model types are referenced for read or write access in a specific domain whose respective access mode is declared for this model type and domain type in the interface that is implemented.

Theorem 3.3.4. *For any expression's inferred type, $\vdash e : c$, model type c must be defined as read-accessible in the respective domain t by the surrounding module's interface, except if access is delegated to another module. It must be write-accessible if features are created or modified. Additionally, for any parameter being part of a mapping or OCL operation's signature, its type c must be defined as accessible with the correct mode (read- or write-accessible for context and input parameters, write-accessible for output and return parameter types) in the respective domain t by the surrounding module's interface.*

Proof. For any expression that is defined in the syntax, a type is inferred by an expression typing rule. There, we can find a precondition in the form of $(c, \cdot) \in \Delta$ for read access checks, and $(c, \texttt{out}) \in \Delta$ for write access checks, depending on the underlying dynamic semantics; exceptions are T-TRACERES and T-MAPPINGINV which delegate to external modules. The same is true for method parameters (rules WF-MAPPINGDECL, WF-MAPPINGIMPL) and assignments (rule WF-ASSIGNMENT). □

Abstraction Safety A program is considered as being well-typed if and only if it does not hurt the information hiding principle.

Corollary 3.3.5. *Let T be a transformation program in valid Core QVT-OM syntax. If* $\vdash T$ WF*, transformation T does not hurt the principle of information hiding as described by rules R1 and R2a to R2c.*

Proof. From the proofs of Theorems 3.3.1 to 3.3.4 immediately follows soundness of our module concept with respect to abstraction safety properties. □

Decidability Because type inference rules are syntax directed, there is only one conclusion for each syntactic form. Evaluation will only get stuck if one of two kinds of premises remains unfulfilled, type conformance or accessibility. If and only if our type system terminates on a program with $\vdash T$ WF, it is well-formed. Hence the type system is decidable, and an efficient implementation exists.

3.3.5. Coq Embedding

The type system and theorems presented in this section have been translated to intuitionistic logic of the automatic theorem prover Coq. Within Coq's formal system, more rigorous and convincing proofs can be provided. The embedding is described in Appendix A.

3.4. Application to Imperative Languages

To demonstrate general applicability of the approach to imperative transformation languages, and for validating the concept on real model transformations, we have integrated the concept into two existing transformation languages, QVT-O and Xtend. QVT-O is an imperative M2M transformation language standard that has been implemented under the Eclipse ecosystem. Xtend is a highly extensible general-purpose programming language suitable for writing M2T transformations. As a sideline, we added a few domain-specific concepts so that M2M transformations can be encoded in Xtend, too.

3.4.1. Implementation in Eclipse QVTo

The QVT-OM approach has been prototypically integrated into the Eclipse QVTo project, a manifestation of the official QVT-O standards. We named the modified version *QVTom*[1]. With QVTo being to the widest extent standards-compliant, adaptation of the language has been carried out without complications.

The example code of the Activity2Process from Listing 3.1 is fully compatible with our QVTom variant. The underlying parser is generated from an LALR Parser Generator (LPG) grammar specification. The parser emits instances of an Ecore modeled Abstract Syntax Tree (AST) using the visitor design pattern. Type checking is done partly by the visitor, partly in a subsequent step. The hereby generated AST model instance is finally interpreted.

We added keywords to the lexical grammar specification and adapted the parser's grammar rules as outlined in Figure 3.2. We had to adjust the generated parser by integrating the type checking rules from Figures 3.3 and 3.4, accordingly. Code has been added that resolves modular dependencies on the fly, eventuating in an AST that can be traversed by the vanilla interpreter.

[1] Sources are available at `qvt.github.io/qvtom`.

The proposed Core QVT-OM is a minimal extension to demonstrate the key concepts. The QVTo project already supports full OCL and QVT-O syntax. For practicability, we implemented several additional features which had not been mentioned so far. First, modules and interfaces can by physically separated in files, and use the import statement to add other files to a file's scope. Second, interfaces can not only declare mapping methods, but also helper methods and query functions.

3.4.2. Implementation in Xtend

We prototypically implemented a transformation language Xtend2m[2] that includes our module concept. Xtend2m augments the *Xtend* language[3] for model-to-model (M2M) and model-to-text (M2T) transformations on EMF-based Ecore models. EMF maps Ecore metamodels to Java types. Xtend is a statically typed language that compiles to ordinary Java code. It features template expressions for M2T and cached methods for M2M, and because it is built with the Xtext framework, it comes with full-featured Eclipse editors and can be easily extended and customized. Extensibility was the primary reason we decided to use the Xtend language for a prototypical implementation of our concepts.

We exploit the fact that Xtend programs are 100% compatible with Java's type system: We utilize Java interfaces as module interfaces and Java classes as module implementations. Mapping operations are Java methods inside a class. As a consequence, Java's type checker automatically ensures that a module conforms to its interface, and enforces that only mappings marked as public are accessed from outside.

However, there are four weaknesses. First, cached methods only take care that, for a certain parameter set, the previously created element is returned instead of a new one. Second, model access restrictions can not be declared for an interface, and implementations are not statically checked

[2] Sources are available at `qvt.github.io/xtend2m`.

[3] Xtend is hosted at `xtend-lang.org`

for violations against restrictions. Third, module implementations must be kept independent from each other. This issue is already tackled by standard dependency injection APIs, but it is not checked if the imported interface is actually a transformation interface. And fourth, Xtend does not prescribe how a transformation's entry point must look like.

To mark classes and interfaces as transformation concepts, and to include access declarations and mapping methods with QVT-O-like tracing, we designed six dedicated Java annotations. Based on these annotations, we were able to make use of an Xtend feature called *Active Annotations*. This mechanism gives language developers the chance to intercept static code analysis and transpilation to Java for two purposes. On the one hand, we can perform static type checking, and in cases of any semantic issues we can create appropriate compiler warnings and errors. These issues are then displayed at the corresponding location in the Eclipse editor. On the other hand, we can manipulate transpilation, for example, we are able to inject code into methods with a certain annotation.

Listing 3.3 again shows the Activity2Process transformation from the introduction, but this time it is implemented in Xtend2m rather than QVTom. All the annotations used there are going to be explained in the following paragraphs.

Interfaces must be indicated with `@TransformationInterface`, and classes with `@TransformationModule`. Control dependencies can be declared via `@Import`, and are mapped by the transpiler to an ordinary `@Inject`. At the same time, transformation modules are automatically injected with a factory for model creation, a module configuration class and a tracing API. Type checking makes sure that an interface implemented or imported by a transformation module is in any case annotated as a transformation interface. A dedicated interface `IMain` constitutes the entry point. A transformation is only valid if this interface is implemented by exactly one module.

We replaced cached methods with our own concept. Methods annotated with `@Create(typeof(T))` automatically create an instance of T that is

```
@TransformationInterface
@ScopeIn(#["activity.Activity", "activity.Action"])
@ScopeOut(#["process.Process"])
interface IActivity2Process extends MainMethod {
  def Process mapActivity2Process(Activity self)
}
@TransformationModule
@Import extension IAction2Step, ICompositeAction2Step
class Activity2Process implements IActivity2Process {
  @Create(typeof(Process))
  override Process mapActivity2Process(Activity self) {
    result.steps = self.actions.map[mapAction2Step]
  }
  override main(List<List<EObject>> input) {
    val activities = input.head.filter(typeof(Activity))
    activities.map[mapActivity2Process]
    doLateResolution
  }
}
```

(a) First module

```
@TransformationInterface
@ScopeIn(#["activity.StartAction", "activity.StopAction"])
@ScopeOut(#["process.Step"])
interface IAction2StepModule {
  def dispatch Step mapAction2Step(Action self)
}
@TransformationModule
class Action2Step implements IAction2Step {
  @Create(typeof(Step))
  override dispatch Step mapAction2Step(Action self) {
    result.name = self.name
    self.next.lateResolveOne [ result.successor = it ]
    result.isStart = self instanceof StartAction
    result.isStop = self instanceof StopAction
  }
}
```

(b) Second module

```
@TransformationInterface
@ScopeIn(#["activity.CompositeAction"])
@ScopeOut(#["process.Process", "process.Step"])
interface ICompositeAction2Step {
  def dispatch Step mapAction2Step(CompositeAction self)
}
@TransformationModule
@Import extension IAction2Step
class CompositeAction2Step implements ICompositeAction2Step {
  @Create(typeof(Step))
  override dispatch mapAction2Step(CompositeAction self) {
    result.name = "Run process " + self.name
    result.successor = self.next.mapAction2Step
    result.isStart = false
    result.isStop = false
    self.mapAction2Process
  }
  @Create(typeof(Process))
  def mapAction2Process(CompositeAction self) {
    result.steps = self.actions.map[mapAction2Step]
  }
}
```

(c) Third module

Listing 3.3: Activity2Process example in Xtend2m

registered at our tracing API. Later on, trace resolution can be conducted in the style of QVT-O, for example by calling `lateResolveOne`. In contrast to QVT-O, late resolution must be triggered by an explicit call to `doLateResolution`. Any referenced model types from inside a method are checked if they are declared as accessible by the interface the surrounding module implements.

Access control can be declared for module interfaces via two annotations, `@ScopeIn` and `@ScopeOut`. These are parameterized by a list of model element classes. All classes in a package can be declared using a wildcard operator, `myPackage.*`.

```
module Activity2ProcessTransformation
Workflow {
  // load metamodels ActivityModel.ecore, ProcessModel.ecore
  // load ActivityModel instance into slot "inputModel"
  ⋮
  component = xtend2m.mwe.ModuleLoader {
    input  = "inputModel"
    output = {
      package = "process"
      slot = "outputModel"
    }
    transformationModule = "Activity2Process"
    transformationModule = "Action2Step"
  }
  // persist ProcessModel from slot "outputModel"
  ⋮
}
```

Listing 3.4: Activity2Process example – MWE2 workflow definition

At this time, the dependency injection framework has not been informed about available implementations. Xtend programs are typically orchestrated from a workflow script written for the Modeling Workflow Engine (MWE). We built a customized workflow component that initiates the wiring and then executes the transformation. So that this can happen, module implementations must be registered. Concerning the introductory *Activity2Process* example, a workflow script must register implementations for two interfaces, `IMain` and `IAction2Step` (Figure 3.4).

As we have shown, transformations written in Xtend2m share all modular concepts of QVT-OM and key QVT-O concepts. Because Xtend already comes with template expressions built-in, not only M2M, but also M2T transformations can be written. One difference concerning our module concept is that no metamodel represents the target, hence access restrictions cannot be declared.

3.5. Applicability to Declarative Transformation Languages

There is a second class of transformation languages that pursues the declarative paradigm: instead of imperatively prescribing how models are transformed into other models, declarative languages describe how elements between multiple models relate semantically. Many of the declarative languages use a first-class concept of a transformation rule to formulate these declarations, hence they are alternatively named rule-based transformation languages. One prominent example for a purely declarative language is QVT-R. Other declarative languages like ATL allow both declarative rule and imperative mapping operations as first-class entities, they are counted to the hybrid transformation languages.

So far it has not been clarified if and how we can transfer our module concept to declarative, rule-based languages. In this section, we are going to demonstrate this for a widely known representative of declarative transformation languages, the QVT-R language. Despite being the only language of its kind that has been described in a standard document, semantics have not been formally described, evidenced by errors and subtle differences in the tools that implement QVT-R. To address this situation, in the consequent subsection we systematically embed a core subset of the formal language standard in constructive type theory under the Coq proof environment. Our embedding is mostly a shallow one, with only a minimum of computational steps, which are fully automatized by code generator templates. We adhere as faithfully as possible to the formal language standard, whilst we confine ourselves to unidirectional, non-updating enforcement semantics. We give justification for any deviation from the official specification.

Having our understanding of QVT-R's core semantics made clear, the next subsection elicits how interfaces and implementations fit into the language.

3.5.1. Semantics of QVT-R

The encoding of QVT-R transformations in Coq is founded on the basic pattern proposed by Poernomo [Poe08], namely

$$\forall s : S.\ Pre(s) \rightarrow \exists t : T.\ Post(s,t),$$

where s is an instance of a source metamodel S, t is an instance of a target metamodel T, *Pre* is a predicate on S that must hold *before* the transformation is applied, and *Post* is a predicate on S and T that must hold *after* the transformation is applied.

Before describing the encoding of a QVT-R transformation, let us first define its abstract syntax, and say what it means for a transformation to succeed.

Definition 3.1 (QVT-R Transformation): A QVT-R transformation T, with source models $m_{S,1}, \ldots, m_{S,r}$, target model m_T, top relations $R_1, \ldots, R_l$, and non-top relations $R_{l+1}, \ldots, R_m$, is given by:

```
transformation T (m_{S,1} : M_{S,1}, ..., m_{S,r} : M_{S,r}, m_T : M_T) {
    top relation R_1 { ... } ... top relation R_l { ... }
    relation R_{l+1} { ... } ... relation R_m { ... } ...
}
```

Definition 3.2 (Successful QVT-R Transformation): A QVT-R transformation is deemed to succeed if all of its top relations hold.

With these definitions in place, we are now in a position to define the encoding of a QVT-R transformation.

Definition 3.3 (QVT-R Transformation Encoding): A QVT-R transformation is encoded as a theorem, whose type is an expression in predicate logic of the following form: for all source models, there exists a target model, so that the encoding of each top relation holds over the models, i.e.

```
Theorem Transformation_T:
forall m_{S,1} : M_{S,1}, ..., forall m_{S,r} : M_{S,r},
```

```
exists m_T : M_T,
  Top_R_1 (m_{S,1}, ..., m_{S,r}, m_T) ∧ ... ∧
  Top_R_l (m_{S,1}, ..., m_{S,r}, m_T).
```

Similarly, before defining the encoding of a QVT-R relation, let us first define its abstract syntax.

Definition 3.4 (QVT-R Relation): The abstract syntax of a QVT-R relation R, which contains a set of local variables, V_{local}, a set of patterns to match on n domains, where $n \geq 2$, a *when* clause C_{when}, and a *where* clause C_{where}, is given by

```
[top] relation R {
    var V_local
    checkonly domain S_1 v_{S_1,root} {
        A_{S_1,1} = (C_{S_1,1} | v_{S_1,1} { (C_{S_1,2} | v_{S_1,2} { ... C_{S_1,k_1} ... }) })
    }...
    checkonly domain S_n v_{S_n,root} { ... }
    enforce domain T v_{T,root} {
        A_{T,1} = (C_{T,1} | v_{T,1} { (C_{T,2} | v_{T,2} { ... C_{T,k} ... }) })
    }
    [when { C_when }]
    [where { C_where }]
}
```

The source model of the i-th domain, $1 \leq i \leq n$, is parametrized by domain variable S_i, and the target model is parametrized by domain variable T. Each domain is required to define at least one pattern, i.e. the root pattern. To ease comprehension in the definition above, the number of attributes A in a domain pattern is restricted to one. Patterns can be nested to an arbitrary depth, until either a pattern is left empty, `{}`, or a constraint C is used, i.e., an OCL expression that may refer to existing variables in R's context.

In QVT-R, relations can appear in two distinct contexts. Firstly, they can appear in a relation's precondition, to check – for a given set of root variables – that the relation holds. This is interpreted as meaning that the relation has already been enforced. Secondly, they can be invoked from a relation's postcondition for a given configuration of the root variables. In this context, a relation is enforced if it does not hold. Recall that top-level relations can never be explicitly called, because they form part of the transformation's principal post-condition, i.e. for any valid match of the checkonly domains, a top-level relation obliges the target model to provide suitable objects to enable it to meet all of its constraints. This is also hinted at by the specification [Obj11, p. 14].

In Coq, we can rely on a single definition for checking both top and non-top relations alike, and for enforcing the non-top relations. However, we cannot use this definition for enforcing top-level relations from the main theorem above, since root variables must be exhaustively bound.

We now define the following short forms of variables in relations, to ease the encoding of relations.

Definition 3.5 (Variable Short Forms): The short forms of variables in relations is given by:

Root variables	V_{root}	$:= \{v_{S_1,root},\ \ldots,\ v_{S_n,root},\ v_{T,root}\}$
Source-bound variables	V_S	$:= \bigcup_{i=1}^{n} \{v_{S_i,root},\ v_{S_i,1},\ \ldots,\ v_{S_i,k_i}\}$
Target-bound variables	V_T	$:= \{v_{T,root},\ v_{T,1},\ \ldots,\ v_{T,k}\}$
All variables	V	$:= V_{local} \cup V_S \cup V_T$
Variables in when clause	V_{when}	$:= \{v \in V \mid v$ is used in condition $C_{when}\}$
Variables in where clause	V_{where}	$:= \{v \in V \mid v$ is used in condition $C_{where}\}$
Source pattern variables	V_{C_S}	$:= \{v \in V \mid \exists\, i \in \{1,\ldots,n\},\ j \in \{1,\ldots,k_i\} :$ v is used in constraint $C_{S_i,j}\}$

Target pattern variables	V_{C_T}	$:= \{v \in V \mid \exists\, j \in \{1,\dots k\} :$ v is used in constraint $C_{T,j}\}$
Target-exclusive variables	$\widehat{V}_T$	$:= (V_{C_T} \cup V_T) \setminus (V_{when} \cup V_{C_S} \cup V_S)$
Source/remaining variables	$\widehat{V}_S$	$:= V \setminus (V_{when} \cup \widehat{V}_T)$

From defined variables, we conclude with our encoding of a QVT-R relation. This definition differentiates between two types of relations, top and non-top relations.

Definition 3.6 (QVT-R Relation Encoding): The encoding of top relations (left) and non-top relations (right) is given by:

(a) Enforcing a top-level relation:

```
Definition Top_R (S_1, ..., S_n,
      T) :=
  forall (V_when ∖ V_T),
  exists (V_when ∩ V_T),
  ( C_when ) →
  forall (V̂_S),
  In S_1,root  S_1 ∧... ∧
  In S_n,root  S_n ∧
  C_S_1,1 ∧ ... ∧ C_S_1,k_1 ∧ ... ∧
  C_S_n,1 ∧ ... ∧ C_S_n,k_n →
  exists (V̂_T),
  ( In T_root  T ) ∧
  ( C_T,1 ∧ ... ∧ C_T,k ) ∧
  ( C_where ).
```

(b) Relation with root variables bound:

```
Definition R (S_1, ..., S_n, T,
      V_root) :=
  ( In S_1,root  S_1 ) ∧ ... ∧
  ( In S_n,root  S_n ) ∧
  ( In T_root  T ) ∧
  forall (V_when ∖ V_root),
  ( C_when ) →
  forall (V̂_S ∖ V_root),
  ( C_S_1,1 ∧ ... ∧ C_S_1,k_1 ) ∧ ... ∧
  ( C_S_n,1 ∧ ... ∧ C_S_n,k_n ) →
  exists (V̂_T ∖ V_root),
  ( C_T,1 ∧ ... ∧ C_T,k ) ∧
  ( C_where ).
```

Note that top relations require both definitions. The definition on the left is used to enforce the relation, whereas the definition on the right is used to check that the relation holds for particular inhabitants of the root variables.

It is easy to see that these definitions differ in two points. First, in the top-level definition, target variables on the *when* condition use *exists* rather than *forall* (Definition 3.6a, line 3 and 3.6b, line 4). At the time that a top relation is enforced (recall that a top relation may depend on other relations, namely those in its *when* clause), for each valid match that is found, witnesses of created objects must exist in the target model. Ultimately, these witnesses are the implementations of the corresponding relations. Knowing about the exact characteristics of created objects facilitates the eventual proof of correctness of the transformation. Second, the binding of root variables differs. Since root variables are expected to be bound at the time a top relation is checked or a non-top relation is called, they already appear as parameters V_{root} in Definition 3.6b, and proper containment of root variables can be pulled up to the top of Definition 3.6b (lines 2–4). On the other hand, when enforcing a top relation, propositions on the containment of root variables must be postponed to the time a variable is introduced (Definition 3.6a, lines 6, 7, and 11).

3.5.2. Conformance with the Language Standard

The semantics of QVT-R according to the language specification are fuzzy, and turn out not to be well-founded when translated to Coq. In this section, we briefly introduce the standard definition, before we compare it to our own variant and give justification for minor modifications and improvements.

In the standard, predicate logic is only given for a single relation. There is an informal description on p. 14, stating that "the execution of a transformation requires that all its top-level relations hold". This informal description correlates with Definition 3.1, and our translation to predicate logic (Definition 3.3).

The standard lists formulas in predicate calculus for both checkonly and enforcement modes. However, because we confine ourselves to non-updating enforcement semantics, only definition `Create` is relevant in this contribution. In fact, it served as the basis for Definition 3.6.

Definition 3.7 (Standardized Enforcement Semantics for Relations): The encoding of non-updating enforcement semantics according to the standard [Obj11, Ann. B, p. 225] is given by:

```
1  Definition Create_R (S_1, ...,
       S_n, T) :=
2    forall (V_when),
3    ( C_when ) →
4    forall (V \ (V_when ∪ V̂_T)),
5    ( In S_1,root  S_1 ) ∧ ... ∧
6    ( In S_n,root  S_n ) ∧
7    C_{S_1,1} ∧ ... ∧ C_{S_1,k_1} ∧ ... ∧
8    C_{S_n,1} ∧ ... ∧ C_{S_n,k_n} →
9    ¬ exists (V̂_T),
10   ( In T_root  T ) ∧
11   ( C_T,1 ∧ ... ∧ C_T,k ) ∧
12   ( C_where ) →
13   assert (V̂_T \ V_T = ∅) ∧
14   forall v : V_T,
15   createOrUpdate
         (v.boundTemplate,
         v,  V \ V̂_T) ∧
16   ( C_where ).
```

Note that variable names have been changed to match those defined earlier, and that the syntax is slightly different from the standard. However, the semantics are the same.

The QVT specification informally explains that domain patterns implicitly include containment checks (cf. [Obj11, p. 223]). We made containment of root variables explicit in our definitions to allow for refactoring steps explained below. Furthermore, domain patterns and conditions are separate terms in the standard, whereas we use constrained terms C that comprise both. The specification remains vague about how these translate to predicate calculus.

In contrast to Definition 3.7, we differentiate between top and non-top relations (Definition 3.6a vs. 3.6b). As already explained, it is impossible to do otherwise because the root variables of non-top relations are already bound upon a call, and are thus input as a parameter set rather than being quantified over.

There is an obvious issue with Definition 3.7 in that some of the variables in V_T may have already been bound in the *when* clause; therefore, line 14 should use $\widehat{V}_T$ instead. An example of where this is relevant is variable s in relation `Class2Table` (cf. ListingB.1).

The standard considers incremental updates, and any logic to define how elements are created or updated is factored out into an (informally described) function `createOrUpdate` (Definition 3.7, line 15). The first parameter is the template expression that corresponds to variable v, the second parameter is variable v itself, and the third parameter defines bound variables that are in scope. Recall that in our definition we do not consider update semantics, including the *key* concept for identifying objects by certain properties. Therefore, we can explicitly use existential quantification to create objects (Definition 3.6a and 3.6b, line 10), instead of a less natural universal quantification (Definition 3.7, line 14). Furthermore, checking for non-existence is not needed (Definition 3.7, lines 9–12). Line 13 assures that variables in the target pattern's expressions are bound at the time of enforcement. Because we decided to exclude type checking, we spared the assertion in line 13, although the same constraint must apply in our case, as well. Line 4 in Definition 3.7 and line 5 in Definition 3.6a and 3.6b are equivalent considering how $\widehat{V}_S$ is defined.

To ease the process of proving, we pull up containment checks right after the corresponding variable is introduced. We further ease proving by using existential quantification rather than universal quantification for any variable on the target domain that is introduced by a when clause.

3.5.3. Creating Standards-Compliant Implementations

The introduced formalism can be used to create functional implementations of QVT-R programs that are provably correct with respect to the program's specification. The first step is to automatically translate the given QVT-R script and the model specifications to Coq. In a second step, an OCaml implementation is written under Coq, which is subsequently, in a third step, manually proven to adhere to the Coq-embedded specification. At last, a Haskell implementation can be automatically derived from the proof, which can then be run on arbitrary model instances. Model instances can be automatically translated from Ecore to Coq and back.

To demonstrate practicability of our formalization, we created from the UML2RDBMS example transformation a Haskell program. Details on the proof, which have been written conjointly with Jeffrey Terrell and Steffen Zschaler from King's College, London, can be found in Appendix B.

3.5.4. Applicability to QVT-Relations

Based on our above described understanding of the semantics of QVT-R's core concepts, we assess the applicability of our module concept to this particular declarative language.

R1: Separation of interfaces from their implementations Compile-time binding of modules is straight-forward, since both QVT dialects share many concepts. We replace the existing structuring concept – one transformation unit can extend other transformation units – by interface-based modularity. In contrast to QVT-O, where an interface declares mapping and query methods, an interface in QVT-R declares the signatures of relations and query methods. The signature of a relation consists of the relation's type (`top` or default type) and name, and the list of domains with kind (`checkonly` or `enforce`) and type,

```
[top] relation R {
    [checkonly | enforce]domain D1
    ⋮
    [checkonly | enforce]domain Dn
}
```

Implementation details including local variables, template patterns, when and where clauses must be omitted (cf. Definition 3.4). Note that, any domain identifier D_i must be declared in the transformation signature of the interface.

R2a: Method provisioning If an implementation is in conformance with its exported interface, it must provide implementation details for any relation and query declared in the interface while adopting types, name and domain parameters. We differentiate between top and non top rules; to keep the runtime behavior of module implementations transparent, any top relation must be kept visible to clients, since at runtime, all top relations are implicitly enforced (see Definition 3.3). Hence, the module system expects that any top relation defined by a module must be part of the module's interface.

R2b: Method access control In QVT-R, relations and query functions are referencable from a relation's when and where clause, but not as part of one of the pattern's expressions. It does not, however, make sense to reference a top rule from a where clause, because it is enforced automatically on any match found. With information hiding modularity, access to relations and queries is controlled. A relation may only reference queries and relations that are either defined locally or by one of the imported interfaces.

R2c: Model access control Model access control mechanisms at the type level can be implemented in a fashion similar to what has been described for operational languages. Classes referenced in an enforceable domain are potentially instantiated or updated and hence must be tagged as write-accessible types. Any other (implicitly or explicitly) referenced type must only be declared as read-only accessible, since QVT-R does not provide instantiation mechanisms or update semantics outside enforced domains.

3.5.5. Interoperability between QVT-Operational and QVT-Relations

Our modularity concept has been originally designed to be resolved at compile-time up to this point. However, binding may be deferred to the runtime of a program. Dynamic binding paves the way for model transformations where the modules of the same program may be implemented in a language by choice, for instance, QVT-R or QVT-O. To facilitate interoperability between declarative and imperative languages, dissimilar language concepts at the interface-level must be integrated. We now discuss a hybrid approach based on a binding mechanism at runtime, where some modules are implemented in QVT's declarative and others in QVT's imperative language.

In an imperative language, there is one single thread of execution that starts at the entry point method and continues with called methods. Contrary to that, a rule-based program does not have a single thread of execution, but rather defines a set of rules which are to be enforced by a rule engine. Typical implementations of a rule-based language apply a depth-first search algorithm to find a valid match of all rules, and reverts the effects of tentatively applied rules of a path that turns out to be non-satisfiable.

Rules correspond to relations in QVT-R, and interaction between rules can be complex, since a rule may refer to itself or another rule as pre or post condition (when and where clauses).An execution engine must always keep track of found matches of a rule, so that rules that refer to rules in their *when* condition can query for a particular match. The domains of a relation are called a trace entry in the QVT specification. A rule is allowed to query another rule only if the rule's module imports the referenced rule's module interface. This check can be done at compile time or at runtime.

The QVT language has been explicitly designed for interoperability. The standard specifies blackbox relations to be used, which can be implemented as QVT-O mappings or procedures in another imperative language:

> Mappings Operations can be used to implement one or more Relations from a Relations specification when it is difficult to provide a purely declarative specification of how a Relation is to be populated. Mappings Operations invoking other Mappings Operations always involves a Relation for the purposes of creating a trace between model elements, but this can be implicit, and an entire transformation can be written in this language

> in the imperative style. (QVT Language Specification [Obj11, Ch. 6.2])

Hence, relations may invoke mappings, and vice versa. However, according to the OMG's understanding of hybrid execution, restrictions apply. A list of these restrictions is given in Chapter 7.8 of the document:

> A relation may optionally have an associated black-box operational implementation to enforce a domain. The black-box operation is invoked when the relation is executed in the direction of the enforced domain and the relation evaluates to false as per the checking semantics. The invoked operation is responsible for making the necessary changes to the model in order to satisfy the specified relationship. It is a runtime exception if the relation evaluates to false after the operation returns. The signature of the operation can be derived from the domain specification of the relation – an output parameter corresponding to the enforced domain, and an input parameter corresponding to each of the other domains. The Relations that may be implemented by Mapping Operations and Blackbox Operations are restricted in the following ways:
>
> - Their domain should be primitive or contain a simple object template (with no sub-elements).
> - The when and where clause should not define variables.
>
> These restrictions allow for a simple call-out semantics, which does not need any constraint evaluation before, and constraint checking after the operation invocation. When clauses, where clauses, patterns, and other machinery can be used in a "wrapper" relation that invokes the simple relation with values constrained by the wrapper. (QVT Language Specification [Obj11, Ch. 7.8])

Specifying a blackbox relation equals a signature declaration in an interface's signature: a reference to an imperative method replaces constraints in the shape of domain patterns or in when and where blocks. The standard remains fuzzy when it comes to additional details on this approach, it mentions rules to reference mappings, and mappings being able to reference other mappings for which a relation (signature) is provided. None of the existing QVT tools implement blackbox functionality this way.

In accordance with the standard, in-place transformation – originally supported by QVT-O – is implemented in QVT-R[4] and hence must be disallowed for interoperability. On the other hand, multi-directional relations, i.e., relations that can be executed in multiple directions, must be implemented in QVT-O for each possible direction. The same applies to update semantics of QVT-R, these are not implicitly provided by operational mappings and must be disallowed.

Contrary to the standard's prescription of "call-out semantics" for blackbox implementations[5], it can be permitted to reference declarative rules from within a mapping's body. If the relation does not hold at the time the statement is executed, execution is triggered. Else, already created instances are returned that are stored in a shared trace model. Using one of QVT-O's trace resolution functions queries the trace model, and execution is deferred when `late resolve` is used. A detailed discussion on how a common QVT model for trace records could like like has been contributed by Willink and Matragkas [WM14].

It is further not clear how the standard implements references to blackbox relations. We suggest to differentiate between references from a when block and a where block: If a mapping is referenced in a when block, the trace model is queried on already mapped elements, and if a mapping is referenced from a where block, the mapping is executed if not done previously.

[4] When source and target domain are bound to the same input model instance, the transformation is ran in-place. In that mode, relations whose target pattern are affected by enforcement-induced modifications are re-evaluated.

[5] Although in Chapter 6.2 quoted before, mappings can invoke relations

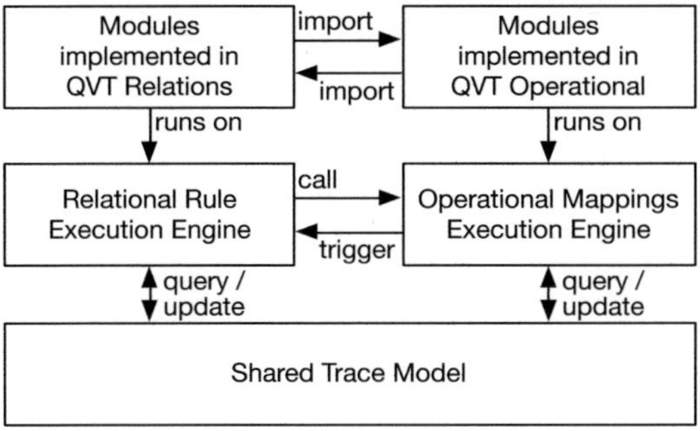

Figure 3.6: Interoperability of QVT-Relations and QVT-Operational

An example architecture for a hybrid transformation engine is described in Figure 3.6. The architecture includes two separate interpreters, one for modules implemented in a declarative language, and another for modules implemented in an imperative language.

3.6. Concluding Remarks

In this chapter, we have introduced a novel module concept that is specially tailored for model transformations. The concept makes data and control dependencies between modules explicit, it provides interface descriptions that can hide implementation details from module users. Implementations are statically checked if they actually meet contractual obligations defined by provided interfaces. We formalized the underlying type system, and, as a proof-of-concept, integrated this approach into the Xtend language.

Type inference does only implement a minimal subset of the OCL and the QVT-O language. In the future, an existing type inference system for OCL [CK01] could be integrated, and static typing of the complete QVT-O language could be included.

Several features of common module systems remain yet unsupported. For example, only implementations can define import dependencies, modules cannot form a hierarchy. Additionally, data dependencies could be augmented with syntactic sugar, e.g. a postponed plus operator could automatically include subclasses of a named class, following a similar feature in Kermeta. Also, behavioral contracts in the spirit of Meyer's Design by Contract could complement our concept, as already proposed by Vallecillo et al. [VGB+12] for monolithic transformations.

Scoping per model parameters (as suggested in the MODULARITY paper) turned out to be impracticable, because (Imperative) OCL expressions only allow to statically infer a type, but not unambiguously the associated *extent* per statement. Ambiguities arise from domains with overlapping model type elements, or with references that link domains. Static dataflow analysis could try to infer the associated domain, and in ambiguous cases, extents would have to be explicitly annotated (e.g., using `@<domain>`).

As we are going to show in a case study on a real-world M2T transformation in Chapter 6, our module system is able to effectively reduce the effort of locating concerns that is involved in typical evolution scenarios.

4. Dependence Visualization for Efficiently Maintaining Model Transformations

In the previous chapter we have ported information hiding modularity, an established technique for software maintenance, to model transformation development. This technique proactively helps to design and implement maintainable transformations. Yet, however, a large number of legacy transformations exists, with many having not been designed with comprehensibility and maintainability in mind. Others could not be properly modularized because the language did not provide a sophisticated module concept. But even if a modular design exists, it often has eroded over time. In any of these cases, gaining an initial understanding of the software for refactoring and repair is a fully manual process that involves much effort.

We propose an interactive visual analytics process that helps in understanding model transformations for maintenance. Data and control dependencies are statically analyzed and displayed in an interactive graph-based view with cross-view navigation and task-oriented filter criteria.

Content of this chapter is based on text that has been primarily created by the author of this thesis alone, and priorly published at the ICMT in 2013 [RNHR13]. Secondary authors of the publication have contributed several ideas and given valuable feedback to the author. Content from the original publication has been comprehensively revised and new content has been added: the running example continues the Activity2Process scenario from the introduction, the mapping from QVT-O to dependence graphs is described in greater detail, and a study on the generality of the approach has been added. Early conceptual work and the implementation prototype have been first described in Per Sterner's diploma thesis [Ste12] which has been created under the author's guidance.

This chapter is structured as follows. First, we evaluate maintenance support of existing transformation development environments by example of Eclipse QVT-O in Section 4.1. In Section 4.2, we introduce our visualization process. Section 4.3 presents a generic model for dependency graphs that is compatible with model transformation languages of any paradigm, and in Section 4.4 we explain a task-oriented filtering technique on dependence graphs that plays a key role in the visualization process. Section 4.5 discusses generality of the approach with regards to transformation languages beyond QVT-O, and Section 4.6 concludes this chapter with a short summary.

4.1. Transformation Editor Support

In practice, transformation developers regularly have to deal with legacy transformations that were designed in a language which offers conceptually weak support for modularity, or available concepts have not been sufficiently utilized. In typical maintenance scenarios, places in the code need to be identified that must be modified, the so-called *locations of concern* (cf. Section 2.4). It is critical for the purpose to possess a sufficient understanding of the procedures (the *control flow*), as well as to know which elements in the models are accessed or changed at which places in the code (the *data flow*).

In the following, we will pick up and go through the maintenance scenarios that have been presented for the Activity2Process example transformation in the introductory chapter in Section 1.2. This time, we evaluate tools and techniques developers use to improve their efficiency and effectiveness. We are able to show for one of the more sophisticated transformation language IDEs, the Eclipse QVT-O environment, that locating concerns involves unnecessarily high manual effort and carries a risk to accidentally miss out on relevant places.

Modifying a module's inner logic. In order to fix an imaginary bug that has been identified to reside in one of the inner methods in module `CompositeAction2Step`, we need to know from which other methods a particular method is called. In our instance, we expect helper method `createProcess` to contain an error that must be fixed, and we would like to know the effects the present bug has on other parts of the transformation. Since QVT-O does not allow to syntactically hide methods from being accessed from outside the module, we must check any module that imports the affected module and check each of the methods if they execute a call to the erroneous method.

In the QVT-O editor under Eclipse, we need to start a text-based search by the method's name. If the transformation is modularized, we need to repeat the search in any other module with an `import` of the rule's containing module. To detect occurrences, it is important to know that in QVT-O, keywords `disjuncts`, `merges`, `inherits` and `map` all have call-semantics.

Identifying locations of concern. In this second scenario, we were assuming that we modified some of the models involved in the Activity2Process transformation. In a first case, we imagined we had not already added another subclass `CompositeAction` of class `Action` to `ActivityModel` (to be placed in a separate package) but rather planned to do so. In a second case, we wanted to add an attribute `name` to classes `Action` and `Step`.

Before we do so, it is useful to know about further locations in the program where class `Action` or possible subclasses are instantiated, or where classes `Action` and `Step` are currently accessed. Again, we need to carry out a text-based search by the class name on all existing modules. Particularly in this first case it is important to know that in QVT-O, there are three ways to instantiate objects: implicitly via a `mapping`, or explicitly via the `object` operator, or by calling the corresponding `constructor` via `new` operator.

Refactoring the modular design. The last scenario was about moving any method that deals with class `CompositeAction` to a separate module `CompositeA2Step2Step`. Just like class `CompositeAction` has been placed into a separate package `CompositeActions`, so it poses an optional extension to the core model in package `ActivityModel`, we want to conceptually isolate transformation logic for this extra part of the ActivityModel.

In this case, a developer must initially find out about the methods privately used by a given method. This requires to track the called method's callers, if there are any available. Similar to the first scenario, we must have an understanding of the import, call and reuse dependencies among modules and methods to isolate methods that are solely reused used by methods that operate on class `CompositeAction`. And similar to the second scenario, we must initially find out about the uses of class `CompositeAction`.

From these three scenarios it is clear that developers, especially those who are less familiar with QVT-O concepts, need to invest a lot of effort to identify relevant control and data dependencies in complex transformation programs. Program analysis techniques can automatically extract dependencies and present these in a graphical form. However, dependency graphs tend to confuse for larger programs without adequate filtering due to their sheer size. In the next section of this chapter, we propose a visual analytics process which takes the burden off developers to visualize only those dependencies that can be considered as relevant for a particular activity.

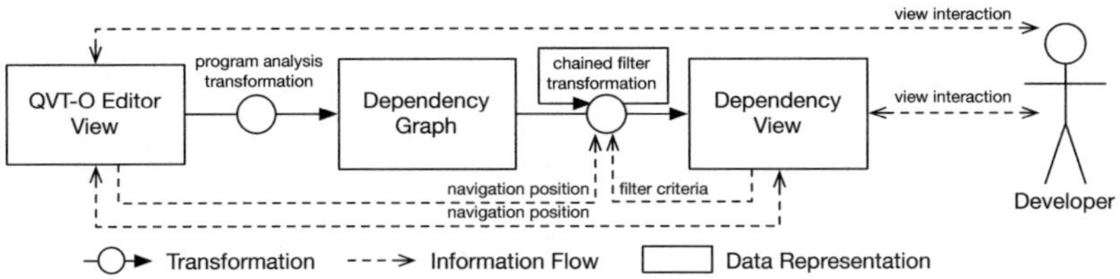

Figure 4.1: Visual analytics process

4.2. Methodology Overview

To solve the information overload problem, *visual analytics processes* combine analytical approaches together with advanced visualization techniques. They can be characterized by four properties [KMS+08]:

> "Analyse First – Show the Important – Zoom, Filter and Analyse Further – Details on Demand"

We define an interactive visualization process which adheres to these principles. In this chapter, we motivate our approach by referring to the QVT-O language. However, the concepts we present here are general enough to be transferred to further declarative and imperative languages. The process contains two transformation steps, a dependency analysis and a filter transformation (Figure 4.1). Code and graph representation are kept in sync regarding navigation position and code modifications. A user can interact with both views in parallel, and she or he can select and configure filters to fit his current task. In the following, we show that our process meets all four properties of a visual analytics process.

Analyze first Eclipse QVT-O features a textual representation, the *QVT editor view*. QVT-O automatically maintains a second representation: a model of the transformation and referenced metamodels. This model adheres to the QVT specification [Obj11], thus offering a standardized interface for code analysis. A so-called *program analysis transformation* extracts data and control dependencies from the QVT model in our process, it is the leftmost transformation in Figure 4.1). Static control and data flow analysis results in an instance of a *dependency graph model*. This model is presented in Section 4.3.

Show the important We already showed in the motivating example that, depending on what kind of maintenance task is performed, a different subset of elements and element types available in the graph is required for reasoning. Which elements will be filtered out is configurable by the user. In Section 4.4, we explain our concept of *task-oriented filters* and we further define a set of useful types of filters.

Zoom, filter and analyse further Humans are capable to only perceive a small subset of information at a time. Thus, we provide filters which remove any information out of focus. Depending on the task to be solved, a user's focus may lie on a certain method in the program, on a particular type of dependencies, or on a higher abstraction level. Since each view is limited regarding the information conveyed, *interaction* is needed. A feedback loop is established by dynamic filters, which can be quickly exchanged and configured, and which react on changes to the editing location. In Figure 4.1, filter dynamics are reflected by information flows leading to the filter transformation. Views are navigable, as pointed out by interactions between the developer and the views.

Details on demand Eventually, maintainers must track an identified location in the graph to the code to perform the actual changes. There also can be occasions when the developer requires more details than those offered by the view. In either case, the dependency view enables users to navigate to the underlying program code of a mapping or the actual definition of a data element. This kind of feature is called *cross-view navigation* and is illustrated in Figure 4.1 by an information flow pointing back to the editor view.

Next, we provide details on what dependence information is included in a graph model and how the dependence graph is built from QVT-O transformations.

4.3. The Dependency Graph

Before we describe the analysis procedure that extracts dependence information from transformation programs, we introduce a generic object-oriented model used to describe dependence information.

4.3.1. Dependency Graph Model

The main idea behind a dependence graph that helps in understanding and maintaining model transformation programs is to provide a high-level structural view on the code, while low-level information that is too implementation-specific is removed. Of course, what classifies as important structural information is arguable and is going to be discussed in the following.

Since we focus on programs that are poorly modularized, particularly because existing transformation languages often do not offer adequate module concepts, we concentrate on the the level of mappings and other methods, common top-level language concepts shared by most if not all transformation languages.

What distinguishes transformation languages from GPLs and other kinds of DSLs is that they are designed to operate on object-oriented models by offering designated syntax or API functions to create, read, update and delete model elements. Thus, another important characteristic is the elements of these models a method operates on, and the structural rewlationships among the model elements. Depending on the use case, classes or even attributes of classes can be important. Therefore we include both types of model elements, classes and attributes, in the graph.

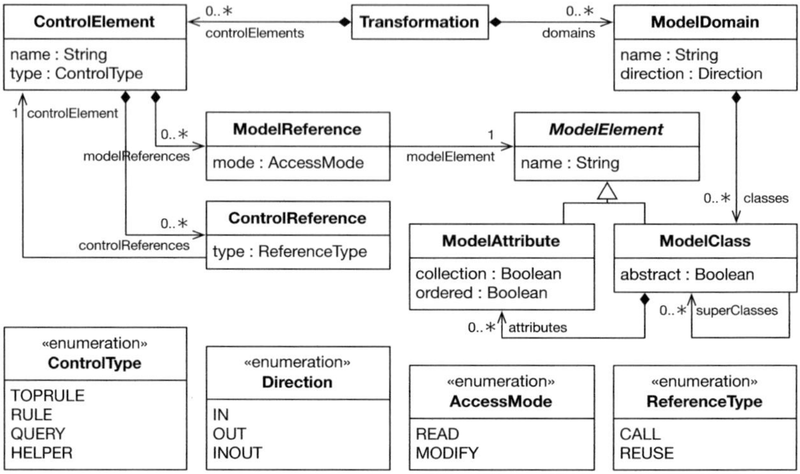

Figure 4.2: Dependency graph model

Figure 4.2 shows how we defined dependence information in the Ecore modeling language. In the model, a transformation (`Transformation`) consists of control elements (`ControlElement`) and metamodel domains (`ModelDomain`). Each domain refers to a metamodel name and has a direction (`IN`, `OUT`, or `INOUT`).

Control elements have references (`ControlReference`) to other rules for reuse purposes, tagged `REUSE`, but also for calls, tagged `CALL`. Control elements are typed. We differentiate mapping rules, tagged `RULE`, methods that form the entry point, tagged `TOPRULE`. Query functions and other helper functions correspond to types `QUERY` and `HELPER`.

A control element can have data dependencies, represented by instances of `ModelReference`. Referencing a model element (`ModelElement`) can be either read-only (`READ`), or the referenced model element can be instantiated or its content modified (`MODIFY` for both cases).

The model differentiates between access to a class and access to an attribute or reference (`ModelClass` and `ModelAttribute`). Like in Java, there is no distinction between references and attributes.

Our model allows for inheritance relationships among classes to be described. For this purpose, classes can further reference super classes in the model (reference `superClasses`). Any model element belongs to exactly one domain.

4.3.2. Dependence Analysis

The dependence graph model is only then of practical use if we can extract dependence information from programs written in preferably any kind of transformation language and build instances of the graph model. The challenge here is to identify language concepts that classify as control element or as control or model use dependency. In this section we will concentrate on two languages, QVT-O and QVT-R. Both languages qualify as good examples, because (a) their syntax and semantics has been described in the QVT specification [Obj11], including a formal MOF-based model of the abstract syntax tree; and (b) they are representatives of distinct programming techniques, the imperative and the declarative/rule-based paradigm, giving us the chance to demonstrate that the graph model is compatible with a wider spectrum of transformation languages.

In the following, we informally describe the various concepts of QVT-O and QVT-R that are represented in the graph. We moreover employ TGG rules (first introduced by Schürr [Sch95]) to formally specify the correspondence between syntactical and graph elements for selected QVT-O concepts (cf. Figure 4.3). We use Kindler's compact notation [KW07] presented in Section 2.1.7.

Control Elements QVT-O implements the imperative paradigm: There is a single method called `main` which forms the entry point. This main method is tagged `TOPRULE`, because it is implicitly executed by the QVT-O

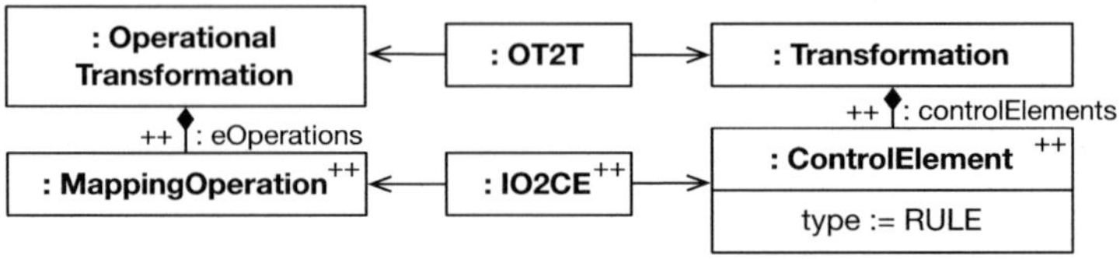

(a) A QVT-O mapping operation corresponds to a `Rule` instance

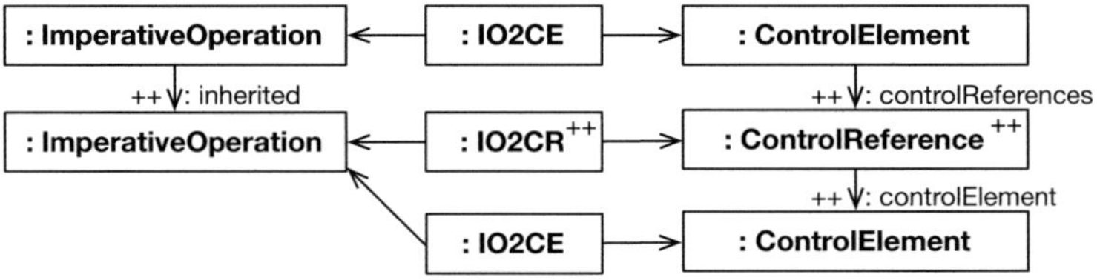

(b) Control references include mappings referenced via `inherits`

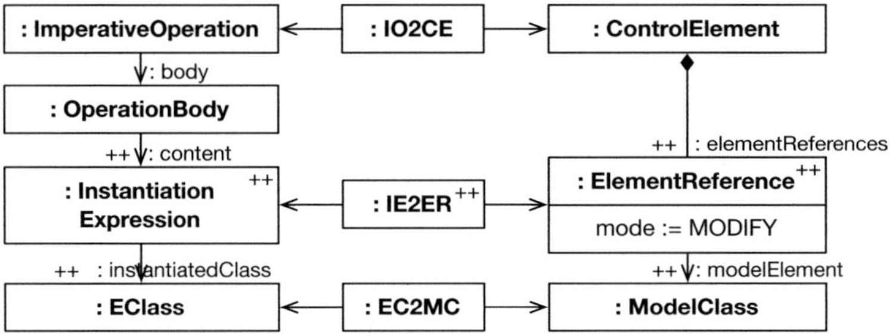

(c) Operator `new` induces a modifying reference

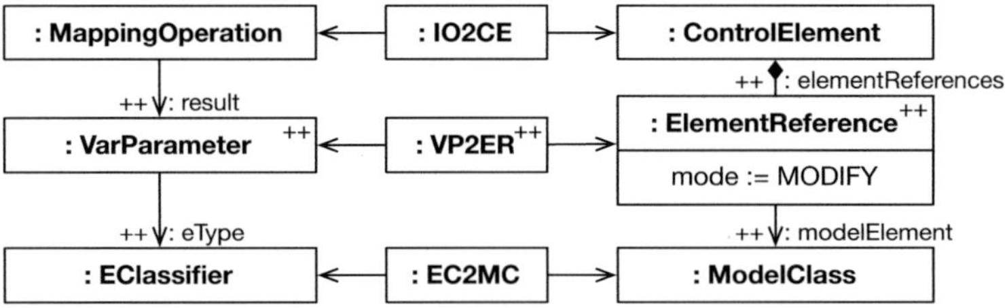

(d) The result parameter embodies a modifying `ElementReference`

Figure 4.3: Constructing dependency graphs from QVT-O code – TGG rules for select concepts runtime. Other types of method concepts comprise mapping, helper, constructor and query methods, all these operations must be called explicitly. Mapping and constructor operations implicitly create the method signature's return type element, whereas helper operations can only instantiate elements explicitly. Query methods in contrast cannot have side-effects. In the graph, mapping operations (defined using keyword `mapping`) are tagged as `RULE`, whereas helper and query operations (defined using statements `helper`, `query`) map to types `QUERY` and `HELPER`, respectively. Custom constructor functions (`constructor`) have a helper-like meaning and thus map to `HELPER`, too. The rule from Figure 4.3a defines how the mapping operation itself corresponds to a control node, i.e., an instance of `ControlElement` that is of type `RULE`.

QVT-R is a rule-based language, where programs declare relations between elements (and patterns thereof) of multiple mapping domains. A QVT-R execution engine operationalizes these unordered rules and implements a pattern matching algorithm. The language knows only three kinds of top-level constructs, relations, top-level relations, and query methods. A relation block (introduced by keyword `top relation`) is recognized as a control element of type `RULE` or, if it is a top-level relation (defined using keyword `top relation`), of type `TOPRULE`. OCL-based query methods are identical to those supported by QVT-O, thus they are typed as `QUERY`, too.

Control Dependencies As usual for procedural languages, mappings in QVT-O programs can refer to other mappings via call or dispatch statements (keywords `map` and `disjuncts` for mappings, and call statements for helper and query methods), or by using one of the features for reuse among mapping methods (`inherits` and `merges`). The transformation rule in Figure 4.3b takes care of mapping operations inherited for reuse, and creates a control reference in any of these cases. Note, that mappings referred to via `inherits` are expressed by a reference `inherited` in the QVT-O syntax tree. Custom constructor functions (`constructor`) replace the default parameter-less constructor, they are called via the `new` operator with the number of parameters and their types matching the constructor's signature.

In QVT-R, relations can invoke relations from when an where clauses. Queries may be invoked from domain patterns and when and where clauses alike, i.e., anywhere OCL expressions may appear. A relation can refine another relation for reuse purposes (keyword `overrides`).

Model Use Dependencies Identifying model use dependencies follows the same approach in both QVT-O and QVT-R: we only need to find OCL expressions in the control constructs' implementation body. Since the type of OCL expressions has been statically inferred by the OCL parser, the list of types (instances of class `Classifier`) must be filtered for those that are defined by one of the metamodels. We are not interested in primitive types provided by the standard OCL library: `Integer`, `Real`, `Boolean`, `String`, and the like. Collection types, i.e. `Sequence`, `Bag`, `Set`, and `OrderedSet`, are reduced to the type they contain.

To determine the access mode of a use dependency, we proceed as follows. If a type occurs as part of a language concept known to create, modify or delete objects in one of the domains, the corresponding use reference is set to mode `MODIFY`. In any other case, `READ` mode is assumed.

In QVT-O, extra rules parse a mapping's body for *imperative* OCL expressions. Imperative OCL is an extension to OCL that adds constructs with side effects. Two commands that are provided by Imperative OCL are `new` and `object`, both can be used to create new instances of a given class in one of the models. The rule shown in Figure 4.3c matches on the `new` operator – represented by `InstantiationExpression` in the QVT syntax tree – and creates a corresponding modifying element reference.

The access mode in QVT-R is determined based on the kind of domain a type is referred to. If a domain has enforced mode (`enforce`), variable types bound by the domain's root variable or contained object template expressions are presumed to be modified. whereas variables that occur in the defining block of a checking or a primitive domain (`checkonly` or `primitive`) are `READONLY`. The same applies to class properties when we parse template property items.

Model types referred to from a control construct's signature definition must be recognized custom to the language. In QVT-O, a mapping's result parameter of a mapping is transformed into a reference that is marked as modifying (the attribute `mode` is set to `MODIFY`), because a QVT-O mapping implicitly instantiates the return type (Figure 4.3d). The context parameter and further input parameters of a mapping or a helper method are read-only (if not explicitly tagged as `out` or `inout`). QVT-R does only support query methods, which are strictly free of side effects in both languages.

4.3.3. Visual Representation

There is no received way of visualizing and laying out graph structures. For our implementation and in this chapter, we decided to visualize dependency graphs as node-link diagrams (NLDs). The advantage in choosing this kind of representation is that we can use the Eclipse Zest framework to visualize and automatically layout the graphs. An illustrative mapping between graph elements and notational elements is given in Figure 4.4.

Control nodes are tagged by different icons depending on the type. Helper and query methods, in contrast to mapping rules, are depicted by an overlaid wrench symbol. Calls are graphically represented by an open arrow in black. Control and model elements can be easily distinguished by color (gray and green, respectively). An overlaid label icon discriminates class properties from classes. Closed and filled arrows stand for inheritance relationships among classes, a notational element referring to the UML. Dashed lines symbolize the ownership relation between attributes and classes. Model use dependencies are represented by open arrows in data flow direction; a green color stands for read and red for write access. Model elements from different namespaces are tagged by label icons in different colors.

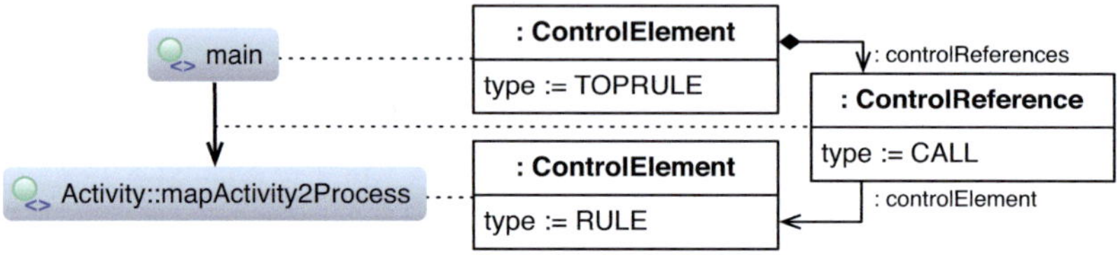

(a) Control elements and call dependencies

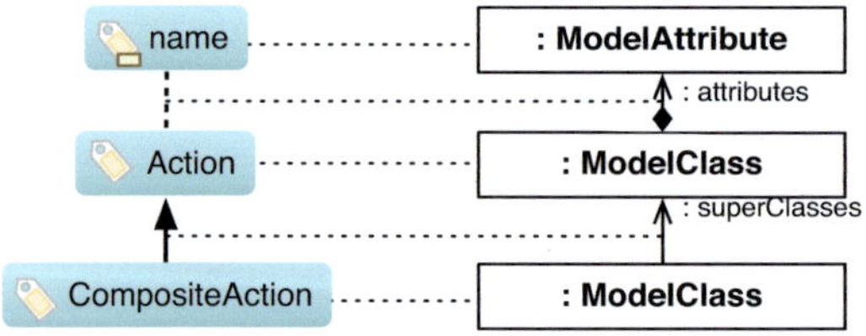

(b) Model elements and structural dependencies

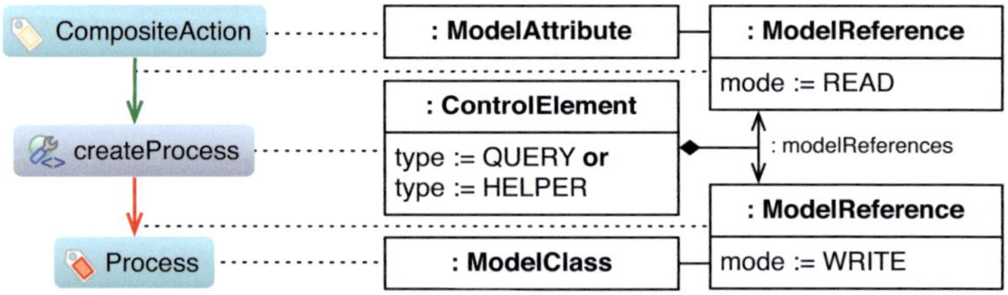

(c) Model use dependencies

Figure 4.4: Notation for dependence graph elements (dashed line marks correspondence)

4.4. Task-Oriented Filtering

Dependency graphs of model transformations can be huge, bearing the danger that useful information gets lost when studied by humans. Our idea is to identify and remove details which are irrelevant for performing a particular task before display. In this section, we present three filter functions and four useful combinations thereof.

As prerequisite for defining the filter functions, we formalize our dependency graph as follows: Let *ControlElement*, *ModelClass*, and *ModelAttribute* be sets that represent instances of metamodel classes of the same name, respectively. Furthermore, let $ModelElement := ModelClass \dot{\cup} ModelAttribute$ denote the set of `ModelElement` instances, i.e., the set containing instances of `ModelClass` and `ModelAttribute`. For referenced instances, let functions *modelReferences*, *modelElement*, *controlReferences*, *controlElement*, *superClasses*, *attributes* be defined by representing sets of instances of their respectively named metamodel reference. When applied to sets, functions are applied element-wise and the result is the union of each mapping.

Then, we create the dependency graph G as a tuple of vertices V and Edges E, i.e., $G = (V, E)$. V and E elements are created using *ControlElement*, *ModelClass*, and *ModelAttribute* elements by defining sets $V^{ControlElement}$, $V^{ModelClass}$, and $V^{ModelAttribute}$, as well as bijective functions ϕ_X (i.e., mapping rules), where

$$\begin{aligned}\phi_{ControlElement} &: ControlElement \rightarrow V^{ControlElement}\\ \phi_{ModelClass} &: ModelClass \rightarrow V^{ModelClass}\\ \phi_{ModelAttribute} &: ModelAttribute \rightarrow V^{ModelAttribute}\end{aligned}$$

We imply $V^{ControlElement}$, $V^{ModelClass}$, $V^{ModelAttribute}$ are pairwise disjunct by construction and define $V := V^{ControlElement} \dot{\cup} V^{ModelClass} \dot{\cup} V^{ModelAttribute}$. We further define $V^{ModelElement} := V^{ModelClass} \dot{\cup} V^{ModelAttribute}$. To obtain E

elements, where $E \subseteq V \times V$, we use the following four derivation rules:[1]

$$
\begin{aligned}
&\forall r_1, r_2 \in ControlElement : \\
&\qquad r_2 \in (controlElement \circ controlReferences)(r_1) \iff \\
&\qquad (\phi_{ControlElement}(r_1), \phi_{ControlElement}(r_2)) \in E \\
&\forall r \in ControlElement, e \in ModelElement : \\
&\qquad e \in (modelElement \circ elementReferences)(r) \iff \\
&\qquad (\phi_{ControlElement}(r), \phi_{ModelElement}(e)) \in E \\
&\forall c_1, c_2 \in ModelClass : \\
&\qquad c_2 \in superClasses(c_1) \iff (\phi_{ModelClass}(c_1), \phi_{ModelClass}(c_2)) \in E \\
&\forall a \in ModelAttribute, c \in ModelClass : \\
&\qquad a \in modelAttributes(c) \iff (\phi_{ModelAttribute}(a), \phi_{ModelClass}(c)) \in E
\end{aligned}
$$

4.4.1. Defining Four Filters

With these definitions in place, we are now able to define three basic filter functions on top of the graph structure G. One that retains control nodes alone, another that retains only a given element and elements that are directly linked to that element, and a last one that drops class attribute.

Filtering control nodes We define a filtering function removing data dependencies by

$$
\begin{aligned}
f^{controlflow}(V,E) := \left(V', E'\right), \text{ where} \\
V' &:= V \setminus V^{ModelElement} \\
E' &:= E \setminus (V^{ControlElement} \times V^{ModelElement}) \\
&\quad \setminus (V^{ModelClass} \times V^{ModelClass}) \\
&\quad \setminus (V^{ModelClass} \times V^{ModelAttribute})
\end{aligned}
$$

[1] The function composition operator "$\circ$" is defined as: $(g \circ f)(x) = g(f(x))$

Filtering direct dependencies. Let $v_{current} \in V$ be the node whose direct dependencies shall be filtered. Contextual filtering is defined by function

$$
\begin{aligned}
f^{context}_{v_{current}}(V,E) := (V',E'), \text{ where}\\
V' &:= \{v \in V \mid (v, v_{current}) \in E \vee (v_{current}, v) \in E\} \cup \\
&\quad \{v_{current}\}\\
E' &:= \{(v_1,v_2) \in E \mid v_1 = v_{current} \vee v_2 = v_{current}\}
\end{aligned}
$$

Filtering classes without attributes. To reduce complexity, attributes of classes and dependencies can be filtered by

$$
\begin{aligned}
f^{classes}(V,E) := \left(V',E'\right), \text{ where}\\
V' &:= V \setminus V^{ModelAttribute}\\
E' &:= E \setminus (V^{ControlElement} \times V^{ModelAttribute})\\
&\quad \setminus (V^{ModelAttribute} \times V^{ModelClass})
\end{aligned}
$$

These basic filter functions can be arbitrarily combined. However, the order in which functions are applied is relevant, and not all combinations can be conceived as useful. We define four filter combinations together with their primary field of application:

$$
\begin{aligned}
F1 &:= f^{controlflow},\\
F2 &:= (f^{context}_{v_{current}} \circ f^{controlflow}),\\
F3 &:= f^{context}_{v_{current}},\\
F4 &:= (f^{context}_{v_{current}} \circ f^{classes}).
\end{aligned}
$$

Next, we describe fields of application for each of the four filter combinations. We go through the Activity2Process maintenance scenarios from the introduction to demonstrate how these maintenance tasks can be solved by choosing the right type of filter. Figure 4.5 illustrates dependency graphs of Activity2Process using distinct filter combinations, configured in a way that aids in locating concerns for the tasks.

F1: *Show control dependencies of the complete transformation.* Resulting view helps to initially grasp the overall control structures of an unknown transformation. Filter F1 is useful for investigating unknown transformations of smaller and medium size.

F2: *Show control dependencies in context of the currently selected control node $v_{current}$.* With an overall understanding of the control structures, this filter reduces the view to direct control dependencies of an element. Filter F2 can be used to incrementally get an understanding of the behavior of larger transformations by progressively navigating the control elements. It is also practical while working within the text editor, as long as data dependencies are of no interest.

F3: *Show control and data dependencies in context of the currently selected control or data node, $v_{current}$.* When reading transformation rules, it makes sense to primarily concentrate on direct dependencies. In contrast to slicing criteria, only direct dependencies are displayed, both in forward and backward directions. This filter helps to cope with change requests where details at the attribute-level are required to locate concerns.

F4: *Show control and data dependencies in context of the currently selected control or data node $v_{current}$, but remove information about accessed class attributes.* The resulting view is the same as that from Filter F3, but further reduces data dependencies to the class-level. If an attribute is modified, the class the attribute belongs to is shown instead. Filter F4 is useful for change requests where details at the class-level are sufficient to locate concerns.

The filters were designed having typical maintenance tasks in mind. They reduce the effort spent by developers to understand transformation logic of previously unfamiliar code, and furthermore, they particularly help to locate concerns more quickly in typical maintenance tasks, as will be pointed out next.

4.4.2. Applying the Filters for Maintenance

At the beginning of this chapter, we have motivated the inferior support of common code editors for transformation languages regarding comprehension and maintenance processes. By the same three maintenance scenarios for the Activity2Process transformation we want to demonstrate benefits of a context-sensitive, interactive dependence view. At the same, Figure 4.5 gives example dependence graphs computed by Filters F1 – F4, configured such that they help to track down the locations of concern in the given three scenarios.

Modifying a module's inner logic. To determine all methods that call helper method `createProcess`, we apply Filter F1, yielding the graph shown in Figure 4.5a; for the user's convenience, we have moved the cursor to method `createProcess` in the text editor. Note that the method currently selected in the code view is highlighted in the graph view with an orange frame, and elements that do not lie in the direct context of the selected element are faded.

Filter F1 is useful in the first maintenance scenario, especially if we first need to get an initial understanding of the transformation logic: It reveals that `createProcess` is indeed only called from method `CompositeAction::mapAction2Step`, therefore the bug is supposed to reside there.

Filter F2's view may have sufficed to track the bug in the previously mentioned scenario, because we were only interested in direct caller dependencies of `createProcess`. In context of this mapping, the filter would yield the exact same graph shown in Figure 4.5a, though with the blurred elements omitted. The filter additionally helps at

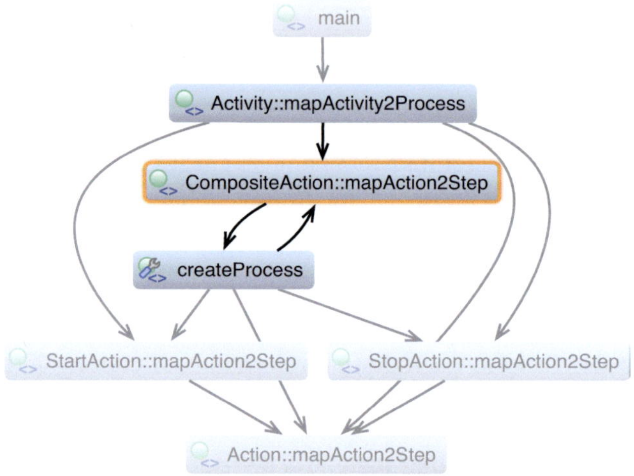

(a) Control dependencies for the transformation, with mapping `CompositeAction::mapAction2Step` highlighted

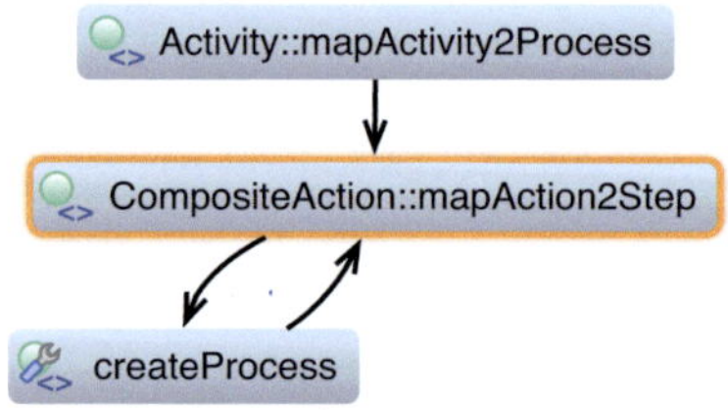

(b) Control dependencies in context of QVT-O mapping `CompositeAction::mapAction2Step`

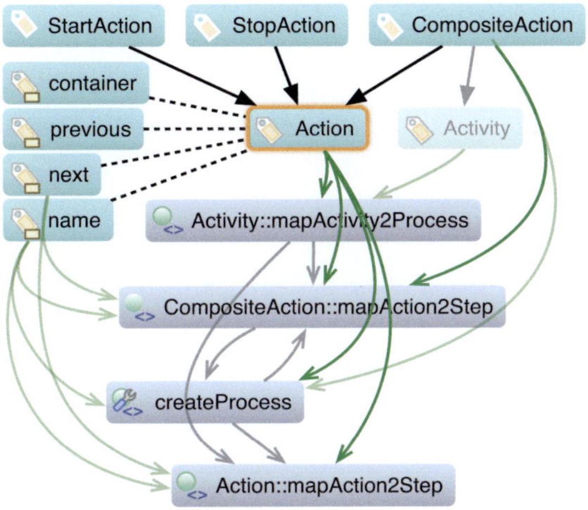

(c) Data and control dependencies for class `Action`

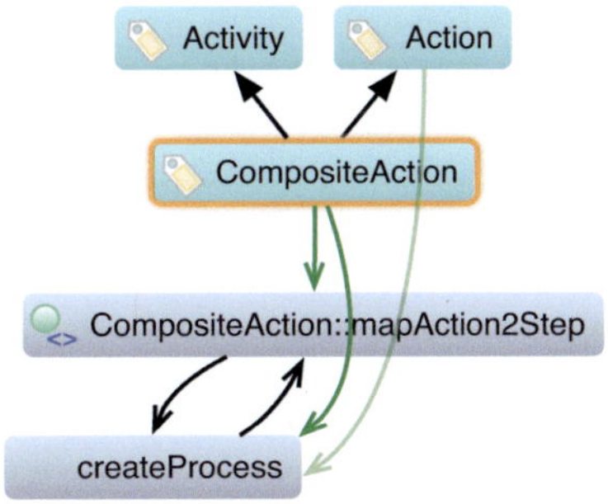

(d) Data and control dependencies for class `CompositeAction`

Figure 4.5: Filtered dependency graphs for the introductory Activity2Process example transformation understanding larger transformation programs by focusing on the portion of the graph that is highlighted in the code view, which can be successively explored by simple clicks. Figure 4.5b shows control dependencies in context of mapping `CompositeAction::mapAction2-Step`. A mouse click would shift the focus in both the code and this graph view to the clicked node. Backwards navigation using Eclipse's navigation history is possible.

Identifying locations of concern. In Section 4.1's second maintenance scenario, we must identify methods that refer to classes `Action` and `Step`. In both cases, we apply Filter F3 in context to show all operations modifying or reading the respective element. Figure 4.5c shows the graph we get with class `Action` in context. There are four mappings reading instances of class `Action`, according to outgoing connections shown in the graph. Notice that subclass `CompositeAction` and attribute `name` are already handled by the transformation at the time the graph was generated.

Refactoring the modular design. The last scenario requires a two-step procedure to locate methods that operate on elements of package `CompositeActions` to be factored out into a separate module accordingly.

In a first step, all methods must be found that operate on class `CompositeAction`, which is the only element in the package. Figure 4.5d depicts dependencies in context of class `CompositeAction` computed by Filter F4. The chosen filter provides enough information to identify methods that handle class `CompositeAction`, the first step in locating concerns for the last scenario. According to Figure 4.5b, there are two mappings that operate on `CompositeAction`, `CompositeAction::mapAction2Step` and `createProcess`.

In a second step, we may use Filter F1 to study control dependencies of methods `CompositeAction::mapAction2Step` and `createPro-`

cess. The filter helps to see if these methods refer to methods that are not referred to elsewhere, and that can be safely moved out as well. We may also judge the quality of this refactoring, because we can quickly see the mappings called. However, according to the graph, the only mappings used by the two candidate methods are the mappings responsible for classes `Action`, `StartAction`, `StopAction`. Hence, a module that would contain both candidate methods must solely import module `IAction2Step`.

By these three example scenarios one can already anticipate that the filters are able to remove much of the information that is irrelevant for accomplishing a particular task. We carried out an empirical study on a real QVT-O transformation to evince an increase in productivity in realistic maintenance scenarios. This study is further described in Chapter 6.

4.5. Applicability to Other Transformation Languages

So far, we have only considered concepts from QVT-O and QVT-R, but we have not yet clarified if dependence graphs can be applied to transformation languages that follow the imperative, declarative and mixed paradigms. For the purpose of demonstrating general applicability, we studied seven different kinds of transformation languages: QVT-O, QVT-R, and further on Xtend, ATL, ETL, Kermeta2, and VIATRA2. QVT-O, Xtend and Kermeta2 are imperative languages, whereas QVT-R is a fully declarative language; ATL, ETL and VIATRA2 combine declarative and imperative features.

We observed that all of these languages technically qualify for our dependence graph, because dependence information can be directly inferred from the available language concepts. Table 4.1 lists for each of the languages top-level control constructs that can be represented as control elements in the dependence graph (in the third column), call constructs that map to dependencies among control elements (in the fourth column), and those that equal model use dependencies (fifth column). As a proof-of-concept, we

Table 4.1.: Control elements and referencing concepts in selected transformation languages

<table>
<tr><th>Language</th><th>Control Constructs</th><th>Control Dependencies</th><th>Data Dependencies†</th></tr>
<tr><td>QVT-O
imperative</td><td>main
mapping M

helper H
query Q
constructor C</td><td>
map M ()
mapping M
inherits|
disjuncts|
merges M'
H (...)
Q (...)
new C</td><td>new B
object B
mapping A::M |
helper H
(..., out b: B,...
..., in a: A,...) : B
statically evaluable type A
of (sub) expression</td></tr>
<tr><td>QVT-R
declarative</td><td>top relation R
relation R
query Q</td><td>when {...R; ...}
where {...R; ...}
Q(...)
rule R overrides R'</td><td>enforce T b:B
checkonly S a:A
statically evaluable type A
of (sub) expression</td></tr>
<tr><td>Xtend
imperative</td><td>@Create(...)
def M (...)
def F(...)</td><td>M(...)
F(...)
override M' | F'</td><td>@Create(B)
def A F(..., a:A,...)
new B
statically evaluable type A
of (sub) expression</td></tr>
<tr><td>ATL
hybrid</td><td>rule R
from a:A to b:B

lazy rule L
helper H
query Q</td><td>implicit cast from A to B
resolveTemp(exp:A, 'b')
rule R extends R'
thisModule.L
H(...)
Q(...)</td><td>rule R
from a:A
to b:B
statically evaluable type A
of (sub) expression</td></tr>
<tr><td>ETL
hybrid</td><td>rule R
primary rule R
lazy Rrule R
operation O</td><td>equivalents()
equivalent()
rule R extends R'
O(...)</td><td>rule R
from a:A
to b:B
statically evaluable type A
of (sub) expression</td></tr>
<tr><td>Kermeta2
imperative</td><td>aspect class A {
operation O(...)
method M(...)
}</td><td>
self.O(...)
M(...)

inheritance mechanism</td><td>B.new
operation O |
method M
(..., a:A, ...) : B
statically evaluable type A
of (sub) expression</td></tr>
<tr><td>VIATRA2
hybrid</td><td>rule main()
gtrule G
rule R
pattern P</td><td>
apply G
apply R
find P</td><td>
gtrule G |
rule R |
pattern P
(..., out B,...
..., in A,...) : B
statically evaluable type A
of (sub) expression</td></tr>
</table>

† Placeholder *A* for type names stands for types from one of the source models (read access), and placeholder *B* stands for types from the target model (write access).

implemented a mapping from QVT-O and QVT-R in the implementations *Eclipse QVTo* and *Eclipse mediniQVT*.

Below, we discuss how concepts from each of the languages could map to our graph model, sparing QVT-O and QVT-R which already have been thoroughly discussed at this point.

Xtend With Xtend being a Java-like GPL, there is no particular concept for mapping methods. However, *active annotations* can be used to augment the language with domain-specific concepts. As mentioned in the previous chapter, we have defined an annotation `@Create` which adds tracing and implicit instantiation of return types. A simpler language concept that is integrated in the language is the cached statement, which can be used in combination with a `new` operator on return types. The graph builder can be made aware of either mapping concept. Xtend is able to use EMF/Ecore-based models when compiled to Java source code.

The language can be, and in practice is more often than not, used as a model-to-text rather than a model-to-model transformation language due to its powerful template expressions. When extracting dependence information from Xtend scripts that incorporate template expressions, we have two choices, ignoring the textual output at all, or statically analysing each method if it uses file-based output library methods, and synthesizing an artificial target model that represents files (for instance, one class per call). The latter technique will be used in Chapter 5, where it is described in greater detail.

ATL The Atlas Transformation Language [JAB+06] unifies declarative concepts with a few imperative concepts, namely called rules and lazy rules which must be invoked imperatively. ATL rules are similarly structured as QVT-R relations, they use/from to instead of checkonly/enforce to denote input/output domains. Lazy rules resemble non-top relations and must be explicitly called, helper and query functions resemble the same-titled QVT-O concepts. On the implementation-level, ATL uses a highly OCL-like expression language. Trace resolution is either done implicitly by coercing a type cast from input to output model elements for which a rule exists, or by calling method `resolveTemp`.

ETL The Epsilon Transformation Language [KPP08] follows a similar approach as the ATL, both offering a mixture of declarative and imperative constructs, and both founded on an OCL-like language – in this case, the Epsilon Object Language (EOL). The concept of primary and lazy rules resembles ATL's concept of ordinary rules and lazy rules. Explicit trace queries are realized by operations `equivalents` and `equivalent`, depending on if the query is executed on a single element or a collection.

Kermeta2 Kermeta2 is a metaprogramming environment based on an object-oriented DSL. The language can be classified as an imperative GPL and thus falls into a similar category as Xtend, with both being usable as a universal programming language. Originally, the language has been designed to add dynamic semantics to object models, but it can be additionally used to implement model transformations [MFV+05]. The recommended design is a source-based visitor pattern. Source classes are annotated by aspect classes that implement traversal operations. Elements are instantiated solely via the `new` operator. A traceability API is not yet integrated.

VIATRA2 In the collection of languages presented here, the VIATRA2 transformation language [VB07] advocates the graph transformation formalism. What differentiates the language from other graph transformation approaches is a textual notation, and further that the ASM formalism complements VIATRA2 with imperative concepts for better practicality. Readers not familiar with graph transformation concepts are referred to Section 2.1.7 for a brief introduction into the concept triple graph grammars. There is only one implicitly triggered rule named `main()`, any other rule must be triggered explicitly using the `apply` statement. Patterns are factored out into a separate `pattern` construct, and the pattern matcher can be invoked by a `find` execution statement. Rules and patterns can have input and output parameters, tagged `in` and `out`; any of the declared input parameters must be passed at invocation time. There is a set of commands for model manipulation in the imperative style not listed in the table, including `new`, `rename`, `move`, `setTo`, `copy` and `delete` among others. VIATRA transformations support MOF standards compliant modeling languages including its own metamodeling environment, the VIATRA Textual Metamodeling Language (VTML).

Discussion of the concepts demonstrates that in the future, additional transformation languages that belong to various programming paradigms can be analyzed for model dependence information. Obtained information can then be visualized in the same way as proposed for QVT languages.

4.6. Concluding Remarks

Regarding model transformations, much complexity is induced by data and control dependencies: The larger input and output metamodels are, the more transformation mappings are required (control dependencies), and the number of referred metamodel elements increases (data dependencies). Call dependencies between mappings can be quite complex, and indirect data dependencies cannot be seen from investigating a mapping without looking at all called or depending mappings. This observation accounts for programs written in transformation languages following any paradigm, be it a declarative, imperative and hybrid language.

In this chapter, we demonstrated a novel approach to visualize data and control flow dependencies of metamodels and transformations using interactive node-link diagrams (NLDs). Interactively navigable dependency graphs are integrated into transformation development IDEs (namely Eclipse QVT Operational Mappings (QVTo) and MediniQVT) as a complementary view to existing textual editors. We expect such a view to ease the effort to understand and maintain model transformations. The view has been integrated into the Eclipse environment and provides adapters for Eclipse QVTmedini and Eclipse QVTo. Adapters for further transformation languages may be easily added, as shown in the previous section.

Our visual analytics approach for model transformations currently provides NLDs for graphical representation. Further information could be attached to this view, for instance warnings and errors emitted by the type checker. Different types of visualizations could offer an improved user experience, for example *filtered hierarchical edge bundlings (HEBs)*. Automatic layout algorithms could be improved and adjusted to better display model transformation mappings and rules. Custom model and transformation refactoring operations could be provided on the graph structure, inspired by Kruse [Kru11]. Additionally, analysis of OCL expressions [JGB11] may be refined, as not all data dependencies are captured yet.

At the moment, the approach uses static type analysis; dynamically typed languages are not supported. However, there are few transformation languages – we only know of RubyTL – that use dynamic typing. Reflective programming can lead to a loss of type information, even in a statically typed language like OCL. OCL since version 2.5 supports reflective programming, e.g. one can select types based on their class name: Instead of using OCL's type selector that explicitly refers to the type, as in Listing 1.1a, line 7,

```
activity.rootObjects()[Activity]
```

we could alternatively use reflective programming,

```
activity.rootObjects()->select(metaClassName() = "Activity")
```

Although reflective programming constructs as the above one can be used in QVT-O and QVT-R, developers are generally discouraged to use reflection capabilities, as they can lead to code with poorer maintainability due to a loss of static type information. Nevertheless, in practical maintenance scenarios, accuracy of a statically derived dependence graph is sufficiently high to provide a significant benefit, as will be revealed in an empirical study presented in Chapter 6. Nevertheless, possible future work could tackle this issue by including dynamic type information into the displayed graph, i.e., types that have been derived when running a program on particular input data, a technique named *footprint estimations* [JGB11].

5. Remodularizing Legacy Transformations with Automatic Clustering

While modeling languages typically provide means to structure classes into packages for improved understandability, transformation programs can be structured into modules to cope with their inherent code complexity. Most transformation languages provide basic module concepts to allow for a fine-grained structuring of the code. In practice, however, the structure of transformations steadily deteriorates as the models evolve, and eventually leads to adverse effects on the productivity during maintenance. This observation has been reported by practitioners from Whittle's studies [WHR+13, p. 9] (cf. Chapter 1), and coincides with our own experiences from the Palladio project. At this point, it remains a manual process to discover concern-based structures of transformation programs, which are essential for understanding and refactoring the programs. Although the preceding chapter's visualization approach reduces the effort to understand transformation programs, it still requires human experts to identify a suitable structure.

In this chapter, we propose to apply clustering algorithms to find decompositions of transformation programs at the method level in a fully automatic manner. In contrast to clustering techniques for general-purpose languages, we integrate not only method calls but also class and package dependencies of the models into the process. We support the three transformation-specific styles identified by Lawley [LDGR04], the source-driven, the target-driven and the aspect-driven decompositional style. The approach relies on the Bunch tool [MM06] for finding decompositions with minimal coupling and maximal cohesion. Extraction of dependence information relies on techniques described in the previous Chapter 4.

Parts of this chapter have been previously published at the AMT workshop, collocated with the MODELS 2014 conference. The present text has been extensively expanded and revised.

Presentation of the approach is organized as follows: We continue this chapter by characterizing three established designs of model transformation programs in Section 5.1. The overall approach which we use to find clusterings of model transformations is described in Section 5.2. The approach comprises four steps described in the next four sections. Section 5.3 gives details on how a dependence graph is extracted from the code. In Section 5.4, we describe how we automatically derive clusterings from the graph. Section 5.5 presents the technique we use to extract an existing modular structure from transformation programs. Section 5.6 gives detail on how results gained from cluster analysis and structural analysis can be used to refactor the transformation at hand. In Section 5.7 we demonstrate applicability to other widely used transformation languages. Eventually, Section 5.8 concludes this chapter.

5.1. Expert Design of Model Transformation Programs

Reconsider the introductory Activity2Process example from Chapter 1. Both maintenance scenarios emphasize the need to keep the scope of models and the number of modules that are imported at a minimum; internally, mappings in a module may have arbitrary references to each other. This relates to two software metrics to measure the quality of a module decomposition, favoring a low degree of method and data interconnectivity between modules and a high degree of intraconnectivity of methods within a module (*low coupling* and *high cohesion*).

In an optimal decomposition, each module encapsulates a single concern with a minimal model scope, and model scopes overlap for as few modules as possible. It is not always as simple as in the Activity2Process scenario, where a mapping references exactly one class including its attributes and references per domain. Depending on the transformation language that is used, mappings may read instances of multiple classes in the source domain and create and/or modify instances of multiple classes in the target domain. Some languages even allow in-place transformations to be defined, where source and target domains overlap.

By observing transformations that have been manually implemented by experts, we can distinguish three classic styles of how a transformation is structured [DGL+05]. Figure 5.1 iconically represents the three design alternatives on the level of mapping rules.

Source-driven decomposition In this case, for objects of each class in the source domain, objects of one or more classes are generated in the target domain (one-to-many mappings). Transformations where models are transformed to models that are equally or less abstract usually fall into this category. The Activity2Process transformation is a typical candidate for a source-driven decomposition. It traverses the tree-like structured activity model, and each node embodies an own high-level concept that is mapped to target concepts. This kind of design often applies to in-place transformations that only modify a small subset of the input model and output the results.

Target-driven decomposition When objects of a particular class in the target domain are constructed from information distributed over instances of multiple classes in the source domain (many-to-one mappings), a target-driven decomposition is deemed more adequate (cf. [DGL+05]). It occurs regularly for transformations from low-level to high-level concepts (synthesizing transformations).

Aspect-driven decomposition In several cases, a mixture of the two applies. Aspect-driven decompositions are required whenever a single concern is distributed over multiple concepts in both domains (many-to-many mappings). In-place transformations (i.e., transformations within a single domain) that replace concepts with low-level concepts

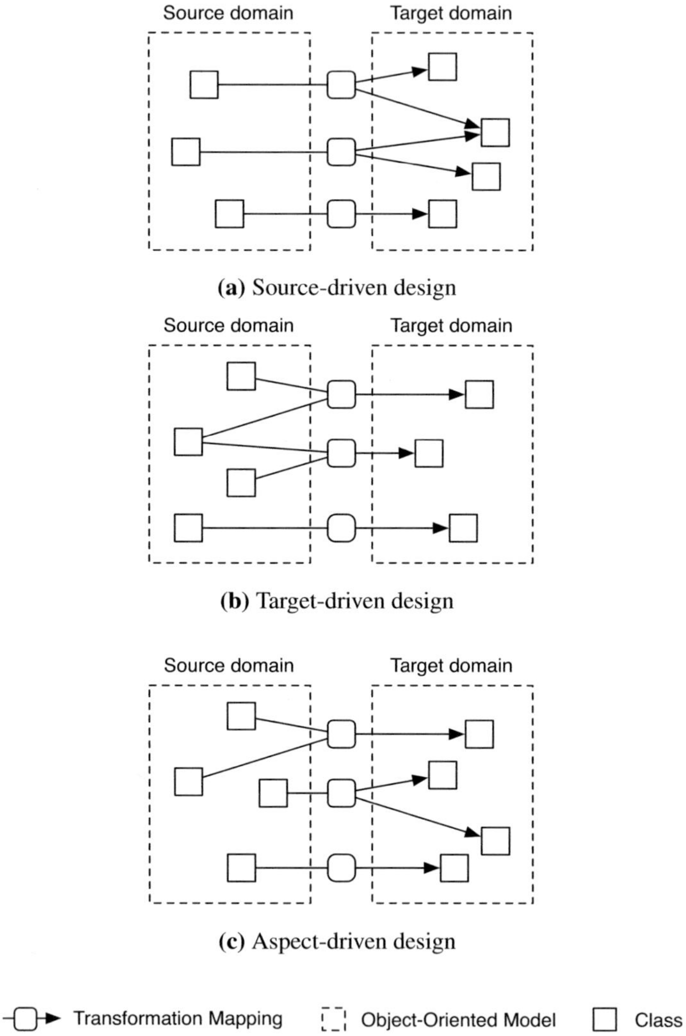

Figure 5.1: Prevalent designs of model transformations

often have to be implemented in this style, particularly if operations are executed per concern and affect multiple elements in the domain. The technique can be used to alleviate an occurent tangling and scattering of the rules, as pointed out by Kurtev et al. [KvBJ06; KvBJ07].

Whilst these styles reflect the design at the mapping level, they affect a modular design accordingly. Note that a single mapping symbolized in Figure 5.1 can be or even has to be implemented by multiple control constructs, depending on the language's capabilities and the underlying logic that is to be implemented. For example, consider a one-to-many mapping from the source-driven decomposition. Such a single concern may require multiple control constructs to implement the mapping in question, one per element created on the target side. A many-to-one mapping, on the other hand, might additionally be accompanied by query functions to collect information from various places in the source model. It is considered a good style to aggregate all top-level constructs that implement a specific concern into a single module. The three design patterns and their ramification on a modular design have been pointed out by Lawley [LDGR04].

Therefore, any of these styles – and preferably also mixtures of the three – must be supported by an automatic decomposition analysis in order to produce meaningful results.

5.2. Overall Approach

We decided to use Bunch, because it uses classic low-coupling and high-cohesion heuristics that match the information hiding property we are heading for, it does not make further assumptions regarding the underlying semantics, and because it has gained a good reputation so far [MB07]. Hill climbing has been reported to produce better results than the genetic algorithm included [SMDM05], which coincides with our own experiences.

The methodology of our automatic clustering approach for model transformations follows to a wide extent the typical procedure of software clustering

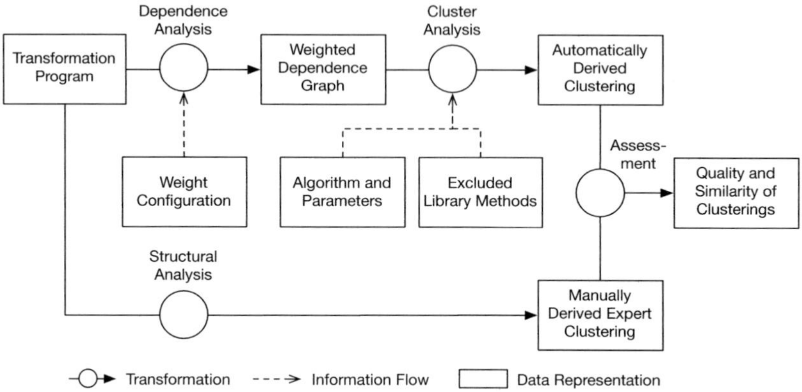

Figure 5.2: Clustering approach

approaches in general. It comprises three steps (Figure 5.2). In the first step, dependence information is statically analyzed and extracted from the source files, resulting in a weighted dependence graph. It is crucial to choose appropriate weights for the types of dependencies that are going to be extracted. The graph serves as input for the cluster analysis. Before running cluster analysis as the second step, an appropriate algorithm must be chosen, and the algorithm's parameters are to be configured. Bunch gives us the ability to identify some of the nodes as globally used library methods ("Excluded Library Methods" in the figure), which can be done in an optional step. In the last step, the automatically derived clustering has to be analyzed. One option is to compare results with the existing modular decomposition that is automatically extractable from the source files, for instance using some of the available similarity measures. As another option, developers may also compare clusterings derived with alternative weights, either manually, or using similarity or quality metrics. This whole procedure can be repeated with different configurations. Developers planning to refactor the present code manually to obtain an improved modular structure can base their decisions on the computed clusterings.

In the following subsections, we will address any of the steps one by one, and elaborate on the peculiarities that appear in light of model transformations. The Activity2Process scenario from the introduction will be used as a running example.

5.3. Dependence Analysis

A preliminary step in any graph-based clustering approach is to extract dependence information from software systems in a graph-based form. When dealing with general-purpose programming languages, various source code analysis tools are available to choose from. However, as we want to extract dependencies from languages specific to the domain of model transformations, we have to build our own structural analyzers, one for each transformation language to be supported.

We use static analysis, i.e., only information is used that is immediately available at the syntactic level, whereas dynamic information that results from (partial) execution of the source code is not used. Here, in the context of transformation programs, we consider not only control constructs and dependencies, but in addition to that the structure of involved models and model use dependencies among control constructs and model elements.

We reuse ideas from the previous chapter's approach that visualizes the obtained dependence graph to aid in the process of transformation maintenance [RNHR13]. The approach presented there is already able to extract method-level dependencies, information on the model structure, and model use dependencies of the methods. In this context, slightly different information is required by the intended clustering algorithm than for visualization. Thus, we are going to define a graph structure that captures relevant information. In this section, we focus on the differences, namely untyped nodes, the option to carry out package-level dependence extraction, and weighted edges configured according to the type of dependence relation.

5.3.1. Implementation Structure

Any method that is present in one of the source files is represented by a single node $v_i \in V$ in the graph $G = (V, E)$. For instance, QVT-O defines four different types of methods, namely helpers, mappings, queries, and constructors; these are all translated to nodes in the graph.

The extraction of top-level constructs and use dependencies among control nodes is equivalent to what has been described in Section 4.3.2, hence we will only give a brief description of the mapping from language to graph concepts.

Method call dependencies are extracted as follows: For any two nodes $v_i, v_j \in V$ in the graph where each node represents a distinct method, $v_i \neq v_j$, a directed edge points from v_i to v_j, $\langle v_i, v_j \rangle \in E$, iff the method represented by v_i calls or otherwise references the method represented by v_j.

Definition 5.1 (Extraction of Method Call Dependencies):

$$\forall\, v_i, v_j \in V_{Methods} : \exists\, \langle v_i, v_j \rangle \in E \Leftarrow v_i \neq v_j \wedge \\ \textit{method represented by } v_i \textit{ references method represented by } v_j$$

In QVT-O, a single call (indicated by keyword `map`) may refer to multiple methods in the case of method dispatching, and references may arise from reuse dependencies (keywords are `disjunct`, `merge`, `override`, and `extend`). The same applies to Xtend, where methods can be annotated with the keyword `dispatch`, and override methods from super classes (keyword `override`).

5.3.2. Model Structure

Any package and class in one of the models that are used by the transformation is represented by a distinct node in the graph.

Package containment is extracted as follows: For any two nodes $v_i, v_j \in V$ in the graph where each represents a distinct model element, $v_i \neq v_j$, a directed edge points from v_i to v_j, $\langle v_i, v_j \rangle \in E$, iff v_i represents a class or package and v_j represents a package that directly contains that class or package.

Additionally, inheritance and reference relationships among classes are defined. For any two nodes $v_i, v_j \in V$ in the graph where each represents a class, $v_i \neq v_j$, a directed edge points from v_i to v_j, $\langle v_i, v_j \rangle \in E$, iff v_i represents a class that inherits from or references instances of another class represented by v_j.

Definition 5.2 (Extraction of Model Structure):

$$\forall\ v_i \in V_{Classes} \cup V_{Packages}, v_j \in V_{Packages} :\ \exists\ \langle v_i, v_j \rangle \in E \Leftarrow v_i \neq v_j\ \wedge$$
$$\textit{model element represented by } v_i \textit{ is directly contained}$$
$$\textit{in package represented by } v_j$$

$$\forall\ v_i, v_j \in V_{Classes} :\ \exists\ \langle v_i, v_j \rangle \in E \Leftarrow v_i \neq v_j\ \wedge$$
$$\textit{class represented by } v_i \textit{ inherits from or references}$$
$$\textit{instances of another class represented by } v_j$$

The same techniques apply that have been described in Chapter 4 to extract this information from MOF compliant modeling languages.

5.3.3. Model Use Dependencies

For any two nodes $v_i, v_j \in V$ in the graph, where node v_i represents a method and node v_j a class or package, $v_i \neq v_j$, a directed edge points from v_i to v_j, $\langle v_i, v_j \rangle \in E$, iff the method represented by v_i implicitly or explicitly refers to one of the classes or packages of the involved models. We distinguish model use dependencies with read access and write access; depending on the access type, a different weight is assigned to the edge, as will be described below.

Definition 5.3 (Extraction of Model Use Dependencies):

$$\forall\ v_i \in V_{Methods}, v_j \in V_{Classes} \cup V_{Packages} :\ \exists\ \langle v_i, v_j \rangle \in E \Leftarrow v_i \neq v_j\ \wedge$$
$$\textit{method represented by } v_i \textit{ references implicitly or}$$
$$\textit{explicitly model element represented by } v_j$$

```
def map2JavaInterface(OperationInterface oi) '''
  public interface «oi.javaName()»
  {
    «oi.interfaceHelperMethodsDeclarationTM»
    «FOR iface : oi.signatures SEPARATOR ";"»
      «iface.operationSignature»
    «ENDFOR»;
  }
'''
```

Listing 5.1: Xtend template method

Extracting model use dependencies is the same as described in the previous chapter with a single exception: the analysis can be optionally carried out on package-level. In this case, if a model use dependency is detected that refers to a class, the containing package is chosen instead as target node.

In QVT-O, read dependencies occur as both context and `in`/`inout` parameters, or within the implementation body for each of the intermediate OCL expression's inferable type; write dependencies occur in the form of a mapping's result parameter and explicit instantiations via `new` or `object` operator. We provide an alternative extraction method that reduces class-level dependencies to package-level dependencies. When using Xtend as a model-to-text transformation language, file system access API is used to generate files at various points in the program.

Transformation programs that generate textual artifacts from models typically use a template-based approach. The Xtend language provides rich string expressions for this purpose. A rich string expression is a multi-line string expression that allows developers to embed model queries, conditionals and loops into the string. Listing 5.1 gives an example for the use of template expressions. The method `map2JavaInterface` from the PCM2SimuCom transformation – further discussed in the validation section below – uses them to maps interfaces of a component model to Java interfaces.

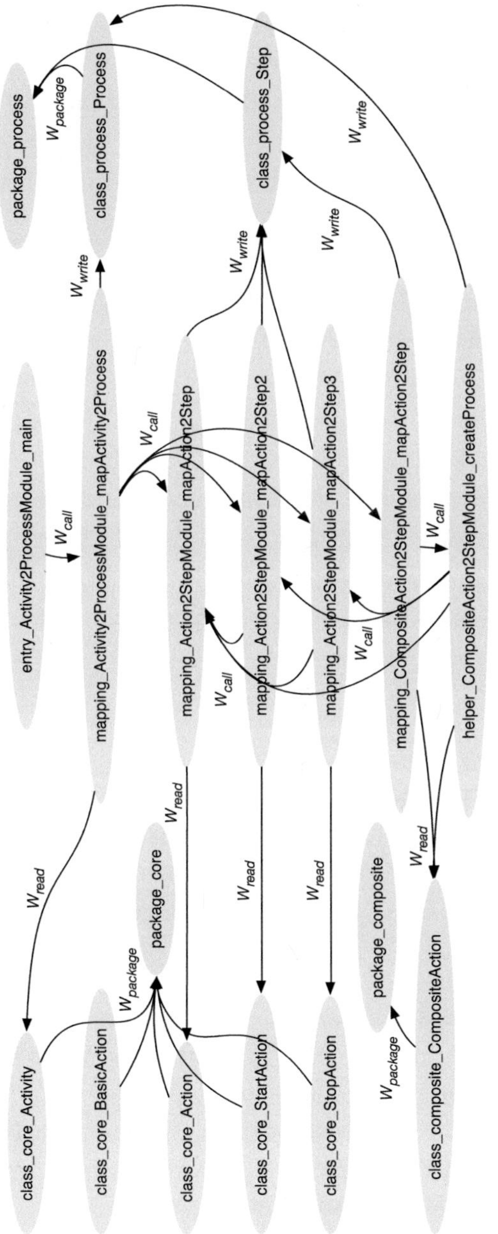

Figure 5.3: Activity2Process transformation – Extracted dependence graph

Rich strings use triple quotation marks, and may contain expressions enclosed by guillemets «... ». The method returns a string that is eventually stored to a file using function `generateFile` from the `FileSystemAccess` API. For any method in an Xtend script that calls `FileSystemAccess::generateFile`, we conceive the method to have a write dependency to a distinct node in the graph that represents the generated file.

Figure 5.3 depicts the graph that has been extracted from the Activity2Process example transformation. The attentive reader should notice that there is no differentiation on the type of nodes; model elements and control nodes are treated the same. Still, dependence relations among the nodes can be assigned different weights depending on their type to prioritize the importance of nodes in the clustering process. Subsequently, we are going to discuss the role these weights play in controlling the clustering algorithm.

Bunch stores dependence graphs in a simple textual form, where each line declares an edge by naming start and end node and an optional weight, separated by whitespace characters. Nodes are uniquely identifiable strings that lack whitespace characters.

5.3.4. Weight Configuration

To guide the clustering algorithm, the influence of dependence relations can be regulated manually. For this purpose, a weighting function $w : E \to \mathbb{N}_0$ assigns positive numbers to the edges in the graph. Depending on the type of dependency represented by the respective edge, we use the following weights:

W_{write} for write-access dependencies to classes and packages,

W_{read} for read-access dependencies to classes and packages from one of the method's parameters,

$W_{navigate}$ for read-access dependencies to classes and packages from within a method body[1],

W_{call} for method call dependencies,

$W_{package}$ for containment of classes and packages to their directly containing package[2],
$W_{reference}$ for associations from one class to another[3],
$W_{contain}$ for aggregations (i.e., containment references) between classes, and
$W_{inherit}$ for inheritance relationships between classes.

These weights constitute a particular weight configuration, vector

$$WC := \langle W_{write}, W_{read}, W_{navigate}, W_{call}, \\ W_{package}, W_{reference}, W_{contain}, W_{inherit} \rangle \in \mathbb{N}_0^8.$$

Since Bunch aims to maximize the MQ value, a higher weighted edge increases the chance that the nodes connected by the edge end up in the same cluster. Choosing a weight of zero naturally results in the respective type of edge being ignored by the clustering algorithm. Choosing values $W_{write} \gg W_{read}$ promotes a mainly target-driven decomposition, whereas values $W_{write} \ll W_{read}$ enforce a mainly source-driven decomposition.

5.4. Cluster Analysis

Once dependence information has been extracted from the source files in form of a graph, and weights have been configured accordingly, cluster analysis can be performed on the obtained graph structure in a follow-up step. With Bunch, we can choose from various algorithms, manually define

[1] It is important to note that our dependence graph model from Chapter 4 does not differentiate between read access dependencies that originate from a method's input parameters and those that derive from the method's implementation body, W_{read} and $W_{navigate}$.

[2] Previous chapter's dependence graph model abstracts away from package elements, whereas at this point we are explicitly interested in them as they expose structural information of the models involved.

[3] We discriminate containment and non-containment associations, because they expose important structural information of the models. Furthermore, bidirectional associations are reduced to a single direction, because Bunch presumes dependence graphs to not contain reflexive edges.

a list of nodes that represent library methods and are excluded from the clustering process, and even predetermine manually derived clusters for a subset of nodes in the graph.

5.4.1. Algorithm and Parameters

Bunch supports three clustering algorithms, exhaustive search, hill climbing, and a genetic algorithm. An exhaustive search is impractical in most realistic scenarios due to graph partitioning being an NP-hard problem. The remaining two search algorithms, hill climbing and the genetic algorithm, are evolutionary search techniques and can be parametrized further. Regarding hill climbing, parameters are the size of the population the minimum percent of search space to consider, the percent of search space that is randomized, and if used, various simulated annealing parameters. Bunch supports variants of the modularization quality index to be used as fitness function.

In this chapter, we solely use Bunch's hill climbing algorithm together with the "Incremental MQ Weighted" metric, since from our experience, this combination appeared to produce more stable results. We use a consistent configuration, with population size set to 100, the minimum search space set to 90%, and randomization to 10%. Simulated annealing has been disabled. This is also preset by Bunch as the default configuration.

5.4.2. Excluding Library Methods

Most software makes use of a set of helper methods that are used by many other methods. Because of their omnipresence, they can be specified for being excluded from the clustering process. Else, the algorithm would try to assign those to one of the clusters, thereby introducing a lot of noise in the output and even distorting the outcome. Model transformation programs, as well, often use common helper and query methods that are usually put into a separate module. However, if helper methods are expected to be useful only for a single module, developers might consider to move such methods into the respective module.

5.4.3. Excluding Model Elements

One could explicitly make the models separate modules on the package-level, but this would not help in minimizing the scope at the class-level.

Thus, we decided to include both model elements and transformation methods into the clustering process, so that classes, packages and mappings are clustered indifferently of their type. Through this, the algorithm will try to group all mapping methods that reference a particular class into the same cluster.

5.4.4. Predefined Clusters

Clustering algorithms must rely on a sufficiently simple metric to find partitions. Such metric can never replace knowledge by human experts, who are able to include sophisticated design decisions and semantics beyond cohesion and coupling. It is commonly accepted by researchers in the field that automatized clustering approaches like Bunch will never replace expert knowledge. Therefore, Bunch gives users the ability to preassign some of the nodes to clusters, and leave the rest of the nodes to be automatically assigned by Bunch.

5.4.5. Clustering the Activity2Process Example Transformation

Figure 5.4 depicts the clustering that has been computed from the Activity2Process's weighted dependence graph. Colored nodes (or darker shaded nodes in a black and white printout) represent the transformation's methods, while light gray nodes mark the transformation's model elements.

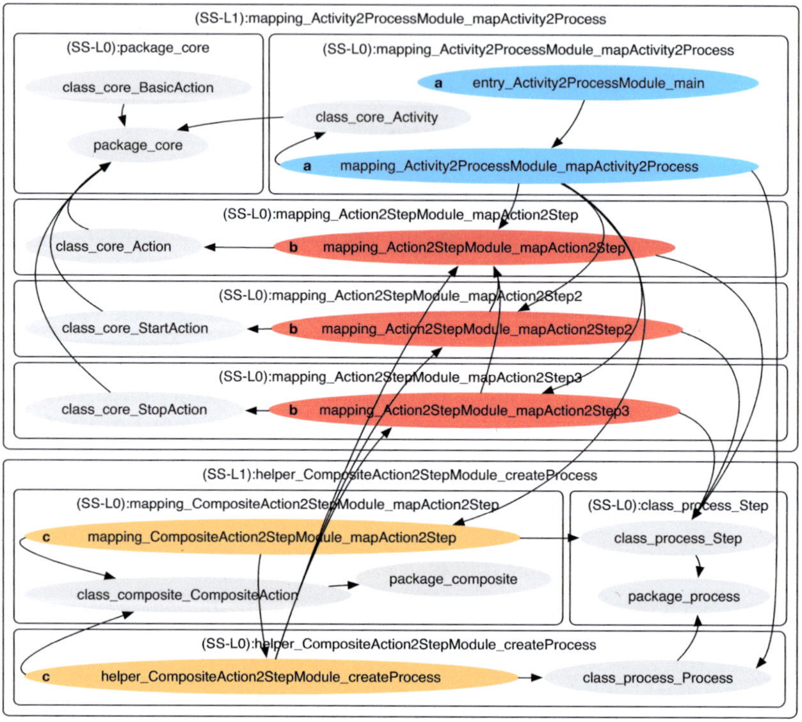

Figure 5.4: Activity2Process transformation – Bunch-derived clustering based on class-level dependencies vs. expert clustering (denoted by small letters in bold)

Boxes mark a two-level partitioning created by Bunch – L0 stands for the lower and more detailed level, whereas L1 partitions subsume one or more L0 partitions. For this clustering, a weight configuration

$$\begin{array}{llllllll} \langle W_{write}, & W_{read}, & W_{navigate}, & W_{call}, & W_{package}, & W_{reference}, & W_{contain}, & W_{inherit} \rangle := \\ \langle 1, & 15, & 0, & 5, & 15, & 0, & 0, & 0 \rangle \end{array}$$

has been used. With a sufficiently higher weight for read than for write dependencies, $15 \gg 1$, a source-driven decomposition has been performed. Therefore, mapping methods have been grouped together with their respective source model elements (`Activity`, `Action`, etc.) on L0. Two of the clusters solely contain model elements and can be ignored. In the L1 partition, two clusters remain: One cluster aggregates `Activity2Process` and `Action2Step` methods, the other cluster aggregates `CompositeAction2-Step` methods. The reference to class `CompositeAction` may have primarily induced the algorithm to correctly group the respective methods together.

When comparing the Bunch-derived L0 partition with our handmade partitioning illustrated by small letters a, b, and c in bold (cf. Figure 5.4), we can observe that both partitions are highly similar. Bunch, however, decided to agglomerate the L0 clusters to a single L1 cluster, whereas the expert decided to put them into two individual clusters a and b. Developers may think about adopting Bunch's recommendation and merge clusters `Activity2Process` and `Action2Step`.

5.5. Structural Analysis

Only few transformation programs are designed completely monolithically. In practice, a given transformation program is likely to already implement a modular design albeit a degraded or obsolete one.

To include the legacy modular structure of the code into a later assessment, an automatized structural analysis can be used that extracts this information. When generating dependence graphs, we have deliberately ignored language concepts used to modularize transformation code. For the purpose of comparing automatically generated partitions with the already encoded partition, it can be helpful to automatically derive modularization information from the program under study.

The Bunch tool that we use here relies on so-called Structural Information Language (SIL) files to persist partition information using a proprietary textual file format. A SIL file comprises one line for each partition declared, where a line names the partition in braces prefixed by keyword `SS` (short

```
SS(mainmodule_Activity2ProcessModule):
    entry_Activity2ProcessModule_main,
    mapping_Activity2ProcessModule_Activity2Process
SS(mainmodule_Action2StepModule):
    mapping_Action2StepModule_Action2Step,
    mapping_Action2StepModule_Action2Step2,
    mapping_Action2StepModule_Action2Step3
SS(mainmodule_CompositeAction2StepModule):
    helper_CompositeAction2StepModule_createProcess,
    mapping_CompositeAction2StepModule_Action2Step
```

Listing 5.2: Activity2Process example – SIL file

for subsystem), followed by a comma-separated list of nodes assigned to that partition. Names of partitions and nodes have to be unique and, like identifiers in Java or C, free of whitespace characters.

Detecting the modular structure is straight forward, yet highly language dependent. In QVT-O, a module is declared using one of keywords `transformation` or `library`. Starting from the main modules, import declarations (keyword `import`) help to recursively identify additionally used modules. Elements in a partition are all control constructs defined in a module, model elements are omitted because in the general case there is no uniquely assigned partition. Listing 5.2 shows the SIL file generated from Listing 1.1.

5.6. Assessment

The main objective of the approach presented in this chapter is to gain a better understanding of the code, but also to agree on a modular decomposition that fosters understandability and that can be used to restructure the code. To achieve this goal, in this last step, the existing modular structure and partitions computed by the algorithm on different parameters are compared against each other regarding their modularization quality and structural differences. Although this is a manual step that requires to find a compromise on two or more partitions and to refine the solution based on expert knowledge, developers can profit from a set of metrics to simplify the process. Metrics support expert decisions by giving objective and repeatable quality measures [KB04]. We require metrics to find answers to two questions:

Is one clustering of inferior quality than another clustering? With regards to cohesion and coupling as a quality measure, one can use Bunch's MQ value to judge the quality by a single value. In the context of this work, the MQ value is also the fitness function by which automatically derived clusterings are judged by.

To what degree are two clusterings similar? There are various metrics to measure the similarity between two graphs, each paying attention to different aspects, e.g., if to consider nodes alone or edges as well, others measurements calculate the distance in terms of modification operations. We use three similarity measures that were already used for comparing Bunch produced clusterings against manually derived clustering [MM08].

5.6.1. Modularization Quality

In context of the Bunch tool, it makes sense to observe the modularization quality index that Bunch uses to assess partitions when searching for a (quasi-)optimal partition. The MQ value can be computed for both method and model dependencies (which it has been optimized for), but also for method dependencies alone. For manually encoded partitions, the MQ value is only available for method dependencies alone, because model elements are not assigned to any clusters. With Bunch's user-driven clustering method, however, one could run Bunch on the preclustered methods to make Bunch cluster the remaining model elements.

5.6.2. Similarity

We use three similarity measures to quantify the similarity of a sample clustering with the expert clustering, Precision/Recall, EdgeSim, and MeCl.

The latter two had been specifically built for the software domain by Mitchell et al. [MM08], all three are supported by the Bunch tool.

Precision and Recall Precision is calculated as the percentage of node pairs in a single cluster of a sample clustering that are also contained within a single cluster in the authoritative clustering. Recall, on the other hand, is defined as the percentage of node pairs within a single cluster in the authoritative clustering that are also node pairs within a single cluster in the sample clustering [ST12]. The metric does not consider edges, and another drawback is the metric's sensitivity to the size and number of clusters [MM01].

EdgeSim The EdgeSim similarity measure [MM01] calculates the normalized ratio of intra and intercluster edges that are present in both partitions. Nodes are not taken into account.

MergeClumps The MergeClumps (MeCl) metric is a distance measure [MM01]. Starting with the largest subsets of entities that have been placed in each of the partitions into the same clusters, a series of merge operations is calculated that is needed to convert one partition into the other. Both directions are considered, and the largest number of merge operations (in a normalized form) is taken as the MeCl distance.

We decided for the three measures due to their good reputation they have gained in the community [ST12]. Other measurements that are used in other contexts include MojoFM [WT04] and the Koschke-Eisenbarth metric [KE00], as surveyed by Shtern et al. [ST12].

5.6.3. Assessing the Activity2Process Example Transformation

We use the above measurements to compare quality and similarity of manually and automatically derived partitions in the Activity2Process example: Results are given in Table 5.2. The expert clustering – the one manu-

Table 5.2.: Activity2Process – Manual vs. derived clustering

Configuration	Statistics		Similarity to expert clustering		
	# Clusters	MQ index wo./w. models	Precision & Recall	EdgeSim	MeCl
Expert clustering					
Derived manually	3	1.067 —	100% 100%	100	100%
Class-level dependencies					
Hill Climbing, Weighted MQ	2	1.083 1.821	33.333% 100%	72.72	85%

ally done – comprises three clusters, whereas the derived clustering comprises two.

The MQ index is at 1.067 for the expert clustering, and 1.083 for the derived clustering (and 1.821 with model elements included in the clusters). This shows that cohesion and coupling cannot be easily improved.

When comparing the expert and the computed partitions without model elements, precision is at 33.333% and recall at 100%. The low precision can be attributed to the fact that two clusters correspond to a single one in the derived clustering. Similarity is at 72.72% according to EdgeSim, and at 85% according to MeCl. Thus, even when taking edges into account as well, Bunch's clustering is highly similar to the expert clustering.

5.7. Applicability to Other Transformation Languages

The approach is universally applicable for any transformation language except for two steps, dependence analysis and structural analysis. So far, we have only looked at two transformation languages in the respective sections, QVT-O and Xtend, because we have implemented the approach only for these two languages.

Regarding the first step, the transformation that extracts dependence information from the code, we already were able to demonstrate applicability of dependence graph analysis to various transformation languages in the

Table 5.3.: Module concepts in selected transformation languages

Language	Modularity Constructs	Module Dependencies
QVT-O imperative	`transformation` T`;` `library` L`;`	`import` $T \mid L$`;` $T \mid L$ `access` $T' \mid L'$ T `extends` T'
QVT-OM imperative	`transformation interface` I `transformation module` M	I `import` I' M `export` I
QVT-R declarative	`transformation` T`;`	`import` $T \mid L$`;` T `extends` T'
Xtend imperative	`class` C	`import` C' C `extends` C' `extension` C

Xtendm
imperative
	`@TransformationInterface`
	`interface` I
	`@TransformationModule`
	`class` C
		`@Import extension` I
		C `implements` I

ATL hybrid	`module` M`;`	M `uses` M'`;`
ETL hybrid	*<file>*	`import "`*<file>*`";`
Kermeta2 imperative	`package` P`;` `[aspect] class` C `package` P	`require "`*<file>*`"` $\mid P$ C `inherits` C' `using` P
VIATRA2 hybrid	`entity` E`;` `machine` M	`import` $N.E$`;` `namespace` $N.E$`;`

previous chapter in Section 4.5. The dependence graph we use here uses only a subset of the concepts reflected by the dependence graph that belongs to the visual analytics approach.

We did not yet, however, discuss to what extent structural information can be extracted from transformation languages other than QVT-O and Xtend. Of course, structural analysis is not a premise to cluster transformations, but if a language already provides a mechanism to structure transformations, it should be supported. In this section, we study the following languages concerning their promoted structuring concept and how they might be supported by our approach: QVT-O and our own extension QVT-OM, QVT-R,

Xtend and Xtendm enhanced by us, ATL, ETL, Kermeta2, and VIATRA2. Table 5.3 delineates modularity concepts for each of the languages[4].

Two questions we would like to answer here is: What are the structuring concepts that represent modules? And how are dependencies among modules defined? Modularity concepts are essential to identify an existing partition. Dependencies are required to resolve the full set of modules starting from the main module, they are not part of the structural model though as it defined above.

QVT-O We have already remarked in Section 5.5 that the QVT-O language distinguishes between transformation and library units. Library units can solely be accessed from other library or transformation units by means of keyword `access`, whereas transformation units can refine other transformation units using superimposition (keyword `extends`). Either way, units must be imported priorly using an `import` statement. For structural analysis, both kinds of units are relevant as they represent valid clusters comprising method implementations.

QVT-OM Our own modularity concept that we have presented in Chapter 3 replaces QVT-O's original concepts to allow for information hiding modularity. There are two types of unit declarations, `transformation interface` and `transformation module`. Only the latter unit type defines method implementations and thus represents clusters. To accumulate required modules when there is only the main module given, analysis can parse `import` declarations, for which a module must be found that exports the respective interface via `export` declaration.

[4] Note that an in-depth discussion of the concepts has already been carried out at the end of Chapter 3, and will again be carried out in the related work section. The former comparison, however, discusses extensibility of existing modularity concepts, and the latter juxtaposes existing concepts in light of their information hiding capabilities and model visibility control.

QVT-R QVT-R is the declarative pendant to QVT-O, which reuses large parts of QVT-R's concepts. Indeed, QVT-R's modularity concepts form a subset of QVT-O's. A transformation unit can only refine another unit through `extends`, no library concept is provided according to the standard documentation. Transformation units pose valid clusters that must be identified during analysis.

Xtend The Xtend language compiles to Java and solely reuses Java's namespace concept, peppered with Google Guice-like dependence injection through the `extension` keyword. Only non-abstract classes should be detected as valid clusters, containing inherited and locally defined methods. A class can reference other classes via composition and inheritance (keywords `extension` and `extends`).

XtendM Our own conceptual extension to Xtend to attain information hiding modularity reuses Xtend's structuring concepts, but uses Java annotations to mark Java interfaces, classes, and class imports as transformation units (cf. the concepts listed in Table 5.3). This alleviates the structural analyzer from distinguishing transformation units from ordinary classes.

ATL ATL's namespace concept is relatively simple, in that it provides `module` declarations that can put into scope of another module via `uses` statements. Hence, modules immediately correspond to clusters.

ETL Modularity in the Epsilon family of languages exploits the physical file system to logically separate declarations, not unlike the C/C++ language. Import statements put definitions from external files into scope. Thus, clusters correlate with ETL and EOL files.

Kermeta2 The Kermeta modeling language uses the same language concepts for both model and transformation definition. Besides using files as physical structuring concepts with the `requires` statement, each file can define the namespace it contributes definitions to via a `package` declaration. External package visibility is then established through `using` statements. Similar to C#'s concept of partial classes [HWG03], portions of a class can be spread out to multiple files by utilizing the `aspect class` mechanism. It is a vitally important feature to separate transformation code from model definitions. A major challenge of static analysis is to separate class definitions that contain transformation operations from those that purely define the models involved in the transformation. Any defined class qualifies as a cluster that defines an operation which is either the transformation's main method, or which is directly or indirectly reachable from the main method.

VIATRA2 The VIATRA language allows developers to split code into physical files. Namespaces are declared using keyword `namespace`, and can be imported into other namespaces using keyword `import`. An abstract state machine is declared in a `machine` block statement, and contains ASM and graph transformation rule definitions. Definitions of model entities are established with `entity` blocks, and can represent packages, classes and objects, thereby attaining MOF compliance. A structural analyzer, similar to the one used for QVT-O in this chapter, could parse for machine statements and identify them as definitions of separate clusters if they appear in different files and namespaces.

5.8. Concluding Remarks

Together with models, model transformations belong to the core assets of software developed according to the model-driven paradigm. Much of the recent work in this area has focused on reuse aspects of transformations, neglecting maintainability as an equally important concern. To manage the inherent complexity of transformation programs, well-approved language concepts can be used, including information hiding modularity. In practice, however, these transformation programs lack structure, or their structure has slowly eroded over time as the transformations evolved.

This chapter proposes to transfer software clustering techniques to the specific domain of model transformation programs. Based on automatically derived clusterings, developers have to spent less effort in understanding, maintaining and refactoring the code. Our aim is to automatically derive clusterings that exhibit high similarity with manual decompositions. To reach this goal, we had to integrate structural information of the models and model use dependencies of the transformation language's concepts, and we had to guide the clustering algorithm by weighting the input dependencies to match the type of transformation at hand.

Despite promising results indicated by the example (Section 5.6.3) and our empirical validation (which will be presented in the subsequent chapter under Section 6.5), a few interesting points for future research arose which we think are worth to be pursued. At the moment, the approach is limited to information that can be automatically extracted from the source code and the models. To achieve an improved partitioning, more expert knowledge could be integrated into the clustering process. We currently extract data dependence information at the type-level, whereas dataflow analysis could help to detect cohesiveness between methods more accurately. Finally, other quality metrics beyond (or in combination with) coupling and cohesion could be explored and tested if they deliver better results.

6. Validation

We already could give evidence for some of the initial objectives stated in the introductory chapter that they have been met (see Section 1.4), whereas it has not been shown yet if efficiency is increased. In this chapter, all three approaches presented in Chapters 3, 4 and 5 are validated in individual case studies.

Results of the case studies had been previously published together with the contribution's paper. Yet, in this thesis we added a few details we originally had to spare off due to size constraints.

The chapter is pre-eminently structured by the case studies that had been carried out. But before, Section 6.1 discusses the overall evaluation goals in greater detail, and Section 6.2 introduces the project where application scenarios for all three studies had been drawn from. Section 6.3 contains the first case study that evaluates our chief contribution, the module concept. Section 6.4 shows practicability for the visual analytics approach in an empirical study. Section 6.5 examines benefits of the clustering approach by two realistic transformations. A final remark in Section 6.6 brings the chapter to a close.

6.1. Evaluation Goals

Three contributions are made by this thesis: a module concept, a visualization methodology, and an automatic clustering technique, all targeted for model transformations. The chief goal of all three approaches is to improve the maintainability of model transformations. To attain this goal, in Section 1.4, we gave a list of success criteria we want to have met for the approaches. Five of the six criteria had already been shown in the respective chapter of the approach:

Soundness The module system is required to be sound regarding the information hiding principle. A sketched proof can be found in Chapter 3, and a Coq embedding of the type system and soundness theorems appears in Appendix A.

Genericity We would like to attain a better maintainability for any transformation language. Applicability to the various types of transformation languages is discussed at the end of contributing chapters (Chapters 3 to 5).

Automation Re-engineering of legacy transformations to a modularized variant should be automated where possible. This goal is obtained by the clustering approach that we presented in Chapter 5.

Efficiency The three principal contributions of this thesis, the module concept, the visualization and the re-engineering approach, are all designed to increase efficiency when carrying out typical maintenance tasks in practical scenarios. We have not shown yet that this is the actual case.

The rest of the chapter aims to demonstrate by a set of case studies that all three contributions are able to meet the last mentioned criterion of efficiency. The case studies focus on real-world transformations from a research project, thus ensuring practicability.

6.2. Application Scenarios

All example transformations used for validation are taken from a larger scientific project, the Palladio Research Project [MKK11]. The project provides a set of methods and tools for predicting the reliability and performance of software architectures.

The *Palladio* approach [BKR09] aims at detecting performance and other quality-related problems at an early stage in the software development process[1]. This is accomplished by modeling the software to be developed already at design-time in the PCM. The Palladio Component Model (PCM) is an architectural modeling language for describing component-based software architectures [BKR09]. The model is then annotated with estimated performance costs and supplemented with expected usage scenarios. A process and event-based simulator, the *SimuCom* simulator, evaluates the performance impact on the hardware resources the components are allocated to. Through this approach, designers can identify performance bottlenecks and other quality issues, and judge design alternatives based on measurements which they obtain from simulation.

6.3. Modularizing an Xtend Transformation Using Information Hiding Modularity

In Chapter 3, we have presented an approach that provides information hiding modularity for model transformation languages. To demonstrate advantages of a thorough module concept over prevalent structuring concepts, we have carried out a case study in order to evaluate if reduced maintenance efforts can be indeed achieved.

We present the experiment design based on Victor Basili's *Goal, Question, Metric* (GQM) plan [Bas92], in alignment with Wohlin's template (cf. [JCP08]): First we set the experiment goal, we formulate questions and hypotheses, and derive metrics (Section 6.3.1). We give details on the experiment setup in Section 6.3.2. We continue to present two scenarios in Section 6.3.3, and for each we describe how we conducted the experiment, including a thorough analysis and discussion of the results (Sections 6.3.4 and 6.3.5). Presentation of the study concludes with a list of potential validity threats (Section 6.3.6) and a summary (Section 6.3.7).

[1] For details on Palladio, see `palladio-simulator.com`.

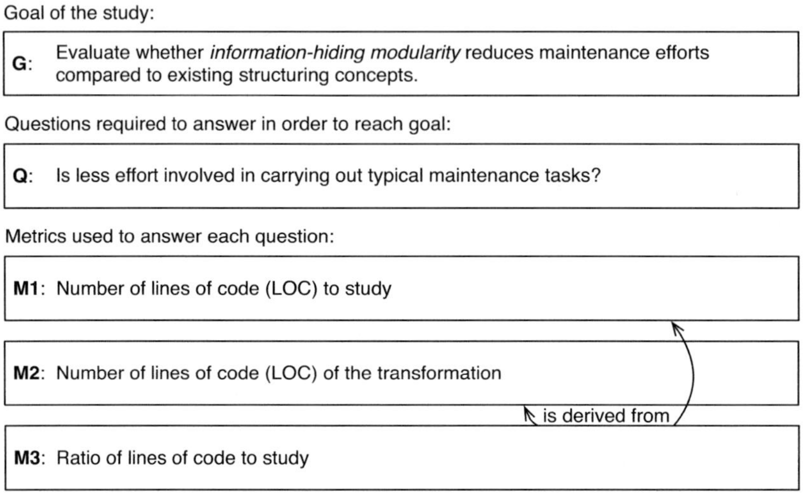

Figure 6.1: GQM plan – Certain metrics (M) are required to answer quantifiable questions (Q), in order to achieve our goal (G).

6.3.1. Validation Goals

The following goal is set to be empirically shown for the approach:

G: "Analyze *information hiding modularity* (object), for the purpose of *evaluation* (purpose), with respect to *process efficiency* (quality focus), from the point of view of *transformation developers carrying out maintenance tasks* (perspective)"

To put it differently, the purpose of the planned study is to find empirical evidence that maintenance costs of transformations are significantly lower (process-related improvement) if the transformation has been thoroughly designed using our novel modularity concept in contrast to regular structuring mechanisms which usually lack explicit interfaces. Note that in this thesis, we perceive process efficiency as a cost-effectiveness ratio, i.e., efficiency is improved if the same effect is achieved at lower costs. Costs may cover arbitrary resources, time, money, perceived strain of the subjects, and so on.

From the goal stated above, we derive a single question and discuss the metrics that are used to answer the question,

Q: "Is less effort involved in carrying out typical maintenance tasks?" The question asks for the effort involved in maintaining a model transformation with versus without information hiding modularity. To give an answer to this question, it is important to clarify what a typical maintenance task exactly is, and how effort can be measured. We decided for two realistic maintenance tasks that belong to distinct classes of maintenance activities. For practicability reasons, we did not carry out a study with human subjects, but rather calculated the amount of code which is required to logically deduce the code spot that is relevant for a particular task (Metrics M1 to M3).

The question relates to the following hypothesis to be observed:

H: Effort A subject who uses information hiding modularity for model transformations requires less effort to carry out typical maintenance tasks.

6.3.2. Experiment Design

The study had been carried out by a single subject. The subject was an experienced transformation developer, familiar with the PCM2SimuCom transformation. We varied the class of maintenance request (control variable). We focused on two important types of maintenance tasks, a perfective and a corrective maintenance request (cf. Section 2.4). To measure the effort, we recorded the number of Lines of Code (LOC) that are required to be read by the subject in order to carry out the respective request (Metric M1). We further computed the number of LOC of the complete transformation under study (Metric M2). The fraction of M1 and M2 forms the percentage of code of the overall transformation program which had to be understood (Metric M3).

6.3.3. Use Case Scenario

To validate our approach, we chose a transformation that is practically used in a larger research project on software architecture simulation, the Palladio approach. The transformation maps the component model to simulation code. For this transformation, we are able to show that maintenance effort is significantly smaller if a transformation is structured based on our module concept.

To identify quality-related issues of a software with the Palladio approach, component-based software architectures and typical usage scenarios are first modeled in the *Palladio Component Model*. Instances of this model are then translated to simulation code that is based on the *SimuCom* simulation framework. Other targets exist as well, for instance mappings to Plain Old Java Objects (POJOs), to Enterprise Java Beans (EJB), and to a performance prototype (ProtoCom).

Technically, *PCM2SimuCom*, the program for translating architectural models to simulation code, had been implemented as a Model-to-Text (M2T) transformation written in Xpand and Xtend1, both being predecessors of Xtend2[2]. M2T transformations are special cases of Model-to-Model (M2M) transformations, where the target model are textual artifacts. Xpand and Xtend2 are both template-based languages, meaning that transformation logic is embedded into static text with the help of meta-tags. The transformation and its design has been described in Becker's doctoral thesis [Bec08b].

We examined two maintenance scenarios from recent maintenance activities. Each activity belongs to a class of activities that typically appear during transformation development at frequent intervals. The first scenario deals with the process of refactoring the modular structure of the transformation. The second scenario is about adapting the transformation for a new requirement. We will demonstrate that the effort involved in identifying bad smells

[2] As we discuss the dated dialect *Xtend1*, we refer to Xtend as *Xtend2*.

and locating concerns can be dramatically reduced with a proper modular structure and descriptive module interfaces.

6.3.4. Scenario 1: Refactoring the Modular Structure

By this first maintenance scenario, we want to evaluate if explicit interfaces specifically help in refactoring the modular structure of a transformation program. This we do by comparing the efforts required to reason about the modular structure of the same transformation program to accomplish a refactoring task, once with and once without explicit interface descriptions.

6.3.4.1. Execution

One of the more recent development tasks in the Palladio project was to migrate the meanwhile deprecated Xpand templates to the Xtend2 language. Transformation templates were already modularized using the template method pattern, with the result that variants share common parts in abstract super classes, and refine implementation details by overriding abstract (template) methods. Yet, former modularizations did not use Xtend/Java interfaces to declare which public methods implementations must provide, and even in Xtend or Java, it is not possible to restrict access to model elements.

As a first step, we took the SimuCom transformation and created a variant that employs interfaces with model use dependencies. We made use of the Xtend2m add-on to declare proper interfaces. We developed Xtend2m as a prototype of our module concept (see Section 3.4.2).

We then analyzed the code for bad smells in the design, e.g., modules with high coupling and/or low cohesion. For each variant, we finally measured the minimal amount of code required to spot the smell just from looking at the code.

Table 6.1.: SimuCom transformation – Data dependencies per module

Xtend Module	reliability.*	resourceenv.*	system.*	seff.*	usagemodel.*	repository.*	**LOC**
M_{1}: Allocation							7
M_{2}: Build			✗			✗	157
M_{3}: Calculators				✗	✗		32
⋮							
M_{10}: Dummies			✗			✗	89
M_{11}: JavaCore				✗		✗	244
M_{12}: JavaNamesExt	✗		✗		✗	✗	278
M_{13}: PCMExt			✗	✗	✗	✗	480
M_{14}: ProvidedPorts						✗	260
M_{15}: Repository						✗	120
M_{16}: Resources				✗		✗	27
M_{17}: SEFFBody	✗			✗		✗	220
⋮							
M_{23}: SimAllocations		✗	✗			✗	111
M_{24}: SimCalculators				✗	✗	✗	86
M_{25}: SimCalls				✗		✗	286
⋮							
M_{32}: SimResources		✗					252
M_{33}: SimSEFFBody	✗			✗		✗	252
M_{34}: SimSensors							35
M_{35}: SimUsage			✗		✗	✗	253
⋮							
M_{39}: SimUsageFactory			✗		✗	✗	91
LOC (Σ)							4987
Modules (Σ)	4	2	11	13	9	30	
LOC (%)	18%	7%	35%	42%	28%	87%	
Modules (%)	10%	5%	28%	33%	23%	77%	

6.3.4.2. Analysis

Results of a precursive analysis of data dependencies are depicted in Table 6.1 in the form of a dependence matrix. The table lists for select modules which of the six PCM packages it references. The PCM is packetized by six modeling aspects, a structural view (repository.*), a behavioral view (seff.*), an assembly view (system.*), a usage view (usagemodel.*), a resource view (resourceenvironment.*), and a view on reliability annotations (reliability.*). For instance, PCM's reliability concepts are handled – and thus referenced –

by four modules: M_{12}, M_{17}, M_{28}, and M_{33} (M_{28} has been omitted in this view). These four modules share 18% of the overall 4987 LOC.

While modules $M_1,\ldots,M_{22}$ act as generic templates for various targets including SimuCom, modules $M_{23},\ldots,M_{39}$ refine these to produce SimuCom target code. For example, M_{23} extends M_1 in order to implement several abstract methods.

According to the table, almost all modules reference model elements from only few packages. This indicates a low coupling regarding data dependencies. Only two modules exhibit a particularly high degree of coupling, JavaNamesExt and PCMExt (M_{12} and M_{13}). Both modules depend on four PCM packages and are called by most other modules. Inspecting their code quickly reveals a low coupling, most methods contained in the modules do not rely on other methods. Background to this is that the two modules had been used to collect helper methods. This design decision issues from Xpand's inability to mix template expressions with utility functions. Both modules used to be implemented in Xtend1. However, with the advent of Xtend2, template expressions and functions are mixable. Almost all methods are only required by single modules, thus they can be moved to the respective module without breaking the code.

H: Effort Determining the two modules M_{12} and M_{13} as the ones with the highest coupling (regarding data dependencies) involves different amounts of effort depending on the variant used. When we use the modules with ordinary interface definitions, we have to carefully read all the implementing classes for model elements used, yielding a full 4987 LOC to examine. Note that studying model import definitions alone is not sufficient, since types might be implicitly accessed from within the module's implementation without the need to import the type. On the other hand, with model use dependencies declared in the interfaces, we immediately get the same results from examining the interface definitions alone, which have 378 LOC. Whilst we have already read the code of modules M_{12} and M_{13} in the first variant's case, it is still required to read them for the second variant, in order to check the code for the degree of cohesion, so we end up with $378 + 758 = 1136$ LOC of the second variant to read. Thus, we end up with a ratio of 100% of code to read regarding the first variant, versus 23% of code to read regarding the second variant. This indicates that, based on statistical significance obtained from a more extensive experiment, hypothesis H might be accepted.

6.3.4.3. Discussion

H: Effort This first scenario demonstrates that there was 67% less code to read with more descriptive interface definitions that have model use dependencies included.

In this example scenario, we identified a bad smell just from studying dependencies declared in module interfaces. Thus, we were able to reduce the coupling and increase cohesion between modules, making the overall transformation presumably easier to understand and maintain. Without descriptive interfaces, we would have to reverse-engineer data dependencies manually, with the risk of missing some dependencies. On the other hand, our type interference system statically analyzes implementations against declared interfaces and identifies violations automatically.

6.3.5. Scenario 2: Locating Concerns

Another important kind of maintenance task is to repair bugs present in a transformation. In this scenario, we study the effort it takes to locate places in the code where the bug potentially resides.

6.3.5.1. Execution

Again, the same two variants of the SimuCom transformation had been used: The original variant that had been structured based on Xtend's class mechanism and the template method pattern, and a second variant that employs interfaces with model use dependencies, but possesses the same modular structure.

In the Palladio model, software components can realize component interfaces. Interfaces in turn can extend other interfaces. When a component realizes such a chain of interfaces, it must provide operations for any interface along that inheritance chain. Until recently[3], our transformations were not aware of inheritance chains. A first step to correct the transformations is to locate places in the code where interfaces are handled. In the PCM, three manifestations of interfaces exist, all being descendants of class `Interface`, namely `OperationInterface`, `InfrastructureInterface`, and `EventGroup`. All four model elements are part of the structural view, and therefore belong to the `repository.*` namespace. Without having data dependencies declared, we must investigate the full code to track down relevant places. Since the SimuCom transformation employs our module concept, we can narrow down possible locations of concern by just studying module descriptions.

We analyzed the code to locate a concern that we were facing in a past maintenance scenario. For each variant, we measured the minimal amount of code required to identify the location of concern from looking at the code.

6.3.5.2. Analysis

By looking at a transformation's module interfaces, we can tell if a module is actually authorized to access these interface concepts. With dependencies declared at the package-level, we would have to check modules with access to the repository namespace, being 30 out of 39 modules (see Table 6.1). Since we already have the transformation's model dependencies declared at the class-level, we can narrow down the number of modules we need to consider even further. Table 6.2 displays for relevant modules if they access

[3] Bug record is `sdqbuild.ipd.kit.edu/jira/browse/PALLADIO-165`, fixed on June 25, 2013.

Table 6.2.: SimuCom transformation – Change impact analysis

Xtend Module	<: repository.Interface	Had to modify?
M_1: Allocation		
M_2: Build	✗	
⋮		
M_6: ComposedStructure	✗	
M_7: ContextPattern	✗	
M_8: DataTypes		
M_9: DelegatorClass	✗	✗
M_{10}: Dummies	✗	
M_{11}: JavaCore	✗	✗
M_{12}: JavaNamesExt		
M_{13}: PCMExt		
M_{14}: ProvidedPorts	✗	✗
M_{15}: Repository	✗	✗
⋮		
M_{19}: Sensors	✗	
M_{20}: System		
M_{21}: Usage	✗	
M_{22}: UserActions		
⋮		
M_{27}: SimContextPattern		
M_{28}: SimDummies	✗	
M_{29}: SimJavaCore	✗	
M_{30}: SimProvidedPorts	✗	
M_{31}: SimRepository	✗	
M_{32}: SimResources		
⋮		
Modules (Σ)	14	4
LOC (%)	40%	14%
Modules (%)	36%	10%

any `Interface`-related class[4] residing in the `repository.*` namespace. There are only 14 modules whose implementation must be examined further. In the end, we had to edit four among these to get our task done.

H: Effort When working with the variant that employs model use dependencies at the class level, the amount of code to read is reduced to the interface definitions plus the implementations of 14 out of the 39 modules, so we end up with 2116 instead of 5298 LOC. This is opposed to the code for all 39 modules when working with the classic variant. Hence, the ratio of code required to read in order to spot the correct places is reduced from 100% to 40%. Again, this is a good indication that hypothesis H might be accepted based on statistical significance from a broader data set.

[4] I.e., references to class `Interface` or subclasses thereof.

6.3.5.3. Discussion

H: Effort Like the first scenario, this second scenario again demonstrates that the amount of code to read can be substantially reduced with model use dependencies being part of interface descriptions, this time defined at the class rather than the package level.

A large portion of maintenance tasks require to locate concerns in the code, particularly corrective maintenance tasks. Having more expressive interface descriptions helps to locate such concerns more quickly and with less effort. Model use dependencies can be stated at the package and class level, giving developers the ability to specify model use dependencies at arbitrary levels. Static type checking frees developers from the burden to check if module implementations strictly abide to model use dependencies declared in the interface implemented. This realistic example scenario demonstrated that class level dependencies can help to locate typical concerns – like in this corrective maintenance scenario – with a much smaller effort.

6.3.6. Threats to Validity

Validity of the outcome is most likely to be threatened by several factors.

Construct Validity Lines of Code (LOC) is often considered as a problematic metric, although it can be – and widely is – used as a rule of thumb to measure code complexity. To reenforce the hypothesis that information hiding modularity actually helps to diminish maintenance efforts, extended case studies are needed that measure the efficiency of experienced developers based on more accurate metrics. It has to be pointed out that the effort required to declare the interfaces by including method and model visibility has not been measured in the experiment.

Internal Validity We had only one subject carry out the tasks, and he co-developed the module concept. As he migrated the original Xpand templates to Xtend, he gained an exhaustive understanding of Xpand and Xtend, and further of the PCM2SimuCom transformation. As a co-developer of the concept, he may have unconsciously worked towards a positive outcome.

External Validity So far, we did just study a single example M2T transformation, thus it is not guaranteed that the results apply to arbitrary transformations of this and other kinds. Additional transformations must be observed in order to obtain statistical significance. An experiment design similar to the one we use to validate our visual analytics approach in Section 6.4 could lead to a more reliable validation in the future.

6.3.7. Evaluation Summary

Without a modular structure based on a descriptive module concept, developers need to fall back to a text-based search. However, a word-based search for "interface" leads to many false positives, because semantics are ignored. With our proposed blackbox module concept, maintenance of model transformations takes less effort than with existing module concepts that do not account for data and control dependencies at the interface-level. Statistical significance remains to be demonstrated in a future study on additional transformations.

6.4. Maintaining a QVT-O Transformation Supported by Visual Analytics

To evaluate how our approach from Chapter 4 supports important maintenance tasks, we carried out an empirical study, where users had to identify code locations affected by typical change requests. For the case study, we implemented our approach for QVT-O under Eclipse.[5]

[5] The tool we implemented can be downloaded from `http://qvt.github.io/tca`.

Next, we are going to give details on the experiment design: We define our validation goals in Section 6.4.1 and derive the hypotheses and variables of the experiment as part of our experimental design in Section 6.4.2, before we present the transformation under study and describe the maintenance scenario in Section 6.4.3. We give details on how the experiment has been conducted (Section 6.4.4), analyze and discuss results (Sections 6.4.5 and 6.4.6), before we expound potential threats that could jeopardize our observations in Section 6.4.7. We then conclude this section with a short summary (Section 6.4.8).

6.4.1. Validation Goals

Formalization of goals is done according to the GQM plan [Bas92], following Wohlin's template. Our experiment's goal can be stated as follows:

G: "Analyze *dependency graphs* (object), for the purpose of *evaluation* (purpose), with respect to *process efficiency, product quality, and user experience* (quality focus), from the point of view of *transformation developers carrying out maintenance tasks* (perspective)"

In other words, the purpose of the study is to empirically evaluate whether our approach makes maintaining model transformations more efficient (process-related improvement), the outcome is of higher quality (product-related improvement), and the developer experiences less effort (improvement regarding user experience).

For each of the three improvements, we define three questions together with suitable metrics, so we can statistically derive answers from measurements (Figure 6.2):

Q1: "Is the product quality improved when the tool is used?" The question can be further refined into "Is there a difference for experts and novices?", for which we observe the results from experts and novices separately. First, we need to find out if the tool has actually been applied; this is done based on objective and subjective observations (active and passive tool usage). The product quality itself is quantified using the f-measure (Metric M3) that is computed from the proportion of right and wrong answers (Metrics M1 and M2).

Q2: "Is the process more efficient when the tool is used?" To give an answer here means to track process resources, i.e., time, money, developers. We focus solely on time (Metrics M4 and M5, because human resources stay constant, and cost is an indirect result of consumed time and developers.

Q3: "Is the user less strained when he uses the tool than without?" An answer to this question is highly subjective to each subject's experience with the tool. We use a questionnaire to record the perceived difficulty and the perceived usability (Metrics M6 and M7). Again, this question can be contemplated for experts and for novices in isolation.

In order to accomplish our set goal, we explored the following three hypotheses:

H1: Effectiveness Subjects who use dependency graphs locate affected places *more effectively* than equally classified subjects who do not use it.

H2: Time expenditure Subjects who use dependency graphs are *faster* in performing the maintenance tasks than equally classified subjects who do not use it.

H3: Perceived strain Subjects who use dependency graphs are *less strained* than equally classified subjects who do not use it.

6.4.2. Experiment Design

We varied the availability of the tool (control variable) and took measurements to assess effectiveness, time consumption and perceived strain (re-

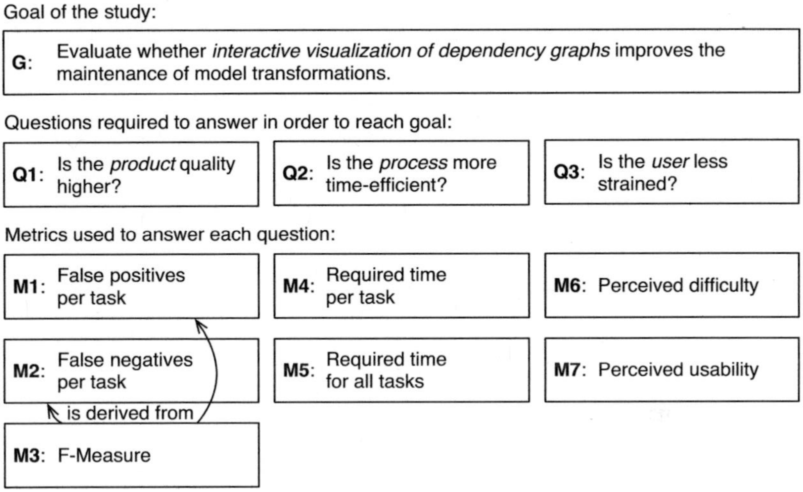

Figure 6.2: GQM plan – Certain metrics (M) are required to answer quantifiable questions (Q), in order to achieve our goal (G).

sponse variables). We used the following metrics: To evaluate the effectiveness, we determined the numbers of false positives and false negatives of each given answer (M1 and M2). Based on these, we used the f-measure with $\beta = 1$ to compute the harmonic mean value of precision & recall (M3). The f-measure is a widely-used measure for assessing quality of information retrieval. It is also suitable for evaluating feature location tasks [WPXZ11].

Subjects were asked to record starting and ending time for each task, so we could calculate the actual time needed (M4 and M5). Regarding the subjectively felt level of strain, we asked for the user's personally experienced difficulty level on six-level Likert items in the post-session questionnaire (M6). We additionally asked tool users for the perceived usability of the tool (M7).

According to a classification scheme by Juzgado and Moreno [JM01], this experiment follows a *between-subjects design*. Its single dimension *tool usage* has two levels (with or without). It is a *quasi-experiment*, since assignment to groups had been done based on information determined from the pre-questionnaire, rather than purely randomly.

The study had been carried out in an exam-style situation on two bachelor students, twelve master students and eight experienced researchers, all of them reasonably trained in the tools and activities of model transformation development.

6.4.3. Use Case Scenario

We decided for the PCM2QPN [MKK11] transformation that is part of the Palladio research project. The transformation PCM2QPN is a QVT-O program that transforms PCM instances to Queuing Petri Nets (QPNs). It encompasses 2886 lines of code, plus 952 lines of code distributed over four library modules. We decided for QVT Operational Mappings because of its stable integration into the Eclipse Integrated Development Environment (IDE), its adherence to a language standard, and its wide acceptance. There is one source metamodel, the PCM, consisting of 154 classes, and SimQPN's Petri net model as target model, consisting of 20 classes.

Each subject was asked to perceive certain aspects, and to locate concerns of a set of change requests to a correct set of code places. In software engineering, there are typically four types of maintenance tasks [Sal09]: preventive, corrective, perfective and adaptive. In accordance to this widely used classification, we name five classes of change requests:

Bug fix request (Corrective): This request is about finding a bug which is present in the transformation, which can cause either the program not to compile, or the output to be incorrect. For instance, as a reaction to modifications to the metamodels, developers need to adapt the transformation accordingly.

Feature request (Perfective): To match new functional requirements, new functionality needs to be added, or existing functionality needs to be changed or removed. Because changes may originate from or have impact on depending artifacts, feature requests may result not only in modification of a transformation but also of metamodels, models and documentation.

Non-functional improvement (Perfective): A perfective task can also target non-functional requirements, it can even have an impact that is orthogonal to code structure.

Refactoring request (Preventive): Refactoring means organizing code structure without adding or removing existing functionality. For instance, a class attribute could be pulled up, which can result in an attribute assignment being pulled up a rule inheritance chain accordingly.

Environmental change request (Adaptive): Transformation programs do not function in isolation. Input metamodels change, or language concepts are updated.

Subjects were asked to *not* perform the actual change, because of the limited time frame, and because people brought a varying level of knowledge and experience with QVT-O and the underlying Object Constraint Language. Subject had to handle the following seven tasks (which can be understood without knowledge of the PCM and QPN metamodels):

T1: Comprehension task / Searching for keywords

"Where does the transformation create elements in the target model? Name one example for each of the three variants for element instantiation."

Subjects had to look for the keywords `constructor`, `object`, `mapping`. They were asked to name one example for each instantiation type, three locations in total. Note that for mappings, non-tool users had to check for a return type, with implicit instantiation semantics. Tool users could check write-access edges in the graph, but still had to check the underlying code for the actual used instantiation type. Filter F4 combined with cross-navigation was the optimal choice. This task served as a warm-up question.

T2: Comprehension task / Analyzing control flow

"Which call trace leads from the entry method to a method creating instances of `ExternalCallAction`*? Do not use the debugger or execute instrumented code."*

A manual depth-first search using the browsing history had to be conducted, in order to find paths in the overall control flow leading from the entry method's node to the target method. Non-tool users had to use text-based search and hyperlink navigation. Tool users could use Filter F2, after identifying the target method as a method having write-access to the named class (Filter F4). The trace was eight methods deep, and included downcasts regarding the contextual type of a mapping.

T3: Refactoring request / Analyzing control flow

"Name all unused methods."

Non-tool users were required to search for occurences of each method's name. The transformation's main file had 41 mappings, 117 helpers, and ten queries. Tool users could check for unreferenced nodes in the general control-flow view (Filter F1). There were twelve unused methods in total, seven mappings and five helpers.

T4: Non-functional improvement / Analyzing data element usage

"Assert statements need to be added to check consistency of created connections. Please name all methods that instantiate objects of type `ConnectionType`*."*

Subjects had to look for the keywords `constructor`, `object`, `mapping`, in conjunction with `ConnectionType`. Non-tool users had to use the search command. Tool users could rely on write-access dependencies (Filter F4). There were 33 instantiating methods in total, 30 mapping rules and three helper methods.

T5: Feature request / Analyzing data element usage

"A new subtype of `AbstractAction` is planned to be added to the source metamodel. Where are `AbstractAction` elements handled? Name all occurrences."

Here, subjects had to check data dependencies. While non-tool users had to use the search command, tool users could select Filter F4 and check outgoing or incoming edges in context of class `AbstractAction`. The correct answer included five mappings and five queries, where two queries were located in an external module.

T6: Feature request / Analyzing data element usage

"Class `ForkAction`, subtype of `AbstractAction`, should be used as blue print for the new subtype of `AbstractAction` to be added. Where does the transformation handle the `ForkAction` element? Name all occurences."

The right answer encompasses eight queries and six mappings. Tool users could check data dependencies in context of `ForkAction` (Filter F4), others had to do a text-based search for the name.

T7: Bug fix request / Analyzing data flow for unused class attributes

"Created target models contain objects of class `Place` with an uninitialized attribute `departureDiscipline`. Identify the buggy lines of code."

Only one single mapping did create elements of type `Place` without proper initialization. Tool users were able to use Filter F3 in context of class `Place`, and check attribute dependencies for each displayed method.

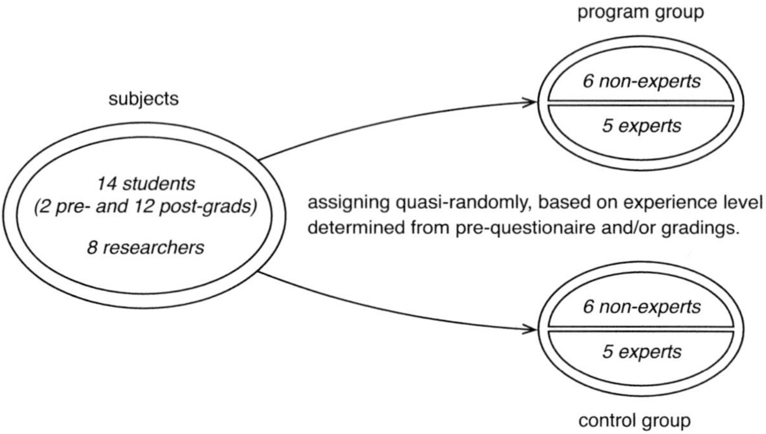

Figure 6.3: Grouping of participants during the experiment

6.4.4. Execution

Students participated in two practical training sessions on transformation development. Training was done by this thesis' author within scope of a practical course on MDSD. Each session ended with graded exercise sheets. We sent our fellow researchers training material to brush up their knowledge of the QVT-O language.

Assignment to one of the two groups happened randomly. Beforehand, participants had to fill out a pre-session questionnaire, where they rated their own expertise level on a five-point Likert item and stated their academic degree. Based on this information, we randomly swapped participants between both groups so that each group had seven students and four researchers, and the mean expertise level for both groups was equally balanced (Figure 6.3).

The experiment started with a 30 minutes tutorial on how to use the tool. Each participant was assigned to one workstation with a preconfigured Eclipse IDE. Then, subjects were handed out the task sheets, they were asked to answer tasks in prescribed order, and to note down when they started and when they ended a task. Subjects could freely partition their available time to the tasks. Subjects could decide to end a task prematurely, without the option to resume later. After 75 minutes total, the experiment closed with a post-session questionnaire. Using a debugger or executing the code was not permitted. Supervisors frequently inspected subjects to ensure that they refrained from using unauthorized tools.

6.4.5. Analysis

For analysis, none of the outliers were removed from the data set to retain the natural results from the study.

H1: Effectiveness For hypothesis H1, we investigated the f-measure. Boxplots in Figure 6.4a contrast program with control group on a per-task level. Applying Welch's one-tailed t-test to the f1-measures at the default significance level of $\alpha = 0.05$, tool users showed a significant improvement over non-tool users for tasks T2-T6 ($p_2 = 0.015$, $p_3 = 0.001$, $p_4 = 0.047$, $p_5 = 0.003$, $p_6 = 0.034$). For tasks T1 and T6, Welch's two-tailed t-test did not reveal a significant difference ($p_1 = 0.160$, $p_7 = 0.283$). We are able to reject H1's corresponding null hypothesis for all tasks but tasks T1 and T7.

H2: Time expenditure For H2 we tested time consumption. Figure 6.4b shows boxplots for the consumed time per task and added up. Welch's t-test had been used to test for significancy. We can confirm hypothesis H2 only for task T3 with a one-tailed test revealing $p = 0.010$. For the other tasks, two-tailed tests did not indicate any significant difference between groups.

H3: Perceived strain H3 was based on subjective data from the questionnaires. All answers were posed using six-point Likert items, ranging from "strongly disagree" to "strongly agree". One question was if subjects would rate the tasks as difficult to solve (see Figure 6.4c for details). Further questions asked tool users if they think that the tool helps in understanding, debugging, refactoring, and extending a previously unknown transformation,

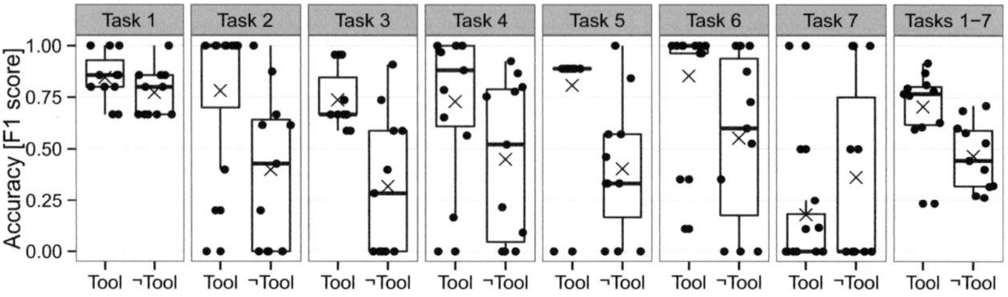

(a) Effectiveness calculated from precision & recall

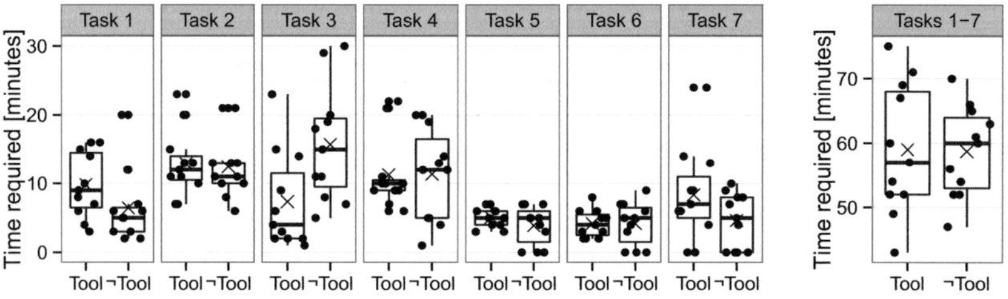

(b) Timing

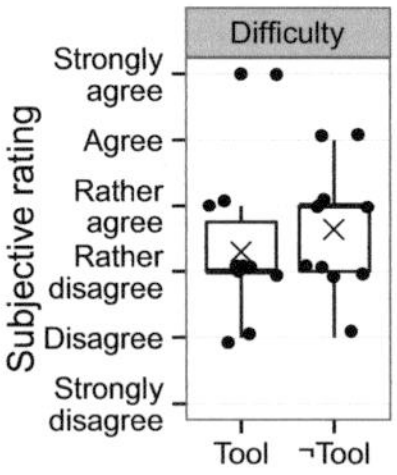

(c) Rating of the overall task difficulty

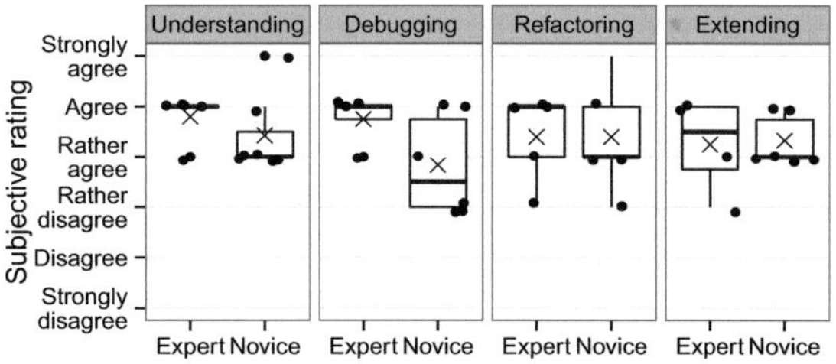

(d) Rating of the tool's ability to assist at one of the tasks, grouped by experts and novices

Figure 6.4: Measured response variables[†]

[†] In the boxplots, individual values are marked as dots jittered horizontally (and for discrete values also vertically) by a random value. A cross marks the mean, and a bar the median value.

based on their experience they gained at the respective task. Figure 6.4d shows respective boxplots. Mean values report that non-tool users found the tasks to be "rather hard", while tool users found the tasks to be "rather easy". Additionally, tool users rated the tool's usability for understanding, debugging, and refactoring a transformation on a six-level Likert item. On average, participants agreed that the tool helps in all four disciplines.

6.4.6. Discussion

H1: Effectiveness Effectiveness is significantly improved for all tasks except the first and the last. For the first task, thought to be a warm-up exercise, we argue that even if tool users could profit from navigating the graph, they would still have to check the underlying code for the keywords, making tool-based navigation only slightly better than a common text-based search. Many users did not find enough time for the last task, four out of eleven non-tool users and three out of eleven tool users did not even begin to process this task. A known problem lies in the tool's inability to detect attributes accessed from within a constructor.

H2: Time expenditure The overall expenditure of time was almost indifferent. Task T3 was solved significantly faster, and with better results. This indicates that for some maintenance tasks our approach produces much better results than for others.

H3: Perceived strain According to the ratings, tool users perceived the same tasks less difficult than non-tool users. Based on their experiences, most tool users found the tool to support understanding, debugging, refactoring and extending transformations, although to a limited extend. Novices were less convinced of the tool's help for debugging tasks. We expect developers to prefer the Eclipse debugging perspective over static analysis for most types of bugs.

Because of a significant improvement of the overall effectiveness, the indifferent overall expenditure of time, and a less perceived strain, we are able to attribute a higher efficiency to tool users. Results show that for some tasks, the abstraction level offered by our tool is too high.

6.4.7. Threats to Validity

Some aspects of our study and its participants may have caused biased results.

Construct validity The study's primary construct is the use of data and control dependencies to locate concerns. The choice of change requests was carefully chosen to represent a real-life situation. We are aware that there are change requests which are not in alignment to data flow and code structure, e.g. cross-cutting concerns, others require finer-grained knowledge, e.g. details of the program code. For instance, the tool's program analysis did miss two dependencies, resulting in a slightly smaller recall value for task T5 (cf. Figure 6.4a). A second threat is due to the metrics we used. In feature location scenarios, using the f-measure is considered as a common method to compare product-related quality [WPXZ11]. Since people could freely partition their available time to the tasks, recorded times are not accurate, particularly towards the end. Subjective ratings need to be treated with care.

Internal validity Blind testing was not possible for the subjects could easily conclude from the experiment setup that the tool was under test, but people were assigned to one group at the latest possible time. Subjects were equally trained, we gave advice for each task on how to optimally use the tool and an alternative IDE feature. None of the subjects were involved in the tool's development. We refrained from asking subjects to perform the actual maintenance task, because we expect the tool to show its particular strength in understanding code and locating concerns rather than in editing code.

External validity Generalizability is threatened by the fact that we investigated only a single transformation written in a single transformation language. We are confident the transformation together with the two incorporated Ecore metamodels, the Palladio Component Model and the Queuing Petri Net, reflect industrial quality standards. Program and model artifacts had been reviewed at least once. We also believe that our mix of novices and experts approximated to a real-world situation. We compared our tool to the bare Eclipse QVT-O environment, as we do not know of similar tools for QVT-O. Yet, by further equipping non-tool users with diagrammatic visualizations as those suggested by van Amstel et al. [vAvB11], we could check if our interactive approach would outcompete a static visualization approach.

6.4.8. Evaluation Summary

Results obtained from the experiment show that subjects using our approach were significantly more efficient and effective carrying out maintenance tasks. Therefore, the experiment is able to demonstrate efficiency of the visual analytics approach. Beyond this, results suggest that it is the large number of dependencies among metamodel elements and transformation rules that hampers understandability of model transformations.

Our study indicates that maintenance processes can be heavily improved by revealing dependency information to maintainers. Instead of utilizing program analysis techniques, transformation languages could proactively provide concepts to let programmers explicitly declare dependencies for program elements, e.g., rules and modules. Since prevalent module concepts are coined towards reuse rather than maintenance [WKK+12b], we recommend to use our module concept from Chapter 3 that allows to declare dependencies upfront.

However, for existing transformations that do not use a module concept with explicit interfaces, a module's dependencies can be derived automatically with our approach. For transformations with non-existent or insufficient module structure, a *clustering algorithm* based on this dependence information can even automatically propose suitable modular structures [DYM+08], as presented in Chapter 5.

6.5. Re-Engineering QVT-O and Xtend Transformations with Automatic Clustering

In this section, we validate the clustering approach from Chapter 5. Two real-world transformations are clustered twice, once manually by an expert, and another time using our automatic approach. Results are compared against each other, and analyzed for their differences.

The approach relies on static analyzers to extract call and model dependencies, as well as the existing modular structure, from parsed syntax trees of programs in the respective transformation language. Dependence and structure analysis (cf. Figure 5.2) are fully automated steps. For the purpose of this case study, we have implemented the steps for two transformation languages: for the QVT-O M2M transformation language as it is available under Eclipse, and for the Xtend language, an extensible language commonly used to build M2T transformations[6]. Both analysis transformations have been implemented in Xtend. As highlighted in Section 5.7, further transformation languages can be added.

To demonstrate applicability and an increased value of our approach, we have clustered two real-world transformations: We use the similarity measures introduced in the previous section to compare automatically derived clusterings with a clustering done manually by an experienced developer. We conceive sample clusterings with a higher similarity to the expert clustering as superior.

We proceed as we did for previously described experiments: Based on Basili's template, we define our validation goals (Section 6.5.1) and derive the hypotheses and variables of the experiment as part of the experimental

[6] Implementations as well as example transformations and data obtained from our studies can be downloaded from `http://qvt.github.io/tca`.

design (Section 6.5.2). Then, we present both transformations under study, one after the other (Section 6.5.3), explaining for each the steps executed to obtain a clustering, analyzing and discussing the results. The section ends with a list of potential validity threats (Section 6.5.6) and an evaluation summary (Section 6.5.7).

6.5.1. Validation Goals

We set our goal for this study as follows:

G: "Analyze *the automatic clustering approach* (object), for the purpose of *evaluation* (purpose), with respect to *product quality and effectiveness* (quality focus), from the point of view of *transformation developers re-engineering the modular structure* (perspective)"

We want to show that the automatic clustering approach produces clusterings which have a comparable or even better modularization quality (equal quality), and which show a higher resemblance to what a human expert developer would have produced by hand (improved effectiveness), when compared to existing clustering approaches. Quality and effectiveness should be assessed from a transformation developer's perspective who is supposed to refactor and maintain the model transformation at hand.

For each of the two aspects, quality and effectiveness, we formulate questions and define metrics that are going to be used to find an answer to the questions (cf. Figure 6.5):

Q1: "Is the outcome of equal or better quality?" The question is to be answered when comparing the approach to existing automatic solutions and a manual clustering. As metrics, the number of clusters (Metric M1) and an objective measure to calculate the modularization quality, with and without model elements (Metrics M2 and M3), are needed.

Q2: "Is the outcome similar to the expert's solution?" Again, similarity to a given manual clustering is observed for automatic clusterings derived using our approach and existing approaches. We chose three established similarity measure, Precision & Recall, EdgeSim, and MeCl (Metrics M4 to M6).

In order to accomplish our set goal, we explored the following two hypotheses:

H1: Quality Clusterings produced by the automatic approach while incorporating model use dependencies are not of *lower quality* than clusterings produced by the automatic approach using control dependencies alone, and manually derived clustering.

H2: Effectiveness Clusterings automatically derived by incorporating control and model use dependencies are *more similar* to an expert clustering than clusterings automatically derived using control dependencies alone.

6.5.2. Experiment Design

The experiment had two control variables. Firstly, we varied the transformation under study, and secondly, we tested three different configurations for the clustering algorithm:

- control dependencies alone,
- control dependencies and model dependencies at the package level, and
- control dependencies and model dependencies at the class level.

We used six different metrics to assess quality and effectiveness (response variables) as follows. Quality (cf. Question Q1) has been measured in three

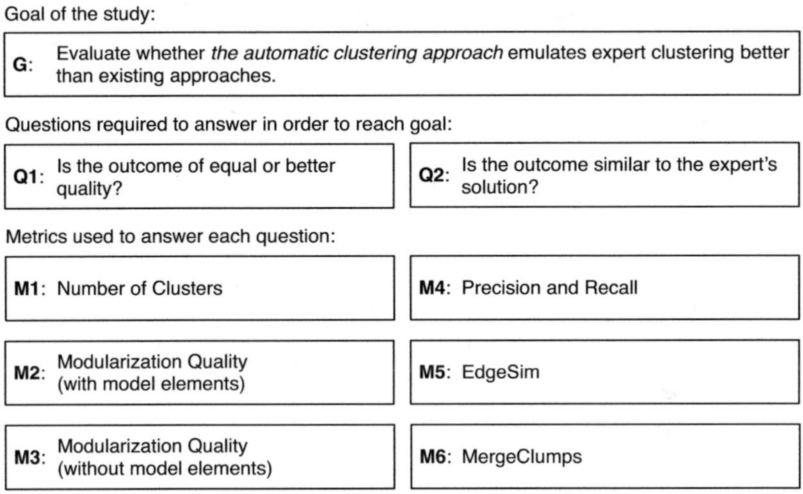

Figure 6.5: GQM plan – Certain metrics (M) are required to answer quantifiable questions (Q), in order to achieve our goal (G).

ways: Metric M1 observes the number of clusters produced. Despite being only a weak reference point, a derived clustering which contains only few or much more partitions than an expert clustering can be deemed as less usable. Metrics M2 and M3 both use the MQ index as a numerical measure for cohesion and coupling. The automatically obtained clustering maximizes the MQ value based on control and model elements (Metric M2), but a manual expert clustering does not take these into account. To compare the quality of automatically and manually derived clusterings an MQ value computed solely on control elements (Metric M3) is required.

To ascertain the effectiveness (cf. Question Q2), we used the same three similarity measures that are utilized by the approach to assess results from different configurations, Precision & Recall (Metric M4), EdgeSim (Metric M5), and MeCl (Metric M6). Their specific characteristics have already been extensively discussed in Section 5.6.

6.5.3. Use Case Scenarios

Both the transformations that we use for this case study, PCMEvents2PCM and PCM2SimuCom, were developed as part of the Palladio approach and play a pivotal role in the approach's implementation. The PCMEvents2PCM transformation is a QVT-O transformation that refines the PCM, and the PCM2SimuCom is an Xtend transformation that maps instances of the PCM to simulation code.

6.5.4. Scenario 1: QVT-O Transformation from PCM with Events to PCM

The first transformation under study replaces high-level concepts for event-based modeling with core concepts in the PCM [RKSK13]. It has been described in greater detail in Rathfelder's doctoral thesis [Rat13]. The PCMEvents2PCM transformation works in-place, meaning that the output model is a modification of the input model. With the transformation executed as a preprocessing step, subsequent transformations (including the one discussed in the second case study below) do not have to deal with event-based concepts. The transformation had been implemented in QVT-O [Obj11], a model-to-model transformation language that augments the OCL with imperative transformation concepts.

The expert decomposition (Table 6.3) has a flat hierarchy of modules: module `Main` imports almost all other modules. The implementation maintains two registries of model parts that are successively added to eventually replace event-based modeling concepts; in the expert decomposition, these are encapsulated by modules `SEFFRegistry`, `OperationSignatureRegistry` and `EventChannelMiddlewareRegistry`. Apart from `Main`, only five modules import modules themselves. There are two helper modules, Finder and Commons, that define general-purpose helper functions to find and manipulate PCM concepts.

Table 6.3.: PCMEvents2PCM – Dependence matrix of expert decomposition (asterisk denotes module with entry point)

	Main	Finder	Commons	VariableUtil	SourcePort	SourceCommunication	Source	SinkPort	SinkCommunication	Sink	SEFFUtil	SEFFRegistry	OperationSignatureRegistry	InterfaceUtil	EventFilter	EventDistribution	EventChannelMWRegistry
***Main (a)**		✗	✗	✗	✗	✗	✗	✗	✗	✗	✗	·	✗	✗	✗	✗	✗
Finder (b)	·		·	·	·	·	·	·	·	·	·	·	·	·	·	·	·
Commons (c)	·	·		·	·	·	·	·	·	·	·	·	·	·	·	·	·
VariableUtil (d)	·	·	✗		·	·	·	·	·	·	·	·	·	·	·	·	·
SourcePort (e)	·	·	✗	·		·	·	·	·	·	✗	·	·	·	·	·	·
SourceCommunication (f)	·	·	✗	·	·		·	·	·	·	✗	·	·	·	·	·	·
Source (g)	·	·	·	✗	·	·		·	·	·	·	·	✗	·	·	·	·
SinkPort (h)	·	·	✗	·	·	·	·		·	·	✗	·	·	·	·	·	·
SinkCommunication (i)	·	·	✗	·	·	·	·	·		·	✗	·	·	·	·	·	·
Sink (k)	·	·	✗	·	·	·	·	·	·		✗	·	✗	·	·	·	·
SEFFUtil (m)	·	·	·	✗	·	·	·	·	·	·		✗	✗	·	·	·	·
SEFFRegistry (n)	·	·	·	·	·	·	·	·	·	·	·		·	·	·	·	·
OperationSignatureRegistry (o)	·	·	·	·	·	·	·	·	·	·	·	·		·	·	·	·
InterfaceUtil (p)	·	·	·	·	·	·	·	·	·	·	·	·	✗		·	·	·
EventFilter (q)	·	·	✗	·	·	·	·	·	·	·	✗	·	·	·		·	·
EventDistribution (r)	·	·	✗	·	·	·	·	·	·	·	✗	·	·	·	·		·
EventChannelMWRegistry (s)	·	·	·	·	·	·	·	·	·	·	·	·	·	·	·	·	

6.5.4.1. Execution

For deriving partitions from this transformation with Bunch, we use a weight configuration of

$$\langle W_{write}, W_{read}, W_{navigate}, W_{call}, W_{package}, W_{reference}, W_{contain}, W_{inherit} \rangle := \langle 15, 5, 0, 10, 15, 0, 0, 0 \rangle$$

Weights for outgoing and incoming model dependencies are at $W_{write} = 15$ and $W_{read} = 5$, respectively. Through this, we achieve a target-driven decomposition, but still respect source elements in case of query methods

Table 6.4.: PCMEvents2PCM – Alternative clusterings

Configuration	Statistics		Similarity to expert clustering		
	# Clusters	MQ index wo./w. models	Precision & Recall	EdgeSim	MeCl
Expert clustering					
Derived manually	17	6.296 —	100% 100%	100	100%
Method-call dependencies only					
Hill Climbing, Weighted MQ	9	4.470 —	14.397% 24.194%	46.73	-1260%
Package-level dependencies					
Hill Climbing, Weighted MQ	7	5.068 3.973	14.224% 31.935%	54.34	-550%
Class-level dependencies					
Hill Climbing, Weighted MQ	16	5.760 6.271	35.461% 32.258%	62.50	-290%
Hill Climbing, Weighted MQ (design. lib. Finder, Commons)	8	2.889 6.271	36.143% 71.935%	78.80	-110%

that miss output dependencies. With W_{call} set to 10, average attention is payed to the method call structure. Because we want to modularize the transformation based on the package structure of the PCM if clustering at the class-level, we weighted package containment dependencies at $W_{package} = 15$. References and inheritance dependencies of classes are omitted. The remaining weights are set to zero. Please see Section 5.3.4 for an explanation of the vector's components.

We derived partitions based on three different levels, on method-level alone, on package-level, and finally on class-level. We configured Bunch's hill climbing with the parameter set from Section 5.4. For each of the partitions we computed modularization quality and similarity metrics when compared to the expert clustering. We use the three measures Precision/Recall, EdgeSim, and MeCl (as discussed in Section 5.6.2) to assess similarity between the automatically derived clustering and a reference clustering that had been done manually by an expert developer. Results of all four runs we carried out are given in Table 6.4.

6.5.4.2. Analysis

When we confined the input graph to methods and call dependencies in the first run, we obtained nine clusters, with an MQ value of 4.470, which is 29% worse than the expert partition's 6.296. All three similarity metrics indicate a relative high dissimilarity.

In a second run, we added model packages and read/write dependencies at the package-level. Bunch produced seven clusters, with a slightly improved MQ value of 5.068 (that is, without considering model elements). With both EdgeSim at 54.34 and MeCl at −550%, the partition showed more similarities with the expert partition than the partition from the first run, because Bunch started to group methods based on the output dependencies. For example, methods that generate elements from the Service Effect Specification (SEFF) package were grouped together, like they had been encapsulated into modules `SEFFUtil` and `SEFFRegistry` by the expert. When looking at the transformation under study, many methods collect data from various places in the input model and therefore depend on multiple packages. Hence, the clustering algorithm can insufficiently group methods by their package responsibilities alone.

Our third run integrated classes and class-level dependencies into the input graph, for which Bunch identified 16 clusters. The modularization quality, according to an MQ index of 5.760, is almost as good as that of the expert clustering. All three measurements agree that similarity is higher than for the previous ones: Precision & Recall, EdgeSim and MeCl are at their highest of 35.461, 32.258, 62.50, and −290%, respectively.

Finally, in a fourth experiment, we marked generic queries and helper methods as designated library methods. With this information, Bunch was able to produce a clustering that is even more similar to the expert's variant. Interestingly, the MQ value without model elements turned out to be the worst of the series (2.889). A very likely reason for this effect is that having outsourced many of the helper methods into a designated library module increases coupling.

Since Bunch uses randomization, results vary on each run. To reenforce our confidence about the added value of class-level dependencies, we repeated the first and fourth runs four times in addition each and applied Wilcoxon's rank sum test in two-sided mode.

H1: Quality The MQ value without model elements is slightly worse for the class-level decomposition due to class dependencies being optimized as well but not considered here. There is no statistically significant difference nevertheless ($p = 0.056 > 0.05$, the typical confidence limit). Therefore, we can reject H1's corresponding null hypothesis.

H2: Effectiveness Precision did also not significantly improve ($p = 0.056$) but Recall, EdgeSim and MeCl ($p = 0.008$ for all three tests). Hence, we are able to reject the null hypothesis of H2.

6.5.4.3. Discussion

In the following, we discuss a partition obtained from the last run (class-level dependencies, designated library methods). Figure 6.6 shows the seven clusters that had been output by Bunch. Nodes of model elements, as well as the eighth cluster that contains the helper methods, had been removed to improve readability. The Bunch-generated clusters had been enumerated for reference; assigned numbers are indicated by circled numbers. The expert clustering has been made visible in three ways for ease of comparison: a small letter in bold (from the enumeration in Table 6.3), a color code, and the prefixed module name.

The most obvious difference is the much smaller number of clusters (8 as opposed to 17). Although Bunch automatically outputs partitions at varying

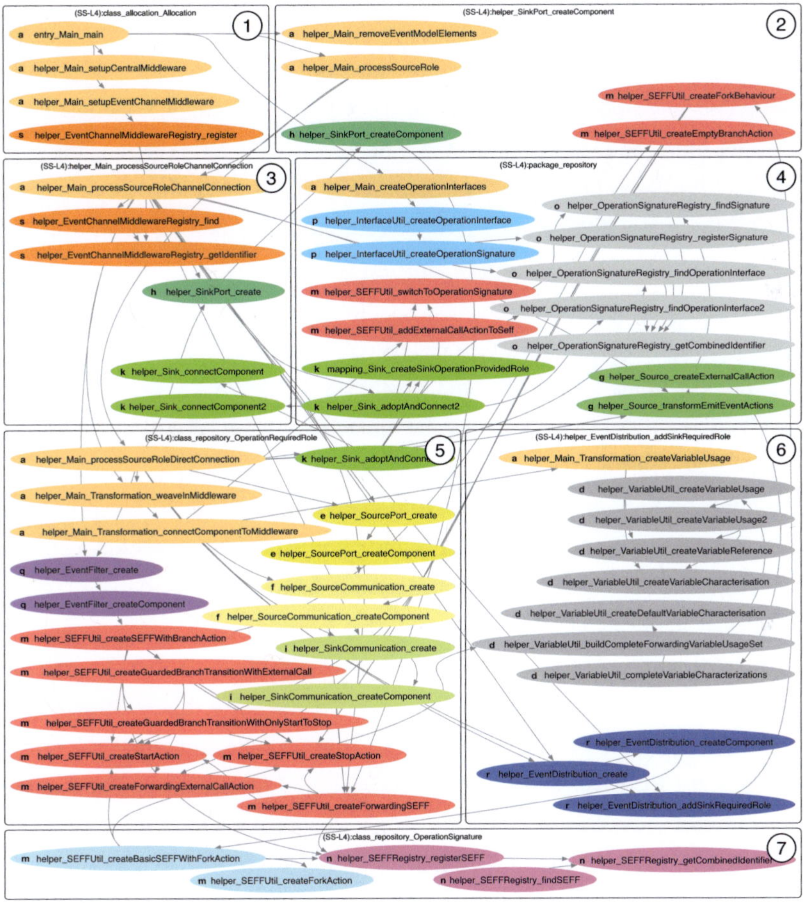

Figure 6.6: PCMEvents2PCM transformation – Bunch-derived clustering based on class-level dependencies (classes and designated library methods removed) vs. expert clustering (denoted by small letters in bold)

levels of detail, this is the level with the most useful average cluster size according to Bunch[7].

Small letters in bold indicate the affinity to clusters in the expert partition. Bunch decided to distribute methods of the main module (depicted in gray) to multiple clusters, leaving only three methods in the main module (cluster one). This has a positive effect on the module use hierarchy, which is much less flat than the expert's partition. The second cluster's responsibility is less clear; `createComponent` of `SinkCluster` should rather be moved to cluster three, and `SEFFUtil`'s methods semantically belong to cluster five. Responsibility of the remaining clusters is more obvious (as indicated by their names): cluster four, for instance, collects methods that modify elements from the `repository` package, clusters five and seven are more specifically concerned with package `SEFF`, and cluster six with class `VariableUsage`.

Many modules (represented by the clusters) contain several methods that are used solely internally. These methods should not be exposed to other modules, as they are implementation-specific. With the newly proposed interface concept for QVT-O, we can hide implementation-specific methods from clients. The dependence information at hand can be used to determine the set of methods relevant for users of a module.

Some common helper functions from `Commons` and `Finder` can be safely moved to a single module if they are used by this module alone. Although helper methods had been put into a dedicated cluster, it could make sense to reassess if they should have global visibility; if a method is expected to be useful only to a single module, it might be reasonable to make it a private method of that module. Some helper methods, like `createAllocationMethod` are only used internally by other common helper methods, in this case `createAssemblyContext`, and can be hidden from client modules. When defining interfaces for each of the modules

[7] The Bunch developers have found the median level of the subsystem hierarchy obtained from hierarchical clustering heuristics to provide a reasonable tradeoff between the number of clusters and the sizes of the individual clusters [Mit02].

Table 6.5.: PCMEvents2PCM – Dependence matrix of class-level clustering (entry point indicated by an asterisk)

	1	2	3	4	5	6	7	8
*1	\	✗	✗	✗	·	·	·	✗
2	·	\	✗	·	✗	·	·	✗
3	·	✗	\	✗	✗	✗	·	✗
4	·	·	✗	\	·	✗	·	✗
5	·	✗	✗	✗	\	✗	✗	✗
6	·	✗	·	·	·	\	✗	✗
7	·	·	·	·	✗	·	\	✗
8	·	·	·	·	·	·	·	\

represented by a cluster, it can be easily checked which of the methods should be public and thus part of the interface definition, and which private to the module.

A downside of Bunch is that many clusters have mutual dependencies. According to the class-level dependence matrix, this partition has five occurrences of direct dependencies (cf. Table 6.5). While cyclic dependencies are possible with our module concept for QVT-O, any good design should avoid them (acyclic dependencies principle [Mar96]). Removing mutual dependencies must be done manually, since Bunch's clustering algorithms cannot ensure acyclicity.

6.5.5. Scenario 2: Xtend Transformation from PCM to SimuCom

The second transformation under study is a model-to-text transformation that is used in context of the Palladio project. It has already been employed in an earlier case study we presented in Section 6.3. Palladio relies upon a transformation that translates instances of PCM models to Java code with references to the *SimuCom* simulation framework. The PCM is translated to different targets as well, for instance mappings to POJOs, to EJB, and to a performance prototype (ProtoCom). Therefore, a componentization of PCM-related transformations is important to ensure reusability of shared functionality.

Reusability has been achieved by the template method design pattern. Target-independent functionality is factored out into abstract classes with abstract methods. Each target does then concretize the abstract classes. The set of subclassing templates for generating the SimuCom target, for example, is prefixed by `Sim`. Mentioned design is further discussed by Becker [Bec08a]. In the following, we abstract away from this reuse technique, because it rests upon inheritance, a whitebox technique – module `SimAllocation`, for instance, is internally implemented by the eponymous class `SimAllocation` and superclass `Allocation`.

Table 6.6 displays dependencies that occur among the 20 modules of the expert clustering. The transformation comprises four separate sub transformations whose entry points are contained in distinct modules, one for each viewpoint of the input model: the component repository (main module `SimRepository`), the system composition (main module `System`), the usage model (main module `SimUsage`), and the resource allocation (main module `SimAllocation`). Modules `Sensors`, `PCM`, and `JavaNames` group query methods that are generally useful for two or more modules. Module `JavaNames` provides 54 methods used by all other modules. Despite the experts endeavor to avoid cycles, there are three occurrences of mutual dependencies, pair `SimJavaCore` and `SimProvidedPorts`, pair `SimUsageFactory` and `SimUsage`, and pair `SimUsage` and `SimUserActions`.

6.5.5.1. Execution

Template-based designs facilitate a target-driven decomposition: methods for generating content of a particular file are often clustered into a single module for optimal coupling and cohesion. To reflect this design principle, we chose a weight configuration of $\langle 40,5,5,20,5,0,0,0\rangle$ for the clustering algorithm. This configuration makes target dependencies the top priority ($W_{write} = 40$), seconded by call dependencies with $W_{call} = 20$ and followed by equal values for source model dependencies and package containment dependencies

Table 6.6.: PCM2SimuCom – Dependence matrix of expert decomposition (asterisks indicate main modules)

	SimAccuracy	SimAllocation	SimCalculators	SimCalls	SimComposedStructure	SimContextPattern	SimDummies	SimJavaCore	SimProvidedPorts	SimRepository	SimResources	SimSEFFBody	SimSensors	SimUsageFactory	SimUsage	SimUserActions	System	Sensors	PCM	JavaNames
SimAccuracy (a)	\	·	·	·	·	·	·	·	·	·	·	·	·	·	·	·	·	·	·	·
***SimAllocation (b)**	✗	\	·	·	·	·	·	·	·	·	·	·	·	·	·	·	·	·	✗	✗
SimCalculators (c)	·	·	\	·	·	·	·	·	·	·	·	·	·	·	·	·	·	✗	✗	✗
SimCalls (d)	✗	·	·	\	·	·	·	✗	·	·	·	✗	·	✗	·	·	·	✗	✗	✗
SimC'dStructure (e)	·	·	·	·	\	·	·	·	·	·	·	·	·	·	·	·	·	·	✗	✗
SimC'tPattern (f)	·	·	·	·	·	\	·	·	·	·	·	·	·	·	·	·	·	·	·	✗
SimDummies (g)	·	·	·	·	·	·	\	✗	·	·	·	·	·	·	·	·	·	·	·	✗
SimJavaCore (h)	·	·	·	·	·	✗	·	\	✗	·	·	✗	·	·	·	·	·	·	✗	✗
SimProvidedPorts (i)	·	·	·	·	·	·	·	✗	\	·	·	·	·	·	·	·	·	·	·	✗
***SimRepository (k)**	·	·	·	·	✗	✗	·	✗	✗	\	·	·	·	·	·	·	·	·	·	✗
SimResources (m)	·	·	·	·	·	·	·	·	·	·	\	·	·	·	·	·	·	·	·	✗
SimSEFFBody (n)	✗	·	·	✗	·	·	·	✗	·	·	✗	\	·	·	·	·	·	·	✗	✗
SimSensors (o)	·	·	·	·	·	·	·	·	·	·	·	·	\	·	·	·	·	·	·	·
SimUsageFactory (p)	·	·	·	·	·	·	·	·	·	·	·	·	·	\	✗	·	·	·	✗	✗
***SimUsage (q)**	·	·	✗	·	·	·	✗	·	·	·	·	·	✗	✗	\	✗	·	·	✗	✗
SimUserActions (r)	·	·	·	✗	·	·	·	·	·	·	·	·	·	·	✗	\	·	·	·	✗
***System (s)**	·	·	·	·	✗	✗	·	·	✗	·	·	·	·	·	·	·	\	·	·	✗
Sensors (t)	·	·	·	·	·	·	·	·	·	·	·	·	·	·	·	·	·	\	·	·
PCM (u)	·	·	·	·	·	·	·	·	·	·	·	·	·	·	·	·	·	·	\	·
JavaNames (v)	·	·	·	·	·	·	·	·	·	·	·	·	·	·	·	·	·	·	·	\

($W_{read} = W_{package} = 5$). Source model dependencies are again considered at both the package and class level, whereas target model dependencies are considered at the file-level.

As we did for transformation PCMEvents2PCM, we initially applied Bunch on method-level dependencies alone, before we added model dependencies and predetermined a set of library methods. We consistently used Hill Climbing with the parameter set from Section 5.4. Table 6.7 shows results for the five automatically derived partitions, and the expert partition

Table 6.7.: PCM2SimuCom – Alternative clusterings

Configuration	Statistics		Similarity to expert clustering		
	# Clusters	MQ index wo./w. models	Precision & Recall	EdgeSim	MeCl
Expert clustering					
Derived manually	20	6.034 —	100% 100%	100	100%
Method-call dependencies only					
Hill Climbing, Weighted MQ	10	4.896 —	13.259% 29.836%	50.63	-6600%
Package-level dependencies					
Hill Climbing, Weighted MQ	12	5.275 5.450	18.442% 23.729%	57.01	-6120%
Hill Climbing, Weighted MQ (design. lib. JavaNames, PCM)	13	7.310 6.600	37.889% 38.278%	84.81	-2380%
Class-level dependencies					
Hill Climbing, Weighted MQ	14	6.560 7.873	16.081% 17.634%	51.91	-6280%
Hill Climbing, Weighted MQ (design. lib. JavaNames, PCM)	25	10.741 15.835	48.695% 59.192%	88.63	-1380%

for comparison. Again, we used MQ to measure modularization quality, and Precision/Recall, EdgeSim, and MeCl to measure the degree of similarity.

6.5.5.2. Analysis

The partition we received from the first run had been derived from method-level call dependencies alone. Ten clusters had been produced, which evaluate an MQ value of 4.9 that is the lowest of all three runs. All four similarity measurements attest a low degree of similarity with the expert clustering.

For the second run, we added model dependencies, at the package and file level for source and target, respectively. This produced a better modularization quality even sans model dependencies ($MQ = 5.275$), and a higher similarity (despite a smaller recall ratio).

In a third run, we considered class level dependencies. Despite a higher rated quality, similarity is worse than for the second run's results. We carried out a fourth and fifth run on the package and class level, respectively, but

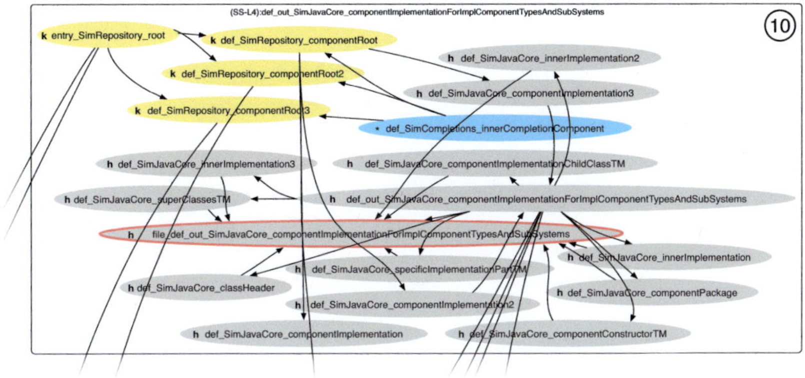

Figure 6.7: PCM2SimuCom transformation – Bunch-derived clustering of cluster #10 based on package and file-level dependencies (packages removed) vs. expert clustering (denoted by small letters in bold)

we explicitly put helper methods from modules `JavaNames` and `PCM` into a dedicated module. Interestingly, both runs produced much better results in terms of quality and similarity. This indicates that crosscutting modules have a strong impact on the outcome.

To demonstrate a significant improvement of class-level clustering over method-level clustering, we again executed each clustering five times and applied Wilcoxon's rank sum test on the observation.

H1: Quality The MQ value improved only insignificantly ($p = 0.952$). Since there is no significant change, we can reject the null hypothesis corresponding to H1.

H2: Effectiveness While the MQ value improved only insignificantly, with a high confidence we can attest a higher similarity to the expert decomposition according to Precision, Recall, EdgeSim and MeCl (p-values are 0.008, 0.008, 0.012, and 0.008, respectively). Therefrom, H2's null hypothesis is rejected.

Table 6.8.: PCM2SimuCom – Dependence matrix of package-level clustering (asterisks indicate modules with entry points)

	1	2	3	4	5	6	7	8	9	10	11	12	13	14	15	16	17	18	19	20	21	22	23	24	25
1		✗	·	✗	✗	·	·	·	✗	·	·	·	·	·	·	·	✗	·	·	·	·	·	·	·	✗
2	✗		·	·	·	·	·	·	·	·	·	·	·	·	·	·	·	·	·	·	·	·	·	·	✗
3	✗	·		·	·	·	✗	·	·	·	·	·	·	·	·	·	·	·	·	·	·	·	·	·	✗
4	·	·	·		·	·	·	·	·	·	·	·	·	·	·	·	·	·	·	·	·	·	·	·	✗
5	✗	·	·	·		·	·	·	·	·	·	·	·	·	·	·	·	·	·	·	·	·	·	·	✗
6	·	·	·	·	·		·	·	·	·	·	·	·	·	·	·	·	·	·	·	·	·	·	·	✗
7	·	·	✗	·	·	·		·	·	·	·	·	·	·	·	·	·	·	·	✗	·	·	·	·	✗
***8**	·	·	✗	·	·	·	✗		✗	·	·	·	·	✗	·	·	·	✗	·	✗	·	·	·	·	✗
***9**	·	·	✗	·	·	·	·	·		·	·	·	✗	·	·	·	·	·	·	·	✗	✗	·	✗	✗
10	·	·	✗	·	·	·	·	·	·		·	·	·	·	·	·	·	·	·	·	·	·	·	·	✗
11	·	·	·	·	·	·	·	·	·	·		·	·	·	·	·	✗	·	·	·	·	·	·	·	✗
12	·	·	✗	·	·	·	·	✗	·	·	·		·	·	·	·	·	✗	·	·	·	·	·	·	✗
13	·	·	✗	·	·	·	·	·	✗	·	·	·		·	·	·	·	·	·	✗	·	✗	·	·	✗
***14**	·	·	·	·	·	·	·	✗	·	·	·	·	·		·	·	·	✗	·	·	·	·	·	·	✗
***15**	·	·	·	·	·	·	·	·	·	·	·	·	·	·		✗	·	·	·	·	·	·	·	·	✗
16	·	·	·	·	·	·	·	·	·	·	·	·	·	·	✗		·	·	·	·	·	✗	·	·	✗
***17**	✗	·	·	·	·	·	·	·	✗	·	·	·	·	·	·	·		·	✗	✗	·	·	·	·	✗
18	·	·	·	·	·	·	·	✗	·	·	·	·	·	·	·	·	·		·	·	·	·	·	·	✗
19	·	·	·	·	·	·	·	·	·	·	·	✗	·	✗	·	·	·	·		·	·	·	·	·	✗
20	·	·	✗	·	·	·	·	✗	·	·	·	·	·	·	·	·	·	·	·		·	·	·	✗	✗
21	·	·	·	·	·	·	·	·	·	·	·	·	✗	·	·	·	·	·	·	·		·	·	·	✗
22	·	·	·	·	·	·	·	·	·	·	·	·	✗	·	·	✗	·	·	·	·	·		·	·	✗
***23**	·	·	·	·	·	✗	·	·	·	·	·	·	·	·	·	·	·	·	·	·	·	·		·	✗
24	·	·	·	·	·	·	·	·	·	·	·	·	✗	·	·	·	·	·	·	·	·	·	·		✗
25	·	·	·	·	·	·	·	·	·	·	·	·	·	·	·	·	·	·	·	·	·	·	·	·	

Next, we take a closer look at one of the five partitions from the last run, where class-level dependencies with predetermined helper methods had been considered.

6.5.5.3. Discussion

With a little over 400 methods and over 200 referenced classes, the partition is too big to be shown as a whole. Figure 6.7 depicts merely one cluster, cluster number ten of this partition[8]. The expert clustering is captured by small letters in bold, by a color code, and by the prefixed name. The shown cluster groups those methods of module `JavaCore` that produce textual output for a generated file (represented by the encircled node). These methods are only used by the `SimRepository` template, and thus cause Bunch to include them to this cluster. A single method belongs to a template that has been omitted in our dependence matrix in Table 6.6, it has been marked by an asterisk.

Without file dependence information, this partition obviously cannot be re-engineered from the method dependence graph automatically, as evidenced by the first run on method-only dependence information.

Table 6.8 exhibits the dependence matrix of the third run's partition. The 25th cluster is the one that collects methods from modules `JavaNames` and `PCM`. Particularly those methods had been grouped differently, for which analysis was either not able to detect any file handle, or the method had been used to generate content for multiple files. This applies to modules with a high reuse rate, indicated by the number of imports.

6.5.6. Threats to Validity

Admittedly, two issues commonly known to apply to clustering algorithms in general remain.

Some modules are not recognized because they serve as a cross-cutting container for helper functions, for instance, `Finder`, `Commons`, `JavaNames` and `PCM` in the case studies above. Yet, few of these helper methods are only used by a single module, and in such cases should be kept local to a component implementation. Here, our clustering approach can help to identify such methods and assign them to a single module.

Because clustering algorithms are NP-hard, we must use heuristics, such as hill climbing or genetic algorithms, to find solutions for realistic programs

[8] The complete partion can be retrieved from `http://qvt.github.io/tca`.

in a reasonable amount of time. Results from heuristics incorporate pseudo-random numbers, making it hard to reproduce the results.

6.5.7. Evaluation Summary

Both case studies demonstrate that the decomposition originally intended by the expert software designer can be significantly better approximated, if we include additional bits of information into the clustering process that go beyond call dependencies. By further extracting model dependencies at the package or class level and integrating them into the dependence graph, a clustering that is substantially more similar to the expert clustering is computed. This, however, requires additional knowledge about the class of transformation to be added, manifested as a weight configuration.

It is generally assumed that automatic clustering results can rarely be taken as is, not only due to the sub-optimality of these solutions, but also due to required simplicity of objective functions. We nevertheless demonstrated that clusterings recommended by Bunch can help to identify misplaced methods, presumed the maintainer brings enough expertise to carefully review the clustering output. With regards to transformation programs, we further demonstrated superiority of results when considering packages and even more so when considering classes versus plain method-level decompositions.

6.6. Concluding Remarks

All of the approaches aim at improving the maintenance processes of model transformations. This chapter exhibited three separate case studies to validate any of the approaches presented in this thesis in terms of their practical efficiency. Our findings from the studies we carried out in here can be summarized as follows:

- An advanced module concept with explicit interfaces that include model use dependencies reduces the effort spent at certain maintenance activities. By one larger transformation we demonstrated that the reasoning on a transformation's modular structure and the locating of concerns can be significantly alleviated. We expect to observe a positive outcome for other transformation languages, as well, yet additional case studies are required to fully ascertain this.

- Interactive visual analytics for model transformations increases the efficiency of development and maintenance tasks by automating much of the work it takes to locate concerns and obtain an understanding of the overall structure for a given transformation program. This may yet be true only for larger transformations that do not make sufficient use of the structuring concepts a given language provides. Studies on further transformation programs must be carried out to answer this question.
- Clustering of model transformations can be significantly improved by incorporating model use dependencies into the optimization heuristics. One caveat, however, is that fundamental knowledge about the kind of transformation – source-driven, target-driven or a compromise between the latter two – must be available. According to our experience, it typically takes several attempts to tare a weight configuration when a transformation should be structured according to more than one domain. Nevertheless can the approach help to refactor the modular structure of model transformations with less effort than a manual approach would demand.

As indicated in the various sections, threats of validity exist which might be tackled in future case studies that were not manageable in the scope of this thesis. So far, only the visual analytics approach had been validated with human participants. In the future, similar experiments could be carried out to test if developers benefit from transformations structured using information hiding modularity. Further on, there is no experiment that studies if an adequately modularized transformation gives a considerable advantage over the visual analytics approach.

7. Related Work

This dissertation relates to three major areas of research in computer science. One area concerns modularization concepts of domain-specific languages and model transformation programs in particular (Sections 7.1 and 7.2) and concerns our module concept from Chapter 3. Another area relates to formal considerations of semantics of transformation languages (Section 7.3), it has been touched by our side contribution from the aforementioned chapter. The third area concerns program analysis, clustering and visualization techniques of model transformation programs (Section 7.4). Contributions to this area have been described in Chapters 4 and 5. This chapter reviews related work in these areas.

7.1. Modularity in Modeling Languages

Model transformations describe how models are transformed. Modeling languages, on the other hand, are languages used to describe the models involved. Our modularity concept for model transformations that we present in Chapter 3 strongly relates to modularity of modeling languages, as it integrates model access control to parts of the models. When structuring a transformation, units of decomposition often conform to the units of the models which are transformed. A particular example for this is the field of *language modularization*, which aims to compose languages from language fragments, in a similar way as models can reuse other models. Each language module contributes its own type checker and generator fragment.

We distinguish here between two intrinsic features of modularity: compositionality and information hiding capabilities. Other extrinsic approaches describe dynamic views on models in a separate language.

7.1.1. Compositionality

Compositionality is about compartmentalizing models to foster comprehensibility, extensibility and reuse. The most prevalent concept to attain compositionality is the packaging mechanism provided by the CMOF modeling language.

The Complete MOF (CMOF) allows to group classifiers, packages and other elements into packages [PPH05; Obj14]. It supports three concepts to relate one package with another: import, access, and merge. A package import makes it possible to refer to the publicly visible package members from the imported package. An import can be public (keyword `import`) or private (keyword `access`), so that imported elements are either again visible for clients, or they remain hidden from clients of the importing package. A package merge creates a new package from the base package and referred packages, it is generally used to extend a model in increments.

The Essential MOF (EMOF) merely defines packages as a means to group elements, import mechanisms are imported from the CMOF. Apart from that, the EMF/Ecore realization of the EMOF standard provides a rudimentary packaging mechanism which resembles the CMOF's default public import described above [SBPM09].

Our model scoping concept adopts Ecore's package construct to establish namespace control, but adds relaxations – if a package is declared as visible, super and subclasses are implicitly visible, even if they are located in packages that are out of scope.

The field of language engineering is related, since the difference between models and languages is quite blurred. Several language workbenches aim for the compositionality of languages from sublanguages. To do so, a language extension must provide means to modularize and compose grammars, type systems, and generators/compilers. A prominent example is JetBrains' Meta Programming System (MPS)[1], a projectional language workbench. Projectional editing means that textual or graphical representations in the editor are projections of the underlying AST. The meta-metamodel of AST representations is close to EMF Ecore. Languages in MPS can be composed from sublanguages, where each language module (called *fragment*) contributes a distinct part of the abstract syntax. To the best of our knowledge, MPS does not allow for visibility control concerning abstract syntax definitions of a language fragment.

7.1.2. Information Hiding

While the MOF provides means to control visibility, as explained, EMF/Ecore does not prevent private elements from being used by importers. There is no notion of access control supported by Ecore, yet annotations may be used to suppress operations or features from being accessed. Either way, the default package import mechanism of Ecore does not respect annotations.

Since most transformation languages are designed to operate on Ecore standardized models, there is no way to reuse visibility information as provided by the Complete MOF and UML language. Thus, we define our own concept on class and package-based visibility control. Just recently, Garmendia et al. [GGKdL14] tackle this limitation with the *EMF Splitter* approach. They introduce modularity concepts (e.g., project, package, and unit) through annotations, and establish rules to control visibility of modeling elements. This visibility, however, addresses extensibility options rather than providing a customized view for transformation units.

The JetBrains MPS does not provide for an encapsulation mechanism for language fragments.

[1] JetBrains Meta Programming System; `https://www.jetbrains.com/mps/`.

7.1.3. Dynamic Views

For the purpose of reuse and interoperability, it can make sense to create a view on one or more larger models, (i) by abstracting from information that is irrelevant for a particular task, and (ii) by linking and pruning information distributed over multiple places in a model. Views are usually created to support modeling tasks carried out by different roles in a software project by creating views on models that omit inadequate information, and transform information to a more appropriate form. Views can also be used to adapt instances of legacy models to overcome versioning problems and foster tool interoperability.

There exists substantial work on creating dynamic views on models independent from the model's intrinsic structure, with the added possibility to conjoin multiple separate models into one single model. Much of this work has been discussed in Goldschmidt's and Burger's dissertations [Gol11; Bur14]. In addition to the approaches mentioned there, Burger presents his own concept of flexible views on a single underlying model.

The scoping of model elements as it is integrated into our approach can be considered a very special case of creating dynamic views on models. Model scoping is an ad-hoc definition of views to provide information hiding at the syntactical level. Views can overlap as well, they do not necessarily have to be pairwise disjoint. For pragmatical reasons, scoping is on the syntactical level, whereas views may define a separate model together with a synchronizing, bijective transformation.

The view-based approach presented by Burger abstracts from the underlying model, at the cost of an additional effort to define and maintain extra transformations, and to ensure that the transformations are semantically preserving. In the end, both our model scoping and the view-based approach establish information hiding regarding models, but on a different level due to different intents: scoping establishes information hiding abilities on the syntactic level with minimal effort, whereas dynamic views establish information hiding on a more abstract (and thus elaborate) level, with the ability to generalize from the underlying models.

7.2. Modularity in Model Transformation Languages

The module concept that we introduce in Chapter 3 is definitely not the first one proposed for transformation languages. Many if not all prevalent transformation languages already include some notion to structure transformations, albeit mostly for the purpose of reuse or as a basic mechanism to physically structure code. In the following, we discuss their properties, primary aims, and how they relate and compare to our own concept.

Early formal treatment of modular concepts as they appear in general-purpose programming languages had been carried out by Burstall and Lampson [BL84]. More recently, modularity has been discovered as beneficial for domain-specific languages as well, for example Kang and Ryu introduced modularity to the JavaScript language [KR12]. Similarly, Bierman et al. proposed a superset of ECMAScript called TypeScript [BAT14] that fosters programming in the large. It does so by adding syntactic sugar in shape of dynamically loadable modules which is statically type checked.

The initial European workshop on composition of model transformations in 2006 marked major interest in the topic for the first time. Since then, compositionality of model transformations has been under steady research, albeit most compositional approaches focus on reusability. In Belaunde's article on QVT-O's compositional abilities [Bel06], the author distinguishes between coarse-grained and fine-grained techniques, also known as internal and external composition. The former work on transformations and whole models, whereas the latter work at the level of mappings and model elements.

This section first overlooks techniques that modularize offer external composability, and finally those that offer internal composability. As will be shown, most of the available techniques aim to leverage reuse, none of them is concerned with maintenance efforts.

7.2.1. Modularization for Reuse

Olsen et al. investigate possible ways to improve reusability of transformations [OAO06], compositional techniques being among them. Among seven different kinds, *as-is* reuse and *opportunistic* reuse (including whitebox techniques like edit, copy & paste) are the most trivial kinds of reuse. Other ways of reuse are *composition* (also known as chaining), *parametrization*, transformations of *higher-order*, *specialization* (e.g., by using inheritance), and *source model filtering* (i.e., limiting the scope to source model subsets). Their experience stems from structuring a library of ATL transformations, as well as development of M2T transformations in MOFScript, a language featuring rule polymorphism, transformation inheritance, and library import.

A more up-to-date survey and far more detailed classification of reuse techniques is given by Wimmer, Kusel et al. [WKK+12b; WKK+12a; KSW+13]. They consider both fine-grained and coarse-grained reuse, which relate to internal and external composability. They observe that no module mechanism so far provides means to define access rights (like `private` vs. `protected` in Java) or restricted inheritance options (`final` in Java) despite the early availability of module concepts. None of the presented fine-grained compositional mechanisms seems to possess blackbox characteristics. We believe the main reason is that techniques which aim at better reuse rely on invasive whitebox mechanisms, whereas we concentrate on improving maintainability. In fact, we deliberately decide in favor of maintainability: Because our approach introduces static dependencies to model elements, we even hinder reuse over metamodels, yet we can improve evolvability, understandability, and type safety.

7.2.2. Internal Composition

Original work on modularity had been carried out in the 1990s in the field of Graph Rewriting Systems, surveyed by Heckel et al. [HEET99]. Hiding of rewrite rules seems to be possible in all of the discussed approaches, but hiding of typed graph structures remains unsupported.

TGG In their article [KKS07], Klar et al. discuss ways to handle problems occurring when dealing with complex transformation specifications. Particularly rule-based languages like QVT-R and TGGs are missing concepts for modularization, composition, specialization, parametrization and reuse. They transfer MOF's concept of structuring models to manage rules in their own TGG dialect named *MOFLON*. Concepts which they reuse and which stem from MOF include packages, nested namespaces, import, merge and rule-based refinement. They have reuse in mind, and although rules can be hidden from imports, there is no explicit interface concept.

Anjorin et al. [ASLS14] set the formal foundations for a refinement mechanism of TGG rules. The matching patterns in TGG rules must be defined for each rule from scratch, although patterns for rules that relate to the same model elements often share similar patterns. To avoid redundancy caused by pattern duplication, they introduce a refinement relation among rules that allows for the flexible composition and reuse of (sub) patterns.

JetBrains MPS Under the MPS language development environment, a language fragment consists of an abstract syntax definition, one or more concrete syntax projections, a type system, and a generator. Language fragments can integrate with other language fragments through one of four design techniques: referencing, extension, reuse, and embedding, according to Voelter's classification of composition approaches [Voe11]. MPS brings its own rule-based language to be used to implement the generator: mapping rules are typically implemented using a template-based mechanism akin to that of Xtend, or a manual approach. There is no dedicated interface definition for language fragments, and none of the concepts provided by a fragment, i.e. syntactical entities, type and mapping rules, can be protected from client access.

Stratego/XT Stratego/XT is another oft-used transformation language in the field of language and compiler engineering. It supports "meta-model extensibility through generator extensibility" [HKGV10], also known as horizontal modularity. Our approach still requires the respective modules to be modified when the models change, yet our descriptive interfaces help to locate the affected modules with less effort.

RubyTL Cuadrado and Molina are the inventors of RubyTL [CMT06; CM06], a DSL for hybrid model transformations embedded into Ruby. They further added a rule organization mechanism called *phasing* [CM08; CM09] to RubyTL, a DSL embedded into Ruby. Phasing is a whitebox technique designed to promote modularity and internal transformation composition. Common code can be factored out, as one phase may refine rules of another phase. A phase has a scope (a pivot point, i.e., an element in the source metamodel from which a rule evolves), a precondition, by-value parameters, and a scheduling script for ordering sub-phases and binding parameters. However, their concept does not include interface descriptions to make data and rule dependencies between phases explicit.

Table 7.1 compares typical modularity features between languages we perceived to be most interesting and our proposed derivate, QVT-OM. A checkmark indicates full support, partial support if bracketed, and either the respective keyword or possible limitations are stated below. All of the observed languages support modularity to some extent.

Xtend The Xtend language is a Java-based general-purpose language, though it can be – and has been – extended by domain-specific concepts. It is already equipped with extensions to write M2M and M2T transformations, namely an OCL-like collection library, cached methods and template expressions. It has to be noted, though, that the concept of mapping methods is very basic compared to "real" transformation languages, e.g., there is no trace resolution API.

Table 7.1.: Comparison of concepts for internal composition

Concept	QVT-OM	Xtend2	Kermeta2	QVT-R	QVT-O	ATL	ETL	VIATRA2
Modules	✓	✓ class	✓ class	✓ library, transformation	✓ library, transformation	✓ module	✓ *files*	✓ namespace
Import mechanisms	✓	✓ extension, extends	✓ inherits	✓ import	✓ access, extend	✓ uses	✓ import	✓ import
Rule inheritance	–	–	–	(✓) *unimpl.*	✓ inherits	✓ extends	✓ extends	–
Rule merging	–	–	–	–	✓ merges	–	–	–
Superimposition	–	✓ override	✓ *implicit*	(✓) *implicit*	✓ extends	✓ *implicit*	✓ *implicit*	✓ *model+ data*
Qualified namespace	✓	✓ package	✓ package	(✓) *models*	(✓) *models*	(✓) *models*	(✓) *models*	(✓) *models?*
Explicit interfaces	✓	✓ interface	✓ abstract class	–	–	–	–	–
Traces	✓	(✓) *only local*	–	–	–	–	–	–
Methods	✓	✓ def	✓ *implicit*	–	–	–	–	–
Model elements	✓	(✓) import	–	–	–	–	–	–
Information hiding	✓	✓ private	–	–	–	–	–	–

Due to its Java heritage, programs can be decomposed into classes. Imports are declarable by the `extension` keyword that translates to an annotation implemented by a dependency injection framework, or by using class-based inheritance (`extends`). Methods may override inherited methods, which paves the way for superimposition. Because Xtend transformations refer to the EMF representation of Ecore models, objects in the model referred to by their type must be imported, either one by one or using a wildcard import. However, types may be still navigated to without an explicit import declaration. Like Java, Xtends supports (but does not require) the use of interfaces and information hiding through private methods. However, in contrast to our approach, interfaces cannot restrict accessibility of traces and visibility of model elements.

Kermeta2 The Kermeta language is an object-oriented (OO) modeling language that allows to imperatively define dynamic semantics with an OCL-like syntax. Kermeta's aspect feature can be used to define model transformations by attaching mapping operations to classes of the source model. Thus, transformations are modularizable using EMOF's class concept and Kermeta's aspect mechanism. Inheritance is possible, and methods are implicitly redefinable. The EMOF-compliant models bring packages as namespace mechanism. There exists support for explicit interfaces through abstract classes. Yet, Kermeta's transformation concept is very rudimentary, as mappings are written as normal operations that must explicitly instantiate target elements. Caching and tracing is so far not provided by Kermeta, and no accessibility control is possible.

QVT-R The declarative transformation language QVT Relations (QVT-R), according to the standard [Obj11], allows transformations to be decomposed into modules, and query methods can be put into separate libraries. Tranformation modules and rule inheritance have not been implemented so far. Wagelaar et al. [WVD10] propose superimposition techniques for both ATL and QVT-R, but this technique remains to be implemented as well. Only complete models can be implemented. Neither explicit interfaces nor information hiding features are regarded by the language definition.

QVT-O The QVT Operational Mappings (QVT-O) language provides two structuring concepts, transformations and libraries. A transformation can either access other transformations and libraries, or it can extend other transformations. The latter mechanism overrides same-named rules from the imported transformation. Rules themselves may reuse imported or local rules in two ways, either by inheritance or by merging another rule's functionality. A transformation has full access to the imported models, no access restrictions apply. There is no possibility to define explicit interfaces, and methods cannot be hidden from clients.

ATL Transformation programs written in the Atlas Transformation Language (ATL) can be structured using the `module` keyword. A module is able to import methods from another module, which can be subsequently called or inherited from (keyword `extends`). Superimposition has been added by Wagelaar [WVD10]. Like in QVT, models can be only imported as a whole. Explicit interfaces are not part of the language.

ETL The Epsilon Transformation Language (ETL) is, just like ATL, a hybrid transformation language, uniting both declarative and imperative concepts. Programs are distributable over multiple files, and one file may import another. Similar to ATL, rules can extend and superimpose other rules. Again, subsets of models, i.e. packages, cannot be imported. It is not possible to declare interfaces.

VIATRA2 The VIATRA language aggregates declarative and imperative features by combining two popular formal techniques, GTs and ASMs. The language's namespace concept makes it possible to decompose programs into modules, which can then relate to each other using import statements. Superimposition is provided, and affects both model and data. To our knowledge, there is no concept that makes it possible to refer to the subpackages of a model, and neither interfaces nor information hiding is supported.

Summary Most of the languages that we discussed concentrate on white-box techniques for reuse matters, for example inheritance, merging, and superimposition of rules. Superimposition was first introduced by Wagelaar to ATL and QVT [Wag08], a technique to overlay sets of rule definitions on top of each other. QVT-O is said to have an OO heritage [Bel06] and thus only supports inheritance and superimposition.

When it comes to interface concepts, only few languages provide concepts to make traces, methods, or model elements explicit. Only internal DSLs are able to hide implementation details by exploiting concepts of high-level languages, for instance Xtend and RubyTL. Rules in Kermeta are defined as class methods in UML, so inheritance, interfaces and other UML concepts can be exploited. To our knowledge, QVT-OM with its existing prototypes QVTom and Xtend2m are the only approaches that introduce blackbox modularity.

7.2.3. External Composition

Several approaches are concerned with compositionality at the transformation level, also known as blackbox composition, mostly aiming at reusability of transformations. The most notable ones are MCC, UniTI [VAB+07] integrated into Eclipse AM3 as a GMM4CT plug-in, PICOTIN, Wires*, TraCo, transML, and MWE. The Model Control Center (MCC) by Kleppe [Kle06] is the oldest approach for transformation composition.

UniTI Universal Transformation Infrastructure (UniTI) is one of the more elaborate composition frameworks. Meanwhile, it has been integrated into AMMA Megamodel (AM3) under the subproject Global Model Management for Composite Transformations (GMM4CT) [Van10], where it builds upon the megamodel registry. The megamodel is a model managing metamodels, models, transformations and arbitrary further types of artifacts, like tools, plus relations among these artifacts. It shares many similarities with the ModelBus approach. In his 2007 publication [VAB+07], Vanhooff additionally defines four roles for transformation development based on UniTI's component concepts: developer, designer, harvester and assembler. The process is roughly explained in the context of his transformation component framework UniTI.

PICOTIN The PICOTIN approach, whose acronym stands for "PICO Transformation INfrastructure", by some sources referred to as the Transformation Composition Framework (TCF), is another component model for the model transformation domain [Mar04]. Picotin defines its own declarative transformation language to be used to specify the basic transformation components, which comprises simplistic forall-exists rules. The component model does not support explicit interfaces, component definitions include both interface and implementation. This work remains a proposal, there is no validation that demonstrates applicability in larger, more realistic MDE scenarios.

Wires* The *Wires** approach is a composition framework for ATL by Rivera et al. [RRLB09]. It is a dataflow-based, graphical description language for ATL-based transformations. Its outstanding feature is the support of higher-order and generic transformations. With the exception of primitively valued extra parameters, components refer to complete models, classifying this as an approach for external composition.

TraCo The *TraCo* approach is a transformation composition framework that showcases safe composition through contractual interfaces [HKA11]. TraCo's interfaces only provide for full models, it has neither built-in support for model access policies, nor does it include mapping operations. A TraCo component is purely data-driven, it cannot refer to external mappings or externally generated traces. A notable field of application is to ensure that only valid transformation variants can be built from available components. With our approach, type-safe configuration of variants could be performed similarly at design-time. There is no runtime validation intended, because our binding is resolved before runtime.

transML Guerra [GdLK+13] et al. present *transML*, a holistic approach to transformation engineering that relies on a family of special-purpose languages for the various phases of the transformation development life-cycle.

The process includes an architectural view at the level of transformation components and interfaces. Metamodels and directions belong to the interface declaration, but no fine-grained access control is possible.

MWE The MWE is a simple orchestration language that belongs to the Eclipse Xtext/Xtend project. It is similar to the *Apache Ant* build tool [TB02], but has been primarily designed for model-based tasks. Components are realized as java beans, where an interface consists of untyped parameters and dynamically typed model slots. The framework already comes with a set of components that serve as facades for EMF-based MDE tools, including model readers, writers, and facades for Xtext and Xtend. Composition of workflows is generally possible, though not very sophisticated.

Summary All of the approaches we discussed follow the data-driven programming paradigm, component instances are executed as soon as models are present at all of the available input ports. None of them offers a language concept for binding model concepts, which has only recently been proposed by Cuadrado et al. [CGdL11; CGdL12] and later refined [SGdL14]. While UniTI supports a shared tracing model, it is not possible to explicitly share single traces based on concepts. As for the other approaches, Cuadrado's component concept as well does not allow transformation fragments to be composed.

7.3. Semantics of Model Transformations

In Section 3.5 we have contributed formal semantics for the QVT-R language based on the official standard's description using first-order logics. Because of the standard's widely accepted impreciseness, many of the formal foundation deviate from the standard's foundation as they investigate bidirectional and update semantics, for which first-order logics have been deemed insufficient.

In addition to first order logic-based semantics in Annex B, the latest version of the QVT-R specification furthermore provides a mapping from QVT-R to the more fundamental language QVT-Core [Obj11, Ch. 10], but is omissive about the exact semantics of QVT-Core. Since there is a general perception that the semantics as they are defined in the specification are not sufficiently formal and rigorous, much work has been done to improve the situation. Most approaches use different formalisms apart from first-order logics to capture semantics of QVT-R.

An embedding of QVT-R into the *Coloured Petri Net* formalism has been explored by de Lara and Guerra to formally define semantics [dLG09], and by Wimmer et al. as a debugging aid [WKK+09]. Stevens applies *game theory* to capture check-only semantics [Ste13]. Bidirectional checking [BS12] and enforcing semantics [BS13] had been formalised in *mu calculus* by Bradfield and Stevens, they forbid unbounded recursion, just as we do in Coq. Macedo and Cunha embed bidirectional semantics into Alloy, a *HOL*-based specification language [MC13]; they use *predicate logic* as well, but pursue ideas from Stevens on bidirectional enforcement semantics [Ste10]. Troya and Vallecillo embed the ATL transformation language in Maude's *rewriting logic* [TV11], but ATL differs from QVT insofar that it mixes imperative with declarative programming concepts. Strecker suggests to deeply embed graph rewriting rules in *Isabelle/HOL* for formal verification [Str08]. Coq4MDE [KCPT11] aims to translate modeling concepts to *constructive type theory*, yet it does not provide an embedding of QVT semantics. Guerra proposes *algebraic semantics* as an aid for translating QVT-R concepts to a formal calculus [GdL12]. Considering the constraint-based nature of QVT-R, instance-based verification instead of program-based verification can be used as an alternative method, as demonstrated by Cabot et al. [CCGdL08], who extract OCL invariants from a QVT specification to verify correctness on an instance-level. Garcia extracts invariants for symbolic analysis using Alloy [Gar08].

All of these works propose their interpretation of the QVT-R semantics, but none of them aims to reuse and improve the first-order logic-based semantics from the QVT standard. At least for the basic case of unidirectional, non-updating enforcement semantics, we are able to translate these to the formal specification language Gallina as faithfully as possible.

Large parts of the OCL have been systematically embedded into HOL by Brucker et al. [BW08]. Brucker's HOL-OCL could have been used to embed the metamodels and OCL expressions into higher-order logics. His approach, however, does not cover transformation logic yet.

7.4. Program Analysis, Cluster Analysis, and Visualization of Transformations

In this thesis, we propose to exploit program analysis techniques twice: Firstly, Chapter 4 additionally applies visual analytics to automatically extracted dependence information to aid the maintenance process, and secondly, dependence information is used in Chapter 5 to re-engineer the modular structure from transformation code. Subsequently, we discuss related work in the context of model transformation engineering on three areas, (i) on program analysis in general, (ii) on cluster analysis, and (iii) on program visualization.

7.4.1. Program Analysis

Program analysis techniques are already applied to model transformations. Varro and his colleagues transfer graph transformations into Petri nets [VVE+06], where they are able to prove termination for many programs. Ujhelyi, Horvath and Varro analyze programs in VIATRA2's transformation language VTCL for common errors in transformation programs [UHV09]. The same authors suggest a dynamic backward slicing approach [UHV12] to understand program behavior for a certain input.

Wimmer et al. [WKK+09] propose to translate QVT-R programs to the QPN formalism, where they are able to reason about the program's properties. Issues which can be detected are violated boundedness properties of output models, and transition errors due to erroneous rules or input models. Termination and confluence can be ensured from state space exploration of the automaton.

Cuadrado et al. [CGL14] perform static program analysis on ATL, in order to detect typing errors that are not detectable by standard tools. They use constraint solving techniques to derive a test model fragment or witness that leads to the problematic statement being executed. Standard ATL tools only support a weak typing system, making it prone to various typing errors.

In comparison, our approach is based on static program analysis, aiming to support both re-engineering and maintenance endeavours rather than reasoning about program properties.

Vieira and Ramalho developed a higher order transformation [VR11] to automatically extract dependencies from ATL transformations. Their objective is similar to ours, namely to assist developers inspecting transformation code by providing dependency information from transformation rules to model elements. The unvalidated approach is specific to the ATL, and it lacks data dependencies and filters. A graphical user interface for the Eclipse-based ATL editor is left for future work.

Further work exists on quality metrics that incorporate the peculiarities of model transformation programs. Code-based quality metrics had been explored by van Amstel et al. for the ASF+SDF term rewriting language and the imperative language Xtend [vALvB08; vAvB11], and by Kapova et al. [KGBH10] for the declarative model transformation language QVT-R. Tolosa defines metrics for the hybrid transformation language ATL [TSG+11], adding relative metrics including the proportion of imperative concepts used. Based on the premise that declarative constructs are regarded to foster a better design and imperative constructs are discouraged, they can give a quick estimation of the quality of designs.

7.4.2. Software Cluster Analysis

Software clustering approaches mainly focus on recovering an architecture from code written in general-purpose programming languages. Hence their view consists of procedures and call relationships, modules and use dependencies, or classes and their relationships.

Other information to discover a modular structure had been put into consideration as well, including the change history [BN05], omnipresent objects [WT05], or transactions (repeated use of a set of classes by other classes indicates that they form a single purpose) [SP07]. Furthermore, a combination of control and data dependencies as a source of information to discover a hidden modular structure in procedural and object-oriented code had been studied over the last three decades [HB85; LW90; CP92; SR99]. We apply a similar technique to model transformation languages, though in our specific case we additionally exploit the subtleties of UML/MOF-compliant modeling languages as data description language, for instance hierarchical structured data elements.

Nevertheless, when it comes to the application of automatic clustering techniques to model transformation programs in particular, no previous work is known to us. Despite some investigations on the architectural design of model transformations [DGL+05; LDGR04; KvBJ06; KvBJ07], there is no work which considers to (semi-)automatically re-engineer such a design from code.

7.4.3. Program Visualization

Software visualization tools had been surveyed by Diehl in his book from 2007 [Die07]. Telea et al. [THER09] make a comparison between HEB visualizations and classical NLDs when used for comprehending C/C++ code. HEBs and NLDs are utilized as paper-based diagrams, yet our dependency graphs can be classified as NLDs.

Regarding general-purpose programming languages, various work can be found on program visualization. Chen and Railich [CR00] proposed abstract system dependence graphs (ASDGs) to help locating concepts in programs. Concepts are given in the form of a change request. An attached case study attests better efficiency to maintainers using their graph variant. ASDGs incorporate data and control dependencies. In contrast to our approach, research is targeting general-purpose programming languages. A retrospective view is given ten years after the initial study [CR10].

The *Stacksplorer* approach [Krä11] is one example for program visualization of GPL code. This approach enhances the Xcode IDE with a demand-driven call graph visualization for inter- and intra-file navigation on ObjectiveC code. The Java IDE under Eclipse, for example, merely allows to navigate the call graph by searching for callers and callees in a tree-based view, without featuring live computation. Still, Stacksplorer misses out on data dependencies, which are highly relevant when dealing with model transformation programs.

Only recently, visualization techniques have been considered for programs from the model transformation domain. Van Amstel et al. have been conquering HEB diagrams for visualizing a transformation's data and control dependencies and metamodel coverage [vAvB11]. They concentrated on ATL, QVT-O, and Xtend. However, data and control dependencies are not integrated into a single view, and effectiveness and efficiency of static HEB diagrams for maintenance tasks remain to be validated.

The VIATRA2 Eclipse integration provides a graph visualization component for model spaces that Zest's automatic layout feature and is editable, but it does not integrate transformation programs into the view.

There is work [JGB11] that proposes to estimate the so-called footprint of model transformation programs. According to the authors, a footprint of a model operation is "the part of a model actually used by an operation". Their main presumption is that transformations typically cover only a small subset of the model and the instance and type level, information which may be used in three scenarios: First, to generate a dynamic view of the relevant subset of a model, second, to optimize the metamodel by removing unneeded elements, and third, to find problems in the transformation. They assess the performance costs and exactness of the results of a static analysis as opposed to that of a dynamic analysis. The approach has been implemented for Kermeta, but is obviously applicable to other transformation languages. Our dependence analysis is similar to a static footprint, in that it creates model slices to hide irrelevant information. Their focus, however, lies on the models, thus they do not, in contrast to our approach, consider control structures of the transformation program, nor do they consider the benefits of an interactive visualization with customizable filters.

Wimmer et al. [WKS+09b; WKS+09a] suggest to employ a graphical debugging method to help developers in understanding QVT-R programs more quickly and thoroughly, and to ease the location of faulty code. They blame the high amount of rules with interrelated data and control dependencies as the main cause for declarative transformation code being poorly understandable. Their debugging framework called Transformations on Petri Nets in Color (TROPIC) translates QVT-R programs into a colored Petri net which is then automatically visualized. All MDE-related artifacts, the transformation, models and instances thereof, are displayed in a single homogeneous view. Users may choose between different levels of abstraction, to hide information not required. The view is designed to make the dynamic operational sequences of the QVT-R language and the actual implementation more transparent. Their approach mainly focusses on the dynamic semantics of QVT-R. Our approach, by contrast, is based on dependence information that can be extracted statically, and is not restricted to declarative transformation languages alone.

In a similar attempt, Schönböck et al. use Petri nets to integrate data and control structures into a graphical view [SKK+10] to foster debuggability. Their approach is designed for declarative rule-based transformation languages alone and lacks validation.

Eclipse editors, including that for QVT-O, support hyperlinked syntax. However, control dependencies are not computed live, and navigation over calls is only possible in the forward direction. Learning about data dependencies from code requires good cognitive abilities and a thorough knowledge of all the relevant language concepts. Still, data dependencies derived from other methods can not directly be seen. Furthermore, it is not possible to directly learn about all the places a particular data element is accessed.

7.5. Summary

This chapter provided an overview of approaches that are closely related to this thesis' contributions. We highlighted shortcomings of existing approaches that have been tackled by our own approaches. These shortcomings, and how they relate to our contributions, can be summarized as follows:

Modularization for Maintainability So far, none of the modularization concepts that had been proposed for model transformation languages are dedicated to mitigate maintenance efforts. Most of the work concentrates on modularity for reuse. Although all of the transformation languages that we studied provide some kind of module concept to structure the code (as shown in the related work chapter), none of them offers explicit interfaces that allow to declare the contextual dependencies of the module at a level of detail sufficient to ease typical maintenance processes.

Semantics of QVT-R Since the standardizing document of the QVT languages has been published in 2008, the normative description of the QVT-R language's semantics have been criticized as incomplete and flawed. There is a substantial body of research work that aims to clarify the exact semantics of QVT-R, mostly focussing on bidirectional and updating semantics. We are obviously the first ones who translated the standard's first-order logics of the non-updating, unidirectional case into a theorem proving engine as faithfully as possible. There, we were able to derive a working implementation with approved standards-compliance.

Automatic Re-Engineering Until now, the re-engineering of model transformation programs had to be performed completely manually. To the best of our knowledge, we are the first who consider to transfer automatic clustering techniques, which are known to reasonably work for general-purpose programs, to model transformation programs. As opposed to general purpose programs, experts tend to structure the programs according to the models involved in the transformation. Hence, input to a clustering intention must include not only control dependence information, but also model use dependencies and a weighting to balance the influence of control and model use dependencies.

Visualization Techniques While several approaches have been proposed up to now that automatically analyze dependence information for visualization, none of them integrates both model and control dependencies, none has been synchronized with the textual editor for improved usability, and none can be interactively navigated and filtered according to preset criteria. Above all, none of the approaches features has been empirically validated in realistic scenarios, which has been done for our own approach with a positive outcome. Existing visualization approaches for GPLs cannot be directly transferred to Model Transformation Languages (MTLs) as they miss out on important details, namely information on model use dependencies.

The three main and one side contributions of this thesis tackle the shortcomings and issues mentioned above. Modularization for maintainability refers to our module concept with information hiding properties that we presented in Chapter 3. The same chapter discusses our improved formalization of the QVT-R language's semantics. The automatic re-engineering approach tailored to the peculiarities of model transformations has been introduced in Chapter 5. Our interactive visualization technique has been explained in Chapter 4.

8. Conclusions

This chapter concludes the thesis with a retrospective view on the research questions and how they have been answered, and further provides a general outlook on the role modularity concepts could play for domain-specific languages.

The chapter is organized as follows. Section 8.1 summarizes the main contributions and validation results, and Section 8.2 outlines benefits gained and scientific findings made. Section 8.3 summarizes assumptions and limitations of our contributions with regard to the initially stated research questions. Section 8.4 suggests questions for short-term and long-term future work. Finally, Section 8.5 ends the thesis by listing the overall benefits.

8.1. Summary

Model-driven techniques promise to make software development more efficient than ordinary engineering methods. Thus, software industries are increasingly interested in model-driven engineering to cope with the ever growing complexity. The domain-specific languages, methods and tools that are used in this field, however, exhibit similar problems as they are not capable to handle the inherent complexity of the models, processes and model transformations [BLW05; HWRK11; HRW11; WHR+13]. In fact, model-driven assets are subject to software evolution to the same extent as traditional software artifacts, and even more so the model transformations, in that they need to co-evolve with the domain models and changes in the target platform.

Programs developed in a domain-specific language can get complex to a degree where one has to think about a sophisticated structure to keep maintenance efforts low. This is not only true for applications designed in general purpose scripting languages, but also for model transformation programs. Many model transformations map between heterogeneous models and platform libraries of increasing size. Moreover, model transformations tend to offer a high degree of variability in terms of configuration parameters or even a feature model.

In this thesis, we presented and validated three approaches to alleviate maintenance costs of transformations, leading to these four contributions:

Domain-specific Modularity for Model Transformations We designed a module concept for model transformation languages that establishes information hiding at the level of mapping methods (or in a declarative context, rules), and model elements. Since transformation modules not only depend on mapping methods/rules provided by other modules, but do further query, modify and create parts of the models that are processed, interfaces must be capable not only to declare the scope of methods/rules, but also the models. With our concept, both of them can be declarable at a sufficient level of detail to allow for a more precise definition of contextual dependencies.

We were able to show that the approach is conceptually compatible with other imperative and declarative transformation languages. For clarification, we formalized the dynamic semantics of a subset of the QVT-R language, as the language standard's description is reportedly incomplete and erroneous. As we found out in Chapter 7, none of the domain-specific transformation languages that have been proposed so far offer explicit interfaces, only those implemented as an internal DSL may hijack the host language's OO concepts. None of the model transformation languages offers a fine-grained access control mechanism for the models involved.

Interactive Visual Analytics for Model Transformations We realized that a lot of transformation implementations which have been designed in the past are not properly structured, or the design has deteriorated over time due to evolution of the models. Not in all cases does it pay off to manually refactor the legacy design, for instance when only few maintenance operations have to be performed. If this is the case, automatic program analysis techniques can provide assistance. We designed an approach that is based on the visual analytics methodology and fitted towards typical maintenance tasks on model transformation programs. In contrast to usual analysis techniques which focus on control dependence information alone, we merge control and model use dependence information into a single graph view. We give developers the ability to interactively apply preconfigured filters. Our navigable graphical view is linked with the textual editor view, so developers get complete details on demand and through this are instantly able to identify the location of concern in the source files.

We showed that the approach is general enough to be useful for both imperative and declarative transformation languages. There are previous approaches on analysis and visualization of model transformations, but none of them integrates control and model dependencies, is synchronized with the textual editor, can be interactively navigated, or offers context-sensitive dynamic filters.

Clustering Analysis for Model Transformations We searched for a method that takes the burden off of developers refactoring legacy transformations with a suboptimal design due to erosion or negligence. Our solution suggests to apply clustering techniques to (semi-)automatically re-engineer the modular structure from the code. In concert with literature, there are three predominant modular designs of model transformations, a source-driven, a target-driven, and a hybrid decomposition. In order to compute clusterings with an optimized cohesion and coupling, it takes information on method call and model use dependencies. Based on a graph representation of the dependence information, we assigned weights to the different types of dependence relationships, so that during clustering analysis, a certain decompositional style is favored.

As we found out at the end of Chapter 5, the approach can be transferred to a variety of transformation languages. We are not aware of previous work that aims to automatically derive clusterings for model transformation programs.

Validation In the scope of this thesis, we have validated the above mentioned approaches in three separate case studies on three different model transformations from the Palladio research project.

For the module concept, we have evaluated realistic maintenance scenarios that were recently carried out on the PCM2-Simu-Com transformation. The study comes to the conclusion that – with a proper modularization based on expressive interfaces – the amount of code that is required to be understood can be reduced by more than 50 percent as opposed to a similar decomposition without interfaces.

Our interactive visual analytics methodology has been validated in an empirical experiment that involved 22 participants. The experiment has been conducted on the PCM2QPN transformation implemented in Eclipse QVT-O. We asked subjects to carry out seven maintenance tasks from all four types of maintenance tasks. Results reveal that subjects using our graphical view achieved significantly higher levels of efficiency and effectiveness than subjects that used the standard Eclipse QVTo editor alone. Various analysis techniques have been proposed for model transformation engineering in the past, yet this is the first one that has been empirically validated in an experiment with human subjects.

Regarding the automatic re-engineering of the module structure, we studied two transformations implemented in QVT-O and Xtend, named PCMEvents2PCM and PCM2SimuCom. We found out that results obtained from automatic analysis are significantly more similar to an expert clustering if we consider model use and structural dependence information in addition to control dependencies. This is because prevalent decompositional styles are driven by the structure of the input and output models of a transformation.

8.2. Lessons Learnt

Assessed from a broader viewpoint, there are two scientific findings made by this thesis, which we are going to point out below.

Applying Language Concepts, Tools and Techniques to Domain-Specific Languages Techniques for complexity and cost reduction known to effectively work for software development in general can be successfully transferred to software artifacts specific to model-driven software development. This includes a sophisticated module concept and automatic program analysis techniques in combination with visual analytics and automatic cluster analysis. In both cases, we had to carefully adapt the generic concepts of modular programming, program analysis and cluster analysis to the domain-specific case of model transformation languages.

What distinguishes model transformation languages the most from imperative GPLs is that they are strongly linked with object-oriented modeling languages. A prominent indication for this bondage is that transformation programs are most often decomposed along one of the model's structure. We had to consider dependencies among code and models in all three approaches, modularity, program and visual analysis, and cluster analysis.

Importance of Modularity for Domain-Specific Languages By example of model transformations, we have seen that programs in domain-specific languages can grow complex to a point where there is a need for a well-designed architecture if we want to avoid high maintenance costs. Most model transformation languages allow programs to be stored across multiple files like any other scripting language. Such a simple modularization mechanism turns out to be insufficient for more complex programs, as evidenced by reports on maintenance problems from larger model-driven software projects. Most model transformation languages provide means to structure transformations, though all of them focus on whitebox reuse, and neglect the benefits of blackbox modularity.

Our solution to this problem is to introduce a structuring concept that minimizes the logical boundaries and makes them explicit through well-defined interfaces. What is exposable through an interface highly depends on the domain concepts used by the language – regarding transformation languages, elements that lie at the logical boundaries are model types and the top level structuring concept. We consider model types at any granularity, reaching from classes, over packages to complete models. Top level structuring concepts are methods and/or rules, depending on if the transformation language uses declarative and/or imperative concepts.

A similar observation can be made for domain-specific languages from other domains: Two prominent examples are JavaScript [CR14; BAT14] and Lua [IdFF07], both had been originally designed for smaller applications. As developers began to use the languages for larger implementations, they began to emulate the information hiding principle using functional programming concepts. At a later time, module systems were integrated into both languages that were more sophisticated, tailored to the particular needs of the domains they were used in.

8.3. Assumptions and Limitations

Not all aspects could have been researched in the context of this thesis. This section briefly looks at the assumptions which have been made and discusses limitations. Some of these have already been mentioned in the concluding remarks of the contributing chapters.

Rule-Level Decompositions We have assumed that decomposing transformations at the level of rules is the optimal choice to attain maintainability. Past research has considered generics and subrule level decompositions, though with the purpose of reuse in mind [KSW+13]. The module concept presented in this thesis does not support the modularization of crosscutting concerns, these would require aspectual techniques to be included.

Limited Portability Applicability and compatibility of the module concept for only a selection of transformation languages has been examined in detail. Although the more prominent languages have been selected, which cover the various paradigms, applicability might not be given for some experimental transformation languages that follow a different paradigm, for instance approaches where transformation rules are semi-automatically derived from a set of interrelated source and target models [Var06].

Upfront Costs of Modular Design Whereas the advantage of a modular design with explicit interfaces has been shown in comparison with the same modular but without explicit interfaces, no comparison of a modular design versus a non-modularized version has been carried out. Model scoping is assumed to be declarable upfront at design time of a model transformation. Fine-grained model access control is an optional feature that allows to set the required scope of a module interface to the full models, to a list of packages, and to a list of classes. As new knowledge about the design is obtained at the later implementation stage, the model scope declarations may be refined accordingly.

Automatic Dependence Analysis vs. Manual Interface Design We present two approaches that help to locate concerns, automatic dependence analysis, and a manual interface design. It remains unknown if our visual analytics method is able to outperform a modularized transformation, particularly when crosscutting concerns must be located that are distributed over multiple modules.

Semi-Automatic Clustering Determining the weight configuration remains an iterative, manual process. The configuration sets used in the case study have been iteratively determined by slight adaptation of a set of starting values and comparing the outcome with the expert clustering. Although we assume that the number of iterations required to reach a configuration that produces clusterings of acceptable quality is low (as it has been the case for the case studies), no general statement can be made.

8.4. Open Questions and Future Work Potentials

While we were conducting this research, some questions appeared that remain unanswered, and ideas for improvements and follow-up research were identified that would have gone beyond the scope of this thesis, but which we consider promising nonetheless. In this section, we point out some of these which pose potential future directions of this work.

General Practicality Up to this point, we were able to show that the structuring concept is compatible with declarative rule-based languages. What we did not demonstrate is the practicability of our approach for this class of transformation languages. As opposed to design patterns for imperative languages, declarative languages are differently structured. Some patterns do not work because the functional character of QVT-R does not include state, hence there is no state to hide. If integrated into a declarative transformation language like QVT-R, does the approach enable developers to create useful decompositions of a program that renders maintenance more effective? To ascertain practicability of the approach for declarative model transformations, declarative transformations from real software projects must be structured and analyzed under realistic maintenance scenarios.

Transformation Language Interoperability Our definition of modularity supports transformation languages from various paradigms, yet we did not treat the case of mixing languages of diverse paradigms. An important, preliminary step would be to agree on language-independent interface descriptions, similar to standardization efforts like Common Object Request Broker Architecture (CORBA) or Microsoft's Interface Description Language (IDL) for imperative, object-oriented languages. This poses the question of what concepts should be supported at the logical boundaries. The semantics of rules specified in the declarative QVT-R language support multidirectionality and updating semantics. If multidirectionality is supported on the interface level, the underlying module concept must make sure that imperative implementations of a bidirectional rule are provided for each possible direction. Romeikat et al. [RRMB08] discuss emerging challenges in context of the QVT language stack, as they translate a subset of QVT-R to QVT-O. General ideas on how to provide interoperability can be drawn from an approach that embeds rule-based programming in the style of PROLOG into Java [CV08].

Aspectual Decomposition Transformations on heterogeneous metamodels are often decomposed by functional aspects, as neither a purely source- nor target-driven decomposition can be applied. In such cases, there are two possible solutions, we may either (i) incorporate aspect-oriented programming techniques, or we may (ii) attempt to refactor the metamodels or introduce appropriate intermediate metamodels. Aspect orientation is currently not supported by the module system in this thesis, but calls for a module concept that allows for fragments of mappings to be declared at the interface level.

Genericity of Transformation Modules The module concept developed in this thesis does hardly facilitate the reuse of transformation logic across different metamodel definitions, as model elements are explicitly referenced.

However, there is some work that applies the concept of *generic typing* to model transformation languages through the binding of generic types to concrete model types [CGdL11]. These approaches, however, do not provide for a proper interface concept as we do. The binding concept suggested by Cuadrado can profit by our module concept: Because our interfaces already declares the elements a module depends on, declarations at the implementation-level for binding accessible elements would only be necessary. We expect the availability of generics at the interface-level to leverage reusability much better than generic definitions without a proper module concept. We believe it is possible that native language concepts can extend the existing module concept in a way type safety can be ensured at compile time by the type checker. A revised form of Cuadrado's model reuse concepts has been proposed by Zschaler [Zsc14], which may leverage reusability if integrated into our module concept.

Variability Mechanism for Transformation Modules While *variability* is easily possible by an additional feature model as input to a transformation, there is no built-in mechanism that selects and binds module implementations according to a given feature configuration.

Typing of Model Transformation Languages Not all transformation languages are strictly typed, making them prone to various typing errors. One example is ATL [CGL14]. Proper typing of model transformations is gaining more and more attention in the community, because it helps to identify errors and ensures that evolving metamodels stay compatible to a transformation. At this time, prevalent transformation languages define proper typing only for a subset of the language, as most rely on the strongly typed OCL.

Verified Transformation Implementations Transformation implementations are currently not verified if they actually provide the demanded functionality. Design by contract as proclaimed by Bertrand Meyer suggests to use pre and post conditions and invariants on the interface level. There is no support for *behavioral contracts* in our interface concept yet. The interface concept of model transformations that has been developed could be augmented by contractual definitions, and implementations of interfaces could be checked using one of the available verification techniques (proof development, model checking, instance-based testing). Another way to improve the concept is to include testing, for example with a native test-case description language for module interfaces.

Fundamental work on this topic has been done by Cariou et al. [CMSD04; CBBD09; CBFB11], who use the OCL to specify contracts at the method level, similar to the Java Modeling Language (JML). Their approach poses a good starting point, although it does not consider benefits gained from specifying contracts at the interface level of transformation modules. An embedding of the ATL and mapping constraints into a SAT-solving engine is provided by Selim et al. [SBC+13]. While their approach demonstrates the importance of correctness and safety in the Automotive industry, it does not consider the fruitful combination of contract-based and modular programming.

Transformation Engineering Process The concepts and tools proposed in this thesis mainly aim to ease maintenance of model transformations. As a future step, it could be interesting to consider other phases of the lifecycle of model transformation development, for instance requirements elicitation, architectural design, validation/certification and testing. Furthermore, co evolution of models and model transformations could be supported by process guidelines.

Formal Verification of Declarative Semantics When safety-critical systems are developed using model-driven techniques, verifiable correctness of model transformations is an important challenge. In this context, an important question is if we can have verified modules. Under verified modules we understand modules whose specification fragment (as part of the interface) is delivered together with not only an implementation, but also a proof that certifies correctness of the implementation with regards to the semantic specification.

Testability of Transformation Modules Another important challenge focusses on unit testing of model transformations. The module concept introduced here is an important premise for automated testing in that it allows to strictly define control and model dependencies. Only instances of those parts of the model must be given as input and tested on the output that are declared in the interface. Such an instance-based test case may be accompanied by mock-up methods that emulate the imported functionality.

Version Control Mechanism Versioning of models is an important challenge that yet remains to be solved. Having modularized transformations, it can be interesting as well to assign separate version numbers to the modules of a transformations. Here, inspiration may be drawn from component models, for instance the Open Services Gateway initiative (OSGi). With the parts of models versioned, for instance at the package level, transformation modules might use available version numbers when resolving dependencies to packages and classes.

Design Patterns for Model Transformations As suggested by Syriani and Gray in their 2012 position paper [SG12], much benefit may be drawn from a catalog of design patterns for model transformations. Not much work can be found on the modular design of model transformations. A study on modularization techniques of rule-based transformation languages was made by Kurtev et al. [KvBJ06; KvBJ07]. Notable advancements on the topic have been published very recently by Lano and Kolahdouz-Rahimi [LK14], who compiled an extensive catalog of transformation-specific patterns. One additional candidate for such a pattern is the model parts registry pattern extensively used in the PCMEvents2PCM transformation presented in this thesis. Future work may explore additional patterns that are based on an adequate modularization constructs, and examine their maintainability enhancements for real transformations.

Automatic Re-Engineering of Model Transformations based on Common Design Patterns In this thesis, only basic design rules are considered by our automatic clustering approach, namely a source and target driven decompositional style. Having identified a set of design rules that are commonly used by transformation developers, these rules could be integrated into our clustering approach to further improve its capabilities. Similar work has been done by Cai et al. who are able to successfully recognize design rules during cluster analysis [CWWW13]. Their approach reveals promising results for the abstract factory design pattern.

8.5. Final Remark

The three approaches presented in this thesis tackle the problem of high maintenance efforts of model transformations. The high complexity induced by large models has been identified as the major cause of a worsened maintainability. This complexity cannot be handled with existing languages and tools: neither do modularity concepts of existing transformation languages provide explicit interfaces with information hiding capabilities of methods and models, nor exist tools to adequately handle the complexity.

Results of this thesis give model-driven software developers new language concepts to proactively develop better maintainable model transformations, as well as new tools that help to understand, maintain and refactor legacy transformations with less effort. Through information hiding modularity and the analysis tools proposed in this thesis, the following benefits are achieved:

Significantly Reduced Maintenance Efforts Maintenance efforts are reduced for previously modularized transformations and legacy transformations alike. Descriptive interface declarations and the visual analytics approach help to identify locations of concern measurably faster.

Significantly Reduced Re-Engineering Efforts Re-engineering the modular structure of legacy transformations can be automated to a large extent, leading to results which reflect the widely accepted transformation designs much better than those obtained from existing clustering methods.

Self-Documenting Transformation Programs Software is easier to understand, use, and reuse, if the program is decomposed into self-contained modules with expressive interface descriptions. Interface declarations are statically enforced by the type checker, reenforcing the confidence in the interface declarations and leveraging modular programming for model transformation engineering.

Collaborative Development Information hiding modularity enables software engineers to subdivide the planned transformation into separate subprograms which are first described by explicit interfaces that enforce the logical boundaries between the modules and models. Based on such a design with minimized dependencies, programmers are able to implement modules in parallel without requiring knowledge of all modules and the complete models. It is easy to identify modules that are affected by anticipated changes to parts of the models, either by reading the interface descriptions, or by using our analytics approach on existing code.

These benefits jointly contribute to reach the primary goal of this thesis, namely a reduction of the costs involved in model transformation development and model transformation maintenance.

From a broader perspective, we demonstrate how a domain-specific language is augmented with a module concept with information hiding capabilities. In contrast to modularity for general-purpose programming languages, one must carefully consider the domain-specific concepts that should be exposed at the module boundaries. As we have found out in this thesis, in case of model transformation languages, not only methods or rules might be published by a module, but also the models – or parts thereof – that are referred to by the internal transformation logic.

With a predicted increase in size and complexity of software, model-driven engineering techniques might reach their limits. Particularly model transformations must be capable to handle increasingly large and complex models without an increase in development and maintenance costs. This research represents a step towards the preparation of software engineering techniques for a lean and cost-effective development of tomorrow's software.

One man's constant is another man's variable.
– Alan J. Perlis [Per82]

A. Type System of Core QVT-OM

In this first of two appendix chapters, we embed language and typing of Core QVTom into the Coq theorem prover. Core QVTom is a dialect of QVT Operational Mappings (QVT-O) which we have extended by information hiding modularity features. This embedding into Coq implements the typing rule from Chapter 3 as faithfully as possible. It reuses ideas and definitions from an embedding done for cast-free Featherweight Java[1] by Bruno De Fraine, Erik Ernst and Mario Sudholt, particularly package `metatheory`.

A.1. Syntax

To begin with, syntactical elements of the language are defined (cf. Figure 3.2 from Section 3.3). To ease proofs, model packages cannot contain further packages. The Activity2Process example does not define subpackages, and without subpackages, no recursion on the package containment hierarchy is needed.

Further on, data structures `genv`, `denv`, and `oenv` are defined, which capture environments Γ, Δ, and Ω, respectively. Inhabitants `PT`, `IT`, and `MT` of lists of packages, interfaces and module implementations are assumed as postulates. They represent the particular set of models, interfaces and modules that is type checked.

```
(** * Syntax *)

(** ** Lexical categories *)

```

[1] Cast-free Featherweight Java, 2008; `http://soft.vub.ac.be/~bdefrain/featherj/`.

```
(** Names of packages, classes, features, interfaces,
     domains, implementations, mappings, variables are atoms
     (their equality is decidable). *)
Definition pname := atom.
Definition cname := atom.
Definition fname := atom.
Definition iname := atom.
Definition tname := atom.
Definition mname := atom.
Definition sname := atom.
Definition vname := atom.

(** The names [self], [result] and [Object], [Boolean],
     [String], [Global] are predefined. We simply assume that
     these names exist. *)
Parameter this : iname.
Parameter self : vname.
Parameter result : vname.
Parameter Object' : cname.
Parameter Boolean' : cname.
Parameter String' : cname.
Parameter Global' : pname.

(** ** Type and term expressions *)

(** Class names are the only form of types. **)
Definition ctype := cname.

(** The expression forms are variable reference, field get,
     method invocation and object creation. Corresponds to
     syntax rule E. *)
Inductive exp : Type :=
| e_trace_resolution_call : exp → cname → exp
| e_mapping_invocation : exp → sname → (*list*) vname → exp
```

```
| e_type_check : exp → cname → exp
| e_feature_access : exp → fname → exp
| e_class_instantiation : cname → (*list exp →*) exp
| e_variable_access : vname → exp (* var includes self *).
Inductive REFTYPE : Type :=
| COMPOSES : REFTYPE
| REFERENCES : REFTYPE.
Inductive REFMULT : Type :=
| ONE : REFMULT
| STAR : REFMULT.
(** Corresponds to syntax rules F, C, and P. *)
Inductive feature : Type := declare_feature : fname → cname →
     REFTYPE → REFMULT → feature.
Inductive class : Type := declare_class : cname → (option
    cname) → (list feature) → class.
Inductive package : Type := declare_package : pname → (list
    class) → (list package) → package.
Inductive TDIR : Type :=
| IN : TDIR
| OUT : TDIR.
(** Corresponds to syntax rules B, S, O, V, I, M and T. *)
Inductive body : Type := declare_body : fname → exp → body.
Inductive methodsign : Type := declare_methodsign : cname →
    sname → ((*list*) cname) → cname → methodsign.
Inductive methodimpl : Type := declare_methodimpl : cname →
    sname → ((*list*) (vname * cname)) → cname → body →
    methodimpl.
Inductive scope : Type := declare_scope : TDIR → pname →
    (list pname) → list (cname) → scope.
Inductive domain : Type := declare_domain : TDIR → tname →
    pname → domain.
Inductive interface : Type := declare_interface : iname →
    (list domain) → (list scope) → (list methodsign) →
    interface.
```

```
Inductive module : Type := declare_module : mname → iname →
    list iname → list methodimpl → module.
(* Transformation definition is covered by axiomatic types
    [PT] [IT] [MT] in this encoding. *)
(*Inductive transformation : Type := declare_transformation
    : list package → list interface → list module →
    transformation.*)
Hint Constructors body.
Hint Constructors methodsign.
Hint Constructors methodimpl.
Hint Constructors scope.
Hint Constructors domain.
Hint Constructors interface.
Hint Constructors module.

(** ** Environments and class tables *)

(** A gamma environment [genv] declares a number of
    variables and their types. A delta environment [denv]
    lists accessible classes together with their respective
    access type. An omega environment [oenv] binds interface
    and mapping identifier to a mapping's signature. *)
Notation genv := (list (vname * ctype)).
Notation denv := (list (TDIR * ctype)).
Notation oenv := (list (iname * methodsign)) (*list ((iname
    * sname) * (ctype * (*list*) ctype * ctype))*).
Inductive ok_genv : genv → Prop :=
| ok_genv_empty : ok_genv nil
| ok_genv_extend : forall Gamma v t,
  ok_genv Gamma →
  (forall (t' : ctype), ¬In (v, t') Gamma) →
  ok_genv ((v, t)::Gamma).
Inductive ok_denv : denv → Prop :=
| ok_denv_empty : ok_denv nil
```

```
| ok_denv_extend : forall Delta d t,
  ok_denv Delta →
  (forall (t' : ctype), ¬In (d, t') Delta) →
  ok_denv ((d, t)::Delta).
Inductive ok_oenv : oenv → Prop :=
| ok_oenv_empty : ok_oenv nil
| ok_oenv_extend : forall Omega i ms cn sn cn' cn'',
  ok_oenv Omega →
  ms = declare_methodsign cn sn cn' cn'' →
  (forall ms_ cn_ sn_ cn'_ cn''_, ms_ = declare_methodsign
      cn_ sn_ cn'_ cn''_ ∧ sn ≠ sn_ ∧ ¬In (i, ms_) Omega) →
  ok_oenv ((i, ms)::Omega).
(** [ptable] maps the names of packages to their
    definitions. A package definition consists of a number
    of contained packages and classes. [itable] maps the
    names of interfaces to their definitions. An interface
    definition consists of a number of domains and method
    signatures. [mtable] maps the names of modules to their
    definitions.  A module definition consists of an
    exported interface, imported interfaces, class and a
    number of methods. *)
Notation ptable := (list package).
Notation itable := (list interface).
Notation mtable := (list module).
(** Predefined objects *)
Parameter Global : package.
Parameter Object : class.
Parameter Boolean : class.
Parameter String : class.
(** We assume fixed tables [PT], [IT], [MT]. *)
Parameter PT : ptable.
Parameter IT : itable.
Parameter MT : mtable.
```

A.2. Auxiliaries

Rule-based definitions for auxiliary methods $classes_C$, $classes_P$, $packages_P$, $features_C$, $mappings_I$, $mappings_M$, $scope_M$, and $scope_I$ from Figure 3.3 directly translate to Coq. For convenience, closures are defined for some of them.

```
(** * Auxiliaries *)

(** ** Lookup of metamodel packages, classes and features *)
(** [classes_c], [classes_p], [packages_p] and [features_c]
      look up inherited classes of a class, contained classes
      in a package, contained packages in a package, and
      features of a class. *)

(** [packages_p p ps] holds if a (root) package named [p]
      defines packages [ps]. *)
Inductive packages_p : package → (list package) → Prop :=
| packages_p_global : packages_p Global nil
| packages_p_other : forall p pn cs ps,
  p = (declare_package pn cs ps) →
  In p PT →
  packages_p p ps
  (* NB: method only works on root packages for now, inner
       packages not used. *).
(** [classes_c c cs] holds if a class [c] maps to list cs
      which contains [c] and super classes of [c]. *)
Inductive classes_c : class → list class → Prop :=
| classes_c_object : classes_c Object nil
| classes_c_boolean : classes_c Boolean nil
| classes_c_string : classes_c String nil
| classes_c_other : forall p cs ps c cn dn fs d cs'' p' cs'
      ps' d' fs',
  (* for any class c that inherits from d *)
```

```
  c = (declare_class cn (Some dn) fs) →
  In (declare_package p cs ps) PT →
  In c cs →
  (* and d is defined as (declare_class d d' fs') *)
  d = (declare_class dn d' fs') →
  In (declare_package p' cs' ps') PT →
  In d cs' →
  (* then we can say that this relation holds *)
  classes_c d cs'' →
  classes_c c (c::d::cs'').
(** [classes_p p cs] holds if a package [p] refers to
    classes [cs] by declaring one of the classes or using
    them as super class. For this we define a closure
    function classes_cs of classes_c. *)
Definition classes_p (p : package) (cs : list class) : Prop
    :=
  exists pn ps, p = (declare_package pn cs ps) ∧ In p PT.
(** [features_c c fs] holds if a class named [c] or its
    super classes define features [fs]. *)
Inductive features_c : class → list feature → Prop :=
| features_c_object : features_c Object nil (* NOTE: we
    could instead define Global as part of ptable *)
| features_c_boolean : features_c Boolean nil
| features_c_string : features_c String nil
| features_c_other : forall p ps cs c cn d dn d' fs fs' fs'',
  In (declare_package p cs ps) PT →
  c = (declare_class cn (Some dn) fs) →
  In c cs →
  d = (declare_class dn d' fs'') →
  features_c d fs' →
  features_c c (fs'++fs)
| features_c_other' : forall p ps cs c cn fs,
  In (declare_package p cs ps) PT →
  c = (declare_class cn None fs) →
```

```
  In c cs →
  features_c c fs.
(** [package_pn pn p] holds if a package named [pn] maps to
    a package [p] of name [pn]. *)
Definition package_pn (pn : pname) (p : package) : Prop :=
  exists cs ps, p = (declare_package pn cs ps) ∧ In p PT.
(** [class_cn cn c] holds if a class named [cn] maps to a
    class [c] of name [cn]. *)
Inductive class_cn : cname → class → Prop :=
| class_cn_object : class_cn Object' Object
| class_cn_boolean : class_cn Boolean' Boolean
| class_cn_string : class_cn String' String
| class_cn_other : forall c cn dn fs p cs ps,
  c = (declare_class cn (Some dn) fs) →
  In (declare_package p cs ps) PT →
  In c cs →
  class_cn cn c.
(** [feature_fn fn f] holds if a feature named [fn] maps to
    a feature [f] of name [fn]. *)
Inductive feature_fn : fname → feature → Prop :=
| feature_fn_other : forall f fn rt rm c cn dn fs p cs ps,
  f = (declare_feature fn cn rt rm) →
  c = (declare_class cn (Some dn) fs) →
  In (declare_package p cs ps) PT →
  In c cs →
  In f fs →
  feature_fn fn f.
(** [interface_in in i] holds if an interface named [in]
    maps to an interface [i] of name [in]. *)
Definition interface_in (in_ : iname) (i : interface) : Prop
    :=
exists ds ss ms, i = (declare_interface in_ ds ss ms) ∧ In i
    IT.
```

```
Inductive interface_ins : (list iname) → (list interface) →
    Prop :=
| interface_ins_nil: interface_ins nil nil
| interface_ins_cons: forall in_ i ins is,
  interface_ins ins is →
  interface_in in_ i →
  interface_ins (in_::ins) (i::is).

(** ** Lookup of declared and implemented mapping types *)
Inductive mappings_i : interface → list (iname * methodsign)
   → Prop :=
| mappings_i_other : forall i in' ds ss ms,
  i = (declare_interface in' ds ss ms) →
  In i IT →
  mappings_i i (List.map (fun m ⇒ (in', m)) ms).
Inductive mappings_is : list interface → list (iname *
    methodsign) → Prop :=
| mappings_is_nil : mappings_is nil nil
| mappings_is_cons : forall i ds is ds',
  mappings_i i ds →
  mappings_is is ds' →
  mappings_is (i::is) (ds++ds').
Inductive mappings_m : module → list (iname * methodsign) →
    Prop :=
| mappings_m_other : forall m mn i is ms ds ss ms',
  m = (declare_module mn i is ms) →
  In m MT →
  In (declare_interface i ds ss ms') IT →
  mappings_m m (List.map (fun m' ⇒ (this, m')) ms').
Inductive mappings_ms : list module → list (iname *
    methodsign) → Prop :=
| mappings_ms_nil : mappings_ms nil nil
| mappings_ms_cons : forall m ds ms ds',
  mappings_m m ds →
```

```
  mappings_ms ms ds' →
  mappings_ms (m::ms) (ds++ds').

(** ** Lookup of model scope, derived from interface signatures and scope declarations *)
Inductive scope_m : interface → list (TDIR * cname) → Prop :=
| scope_m_other : forall i in' ds ss ms,
  i = (declare_interface in' ds ss ms) →
  In i IT →
  scope_m i (List.flat_map
    (* for a given (exported) interface, parameter types of all the methods are in scope *)
    (fun m ⇒ match m with (declare_methodsign c s c' c'') ⇒
      (IN, c)::(IN, c''):: (IN, c')::nil
    end)
    ms).
Inductive scope_i : interface → list (TDIR * cname) → Prop :=
| scope_i_other : forall i in' ds ss ms m is ms' cs' ss' c' p' i' cn',
  i = (declare_interface in' ds ss ms) →
  In i IT →
  In (declare_module m in' is ms') MT →
  scope_i i (
    (* primitives are always accessible *)
    (OUT, Object')::(OUT, Boolean')::(OUT, String')::
    (* for each scope declaration, make declared packages and classes accessible *)
    (List.flat_map (fun s ⇒ match s with (declare_scope d p ps cs) ⇒
      (* get declared class/package from class/package name, compute super/contained classes, return respective name + scope directive as tuple. *)
      (List.map (fun c ⇒ let x := (class_cn cn' c) in (d, cn')) (List.flat_map (fun cn ⇒ let x := (class_cn
```

```
            cn c') in let y := (classes_c c' cs') in cs') cs))
            ++
      (List.map (fun c⇒ let x := (class_cn cn' c) in (d,
            cn')) (List.flat_map (fun pn⇒ let x :=
            (package_pn pn p') in let y := (classes_p p' cs')
            in cs') ps))
    end) ss) ++
    (* iterate over all exported interfaces (is) *)
    (List.flat_map (fun in'⇒ let x := (interface_in in' i')
        in let y := (scope_m i' ss') in ss') is)
  ).
```

A.3. Typing

Core QVT-OM's typing and well-formedness rules are implemented as one inductive definition `typing` and several additional definitions commencing with `ok_` under Coq, as presented in Figures 3.4b and 3.4a. Subtyping rules (cf. Figure 3.3) are declared by definition `sub`.

```
(** * Typing *)

(** ** Well-formed types *)

(** [ok_type t] holds when [t] is a well-formed type. *)
Inductive ok_type : class→ Prop :=
| ok_object: ok_type Object
| ok_boolean: ok_type Boolean
| ok_string: ok_type String
| ok_in_pt:
  forall p pn cs ps c cn dn fs,
  p = (declare_package pn cs ps)→
  In p PT→
  c = (declare_class cn dn fs)→
```

```
  In c cs →
  ok_type c.
Inductive ok_types : list class → Prop :=
| ok_type_nil : ok_types nil
| ok_type_head : forall c cs,
  ok_types cs →
  ok_type c →
  ok_types (c::cs).
Hint Constructors ok_type.
Hint Constructors ok_types.

(** ** Subtyping *)

(** [extends C D] holds if [C] is a direct subclass of [D].
    *)
Definition extends (C D : cname) : Prop :=
  exists pn cs ps fs, In (declare_package pn cs ps) PT ∧ In
      (declare_class C (Some D) fs) cs.
Hint Unfold extends.
(** [sub s u] holds if [s] is a subtype of [u]. The subtype
    relation is the reflexive, transitive closure of the
    direct subclass relation. *)
Inductive sub : ctype → ctype → Prop :=
| sub_reflexive : forall t, sub t t
| sub_transitive : forall t1 t2 t3, sub t1 t2 → sub t2 t3 →
    sub t1 t3
| sub_extends : forall C D, extends C D → sub C D
| sub_object : forall C, sub C Object'.
Hint Constructors sub.

(** ** Term expression and declaration typing *)

```

```
(** [typing E e t] holds when expression [e] has type [t] in
    environments [Gamma, Delta Omega]. [wide_typing E e t]
    holds when [e] has a subtype of [t]. *)
Inductive typing : genv → denv → oenv → exp → ctype → Prop :=
| T_Variable :
  forall Gamma Delta Omega x cn tdir,
  ok_genv Gamma →
  ok_denv Delta →
  In (x, cn) Gamma →
  In (tdir, cn) Delta →
  typing Gamma Delta Omega (e_variable_access x) cn
(* self is just an ordinary variable in this encoding
| T_Context: ... *)
| T_ClassInst:
  forall Gamma Delta Omega cn,
  In (OUT, cn) Delta →
  typing Gamma Delta Omega (e_class_instantiation cn) cn
| T_Feature:
  forall Gamma Delta Omega e0 c0n c0 fs fi ci tdir fin c rt
      rm,
  typing Gamma Delta Omega e0 c0n →
  class_cn c0n c0 →
  features_c c0 fs →
  In fi fs →
  In (tdir, c0n) Delta →
  In (OUT, ci) Delta →
  fi = (declare_feature fin c rt rm) → (* extract feature
      [fi]'s name [fin] *)
  typing Gamma Delta Omega (e_feature_access e0 fin) ci
| T_TypeCheck:
  forall Gamma Delta Omega e0 c0n tdir cn,
  typing Gamma Delta Omega e0 c0n →
  In (tdir, cn) Delta →
  typing Gamma Delta Omega (e_type_check e0 cn) Boolean'
```

```
| T_MappingInv:
  forall Gamma Delta Omega e0 c0n c0 vn vc in' sn c vc' c'' in'' c' tdir tdir' tdir'',
  typing Gamma Delta Omega e0 c0n →
  typing Gamma Delta Omega (e_variable_access vn) vc →
  In (in', declare_methodsign c sn vc' c'') Omega →
  ((In (in'', declare_methodsign c' sn vc' c'') Omega) → sub c c') →
  sub c0 c →
  sub vc vc' →
  In (tdir, c0) Delta →
  In (tdir', c'') Delta →
  In (tdir'', vc) Delta →
  typing Gamma Delta Omega (e_mapping_invocation e0 sn vn) c''
| T_TraceRes:
  forall Gamma Delta Omega e0 c0 c tdir tdir',
  typing Gamma Delta Omega e0 c0 →
  In (tdir, c) Delta →
  In (tdir', c0) Delta →
  typing Gamma Delta Omega (e_trace_resolution_call e0 c0) c
(* wide_typing implicitly adds super types of a type: typing E C ∧ C :> D → typing E D *)
with wide_typing : genv → denv → oenv → exp → ctype → Prop :=
| wide_typing_sub : forall Gamma Delta Omega e t t',
  typing Gamma Delta Omega e t → sub t t' → wide_typing Gamma Delta Omega e t'
with wide_typings : genv → denv → oenv → list exp → list ctype → Prop :=
| wide_typings_nil : forall Gamma Delta Omega,
  ok_genv Gamma →
  ok_denv Delta →
  ok_oenv Omega →
  wide_typings Gamma Delta Omega nil nil
```

```
| wide_typings_cons : forall Gamma Delta Omega E0 es e t,
  wide_typings Gamma Delta Omega es E0 →
  wide_typing Gamma Delta Omega e t →
  wide_typings Gamma Delta Omega (e::es) (t::E0).

(* We do structural recursion, and there is exactly one rule
     applicable to the residual syntactical expression (in
     contrast to expression typing). Thus, we can refer to
     the next rule directly. *)
Definition ok_assignment (Gamma : genv) (Delta : denv)
     (Omega : oenv) (b : body) : Prop :=
  exists b e0 c0 c cn c' tdir fn f fs rt rm,
  b = declare_body fn e0 →
  In (result, cn) Gamma →
  In (OUT, cn) Delta →
  sub c0 c' →
  In (tdir, c0) Delta →
  features_c c fs →
  In f fs →
  f = (declare_feature fn c' rt rm) → (* extract feature
       [f]'s name [fn] and type [c'] *)
  typing Gamma Delta Omega e0 c0.
Definition ok_mappingimpl (Delta : denv) (Omega : oenv) (m:
     methodimpl) : Prop :=
  exists m cn sn pn cn'' b vn cn' tdir tdir',
  m = declare_methodimpl cn sn pn cn'' b →
  pn = (vn, cn') →
  In (tdir, cn) Delta →
  In (tdir', cn') Delta →
  In (OUT, cn'') Delta →
  ok_assignment ((self, cn)::(vn, cn')::(result, cn'')::nil)
       Delta Omega b.
Definition ok_module (m: module) : Prop :=
  exists m mn in_ jns js mis i ds ss ms ss' os' os'',
```

```
  m = declare_module mn in_ jns mis →
  i = declare_interface in_ ds ss ms →
  In i IT →
  scope_i i ss' →
  interface_ins jns js →
  mappings_is js os' →
  mappings_m m os'' →
  (forall mi, In mi mis → ok_mappingimpl ss' (os' ++ os'') mi).
Inductive ok_modules : list module → Prop :=
| ok_modules_nil: ok_modules nil
| ok_modules_cons: forall m ms,
  ok_module m →
  ok_modules ms →
  ok_modules (m::ms).
Definition ok_mappingdecl (Delta : denv) (in_ : iname) (ms: methodsign) : Prop :=
  exists cn sn cn' cn'' m mn jns mis os tdir tdir' ms0 cn0 cn0' cn0'',
  ms = declare_methodsign cn sn cn' cn'' →
  m = declare_module mn in_ jns mis →
  In m MT →
  mappings_m m os →
  In (in_, ms0) os →
  ms0 = declare_methodsign cn0 sn cn0' cn0'' →
  In (tdir, cn) Delta →
  In (tdir', cn') Delta →
  In (OUT, cn'') Delta →
  sub cn0 cn →
  sub cn' cn0' →
  sub cn'' cn0''.
Definition ok_interface (i: interface) : Prop :=
  exists in_ ds ss mss ss',
  i = declare_interface in_ ds ss mss →
```

```
  scope_i i ss' →
  (forall ms, In ms mss → ok_mappingdecl ss' in_ ms).
Inductive ok_interfaces : list interface → Prop :=
| ok_interfaces_nil: ok_interfaces nil
| ok_interfaces_cons: forall i is,
  ok_interface i →
  ok_interfaces is →
  ok_interfaces (i::is).
Definition ok_program : Prop :=
  ok_interfaces IT ∧ ok_modules MT.
```

A.4. Properties

At this point, we are able to translate the theorems that postulate abstraction safety from Section 3.3.4 into Coq propositions. Abstraction safety (Rule 1) is captured by parameter `representation_independence`. Representation invariants (Rules 2a to 2c) are captured by parameters `method_provisioning`, `method_access_control`, and `model_access_control`. The actual proofs under Coq, which give evidence that the four theorems apply to the previously translated type system, are left for future work.

```
(** * Properties *)

(** Abstraction safety *)

Definition parameters_match (mi : methodimpl) (ms :
    methodsign) : Prop :=
  exists cn sn vn cn' cn'' b cn_ cn_' cn_'',
  mi = declare_methodimpl cn sn (vn, cn') cn'' b ∧
  ms = declare_methodsign cn_ sn cn_' cn_'' ∧
  sub cn_ cn ∧
```

```
  sub cn_' cn' ∧ (* this must be done recursively for
      multiple parameters *)
  sub cn'' cn_''.
Function method_call_in_scope (e : exp) (ins : list iname)
    (mis : list methodimpl) : Prop :=
  match e with
  | e_trace_resolution_call e' cn ⇒ method_call_in_scope e'
      ins mis
  (* for any invocation of method [sn] in the method body of
      [mi] *)
  | e_mapping_invocation e' sn vn ⇒
    method_call_in_scope e' ins mis →
    (* [s] is either defined locally, then *)
    ( (* there must be exactly one method implemented by the
        given name, where *)
      exists! mi, forall cn vn cn' cn'' b,
      In mi mis →
      mi = declare_methodimpl cn sn (vn, cn') cn'' b →
      (* It remains future work to infer typing of... *)
      (* * context type [e] |- [cn_] matches type of context
          parameter [cn] *)
      (* * variable [vn] |- [cn'_] :> input parameter [cn']
          *)
      (* * return type = return type of surrounding method
          implementation) <: return type [cn''] *)
      True
    (* else, there is an [s'] defined in exactly one
        imported interface [in_] with *)
    ) ∨ (
      exists! i ms, forall in_ ds ss mss cn cn' cn'' ,
      In in_ ins →
      In i IT →
      i = declare_interface in_ ds ss mss →
      In ms mss →
```

```
      ms = declare_methodsign cn sn cn' cn'' →
      (* parameter types of [ms] and [ms'] match (according
          to Liskov's principle) *)
      True
    )
  | e_type_check e' cn ⇒ method_call_in_scope e' ins mis
  | e_feature_access e' fn ⇒ method_call_in_scope e' ins mis
  | e_class_instantiation cn (*es*) ⇒ True
  | e_variable_access vn ⇒ True
  end.
Definition model_access_in_scope (td : TDIR) (cn : cname)
    (ss : list scope) : Prop :=
  (* class [cn] is either declared directly, *)
  exists s, forall pn pns cns,
  In s ss →
  s = declare_scope td pn pns cns →
  In cn cns ∨ (
    (* or one of the declared packages [pns] contains [cn] *)
    exists pn', forall p cns' pns' c scn fs,
    In pn' pns ∧
    In p PT ∧
    p = (declare_package pn' cns' pns') ∧
    In c cns' ∧
    c = (declare_class cn scn fs)
  ).
Function expression_model_access_in_scope (e : exp) (ss :
    list scope) : Prop :=
  (* for any expression [e] in the method body of [m], the
      inferred type [t] must be (read/write) accessible. *)
  match e with
  | e_trace_resolution_call e' cn ⇒
      expression_model_access_in_scope e' ss ∧
      model_access_in_scope IN cn ss
```

```
  | e_mapping_invocation e' sn vn⇒ expression_model_access_in_scope e' ss ∧ True
  | e_type_check e' cn⇒ expression_model_access_in_scope e' ss ∧ model_access_in_scope IN cn ss
  | e_feature_access e' fn⇒ expression_model_access_in_scope e' ss
  | e_class_instantiation cn⇒ model_access_in_scope OUT cn ss
  | e_variable_access vn⇒ True
  end.

Module Type AbstractionSafety (H: Hypotheses).
  Parameter representation_independence:
    (* for any transformation built from list of models [PT], interfaces [IT] and implementations [MT], and interface i and implementations [m], [m'] *)
    forall i m m' MT' in_ ds ss mss mss' mn mn' is is' mis,
    (* interface [i] is implemented by [m] and [m'] *)
    i = declare_interface in_ ds ss mss→
    m = declare_module mn in_ is mis→
    m' = declare_module mn' in_ is' mss'→
    ok_interface i→
    ok_module m→
    ok_module m'→
    (* if the program is wellformed with [m], then it must also be wellformed with [m'] *)
    (MT = (m::MT') → ok_program) →
    (MT = (m'::MT') → ok_program).
  Parameter method_provisioning:
    ok_program→
    (* for any interface [i] *)
    forall i in_ ds ss mss,
    In i IT→
    i = declare_interface in_ ds ss mss→
```

```
  (* there exists exactly one module [m] that implements
      interface [i] *)
  exists! m, exists mn is mis,
  In m MT ∧
  m = declare_module mn in_ is mis →
  (* and a bijective mapping between signatures of [i] and
      [m] with names, parameter names and types matching *)
  forall ms, In ms mss → exists! mi, In mi mis ∧
      parameters_match mi ms.
Parameter method_access_control:
  ok_program →
  (* for any module [m] *)
  forall m mn in_ ins mis i ds ss mss mi cn sn vn cn' cn''
      b fn e,
  In m MT →
  m = declare_module mn in_ ins mis →
  (* that implements interface [i] *)
  In i IT →
  i = declare_interface in_ ds ss mss →
  (* for any method [mi] implemented by [m] *)
  In mi mis →
  mi = declare_methodimpl cn sn (vn, cn') cn'' b →
  b = declare_body fn e →
  (* method invocations in implementation [mi]'s body [b]
      must be in scope *)
  method_call_in_scope e ins mis.
Parameter model_access_control:
  ok_program →
  (* for any module [m] *)
  forall m mn in_ ins mis i ds ss mss mi cn sn vn cn' cn''
      b fn e,
  In m MT →
  (* there exists exactly one module [m] that implements
      interface [i] declaring scope [ss] *)
```

```
    m = declare_module mn in_ ins mis →
    In i IT →
    i = declare_interface in_ ds ss mss →
    In mi mis →
    mi = declare_methodimpl cn sn (vn, cn') cn'' b →
    (* for any expression [e] in the method body of [m], the
        inferred type [t] must be (read/write) accessible. *)
    b = declare_body fn e →
    expression_model_access_in_scope e ss →
    (* for any parameter in the method signatures of [m],
        the defined type [t] must be (read/write)
        accessible. *)
    model_access_in_scope IN cn ss ∨ model_access_in_scope
        OUT cn ss →
    model_access_in_scope IN cn' ss ∨ model_access_in_scope
        OUT cn' ss →
    model_access_in_scope OUT cn'' ss.
End AbstractionSafety.
```

B. Standards Compliant Implementations of QVT-R Transformations

In this second and last appendix chapter, by example of the UML2RDBMS example transformation, we demonstrate how to create unidirectional, non-updating implementations of QVT-R specifications that are verifiably correct with respect to the intended semantics of the language.

B.1. The Approach

Ideas from several different proposals went into the QVT standard, making QVT-R a universal language with advanced mapping features. For instance, the same transformation can be executable in multiple directions (*bidirectionality*), and either be used to check if models are consistent (*check-only mode*) or to update an existing model (*check-before-enforce mode*). The standard uses predicate logic to specify the semantics, but these are incomplete and ill-formed with respect to the bidirectional use case. Thus, most work on QVT [Ste13; BS12; BS13; MC13; dLG09; Gar08] exploits better suitable formalisms to capture the semantics of advanced features. Standards conformity is demonstrated for none of them, probably due to known errors.

To address this situation, in this chapter we systematically embed a core subset of the formal language standard in constructive type theory under the Coq proof environment. Our embedding is mostly a shallow one, with only a minimum of computational steps, which are fully automatized by code generator templates. We adhere as faithfully as possible to the formal language standard, whilst we confine ourselves to unidirectional, non-updating enforcement semantics. We give justification for any deviation from the official specification.

The embedding can be used to systematically create implementations of QVT-R specifications that conform to the standard. The essential steps of our approach are as follows:

1. We encode a QVT-R specification in Constructive Type Theory (CTT) using ideas from Lano [LKP+12] and Poernomo [Poe08];
2. We prove implementability of the CTT specifications using the Coq interactive proof assistant [Pau12];
3. Using the Curry-Howard Isomorphism [Pau12], we extract a functional and verified – albeit not necessarily very efficient – implementation of the transformation specification from our proof.

Implementation and proof that follow emerged from a collaboration with Jeffrey Terrell and Steffen Zschaler from King's College, London.

B.2. Example Implementation and Proof

As a running example, we use the well-known UML2RDBMS transformation, which transforms UML class diagrams (Figure B.1a) into relational schemata (Figure B.1b). There is a standard encoding of this transformation in the QVT standard [Obj11, Annex A.1.1], which demonstrates many of the key concepts.

Although the transformation is relatively small and well studied, it is a good example for our purposes as it exercises all of the features of QVT-R. In particular, it consists of a number of *top* and *called* relations, with *when* and *where* clauses. Some of these relations invoke each other recursively, giving grounds to a recursive specification of the transformation. The relations use extensive pattern matching and variables in different contexts, such as at the top of a relation or as part of a matched pattern, giving grounds

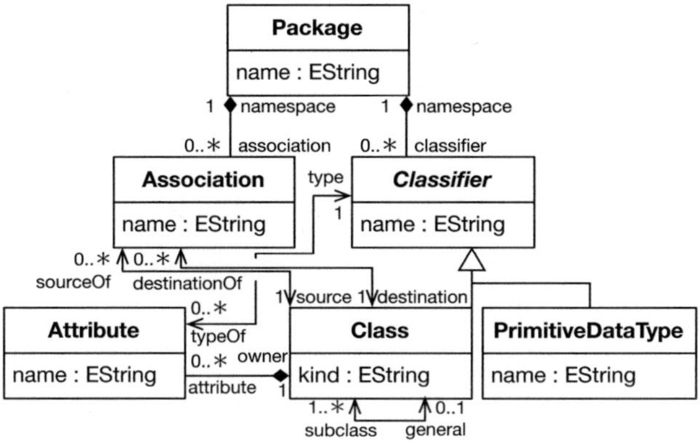

(a) Simplified UML

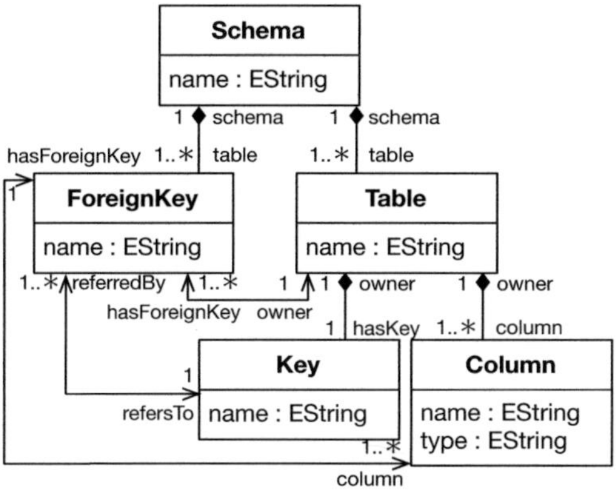

(b) Simplified RDBMS

Figure B.1: Metamodels used by the UML2RDBMS example

to different forms of specification. We will discuss the transformation in more detail in the next section.

The UML2RDBMS transformation is specified as a set of relations between the elements of two typed models, `uml` and `rdbms`. Identifiers `UML` and `RDBMS` stand for their respective types.

```
transformation UML2RDBMS (uml : UML, rdbms : RDBMS) { ... }
```

```
top relation Class2Table {
  cn, prefix: String;
  checkonly domain uml c:Class {
    namespace = p:Package { },
    kind = 'Persistent',
    name = cn };
  enforce domain rdbms t:Table {
    schema = s:Schema { },
    name = cn,
    column = cl:Column {
      name = cn + '_tid', type = 'NUMBER' },
    hasKey = k:Key { name = cn + '_pk', column = cl } };
  when { Package2Schema(p, s); }
  where { prefix = ''; Attribute2Column(c, t, prefix); }
}
```

Listing B.1: UML2RDBMS example in QVT-R – Relation Class2Table

The official UML2RDBMS transformation used here comprises eight relations, `Package2Schema`, `Class2Table`, `Class2PKey`, `Attribute2Column`, `PrimitiveAttribute2Column`, `ComplexAttribute2Column`, `SuperAttribute2Column`, and `Association2FKey`. In addition, there is also one query function for mapping primitive type identifiers from MOF to Structured Query Language (SQL), `PrimitiveType2SqlType`. Relation `Attribute2Column` and the other three relations on subtypes of class `Attribute` form a potentially recursive chain of invocations. The mapping of attributes is initiated by top relation Class2Table, which is specified in Listing B.1.

The rule obviously relates classes with tables, it checks some of the properties on either domain. The relationship can only be enforced to hold in direction of the RDBMS model, noticeable from keyword `enforce` attached to the respective domain. According to the relation's *when* section, relation `Package2Schema` must hold on the containing elements of matched classes and tables. If it holds, attributes and columns are matched, accordingly, as denoted by the expression in the *where* section.

B.3. Encoding QVT-R Transformations in Coq

As part of defining standards-compliant semantics, we developed a tool for automatically translating QVT-R transformations, along with the Essential MOF (EMOF) metamodels on which they are based, into Coq. In this section, we describe the core mapping rules.

B.3.1. Encoding Metamodels

We start by describing how classes, attributes, containment references, associations and inheritance are encoded in Coq. We are specifically using EMF/Ecore [SBPM09], EMOF's most prevalent dialect. We complement the work of Calegari et al. [CLST10] with an essential prerequisite for capturing the semantics of QVT-R transformations correctly, namely an encoding of bidirectional associations.

A class is encoded as an inductive type, with its attributes and immediate super class (if any) encoded as members. Since containment references cannot be cyclic, they can be encoded inductively just like an attribute, with the attribute's type equal to that of a previously defined class. For instance, class `Table` in the RDBMS metamodel is encoded as follows.

```
Record Table_OID : Set := Build_Table_OID {
  Project_Table_OID_nat : nat }.
Record Table : Set := Build_Table {
  Project_Table_oid : Table_OID;
  Project_Table_super : ModelElement;
  Project_Table_columns : list Column;
  Project_Table_hasKey : option Key }.
```

Clearly, the order in which classes are defined is important. Where there is a need to support recursive relations, as is the case in the running example, Coq demands to be able to syntactically determine whether the recursion will terminate. In such situations, a suitable subset of the classes is encoded as a set of mutually inductive types. This is discussed further in Section B.3.2.

Most primitive data types in the EMOF have a direct correspondence in Coq, e.g., `string` for `String`, `nat` for `Integer`, and `bool` for `Boolean`. Further, a multiplicity of `0..1` is encoded as an `option` type, and a multiplicity of `0..*` is encoded as a `list` type.

In contrast to containment references, associations can form cycles. We encode associations so that the tree structure of inductive types is preserved. Instead of directly referencing an associated object, its object identifier (OID, a unique natural number) is referenced as a proxy value[1]. For example, in order to resolve reference `ForeignKey`::`owner` (cf. Figure B.1b), two auxiliary functions are employed: `AllInstances_Table` builds a list of all `Table` objects in the model's containment tree, and `Find_Table` looks up the matching `Table` object for a given OID.

```
Definition AllInstances_Table (rdbms : RDBMS) : list Table :=
  flat_map Project_Schema_tables (AllInstances_Schema rdbms).
Definition Find_Table (rdbms : RDBMS) (oid : Table_OID) :
    option Table :=
  find (fun oid' ⇒ beq_nat
    (Project_Table_OID_nat (Project_Table_oid oid'))
    (Project_Table_OID_nat oid)) (AllInstances_Table rdbms).
Definition Resolve_ForeignKey_owner (rdbms : RDBMS) (fk :
    ForeignKey)
       : option Table :=
  (Find_Table rdbms (Project_ForeignKey_owner fk)).
```

Attentive readers will have noticed that `hasForeignKey` and `schema` are not part of class `Table`'s record definition. This is because they are computationally derived from their opposing reference. We illustrate this by example of `hasForeignKey`.

```
Definition Resolve_Table_hasForeignKey (rdbms : RDBMS) (t :
    Table)
```

[1] Whilst coinductive representations are generally possible (for example, see Picard and Matthes [PM11]), they are more difficult to prove than inductive representations.

```
        : list ForeignKey :=
  (filter (fun t' ⇒ match (Resolve_ForeignKey_owner rdbms t')
      with
    | Some t'' ⇒ beq_nat
      (Project_Table_OID_nat (Project_Table_oid t''))
      (Project_Table_OID_nat (Project_Table_oid t))
    | _ ⇒ false
    end) (AllInstances_ForeignKey rdbms)).
```

This method exposes a limitation in that only the forward direction can be assigned a value, i.e. the backward direction must be derived. By default, we choose the forward direction to be the one that targets the class that is lowest in the containment hierarchy.

For our approach to work, we have to assume that the OIDs of each class are unique. A transformation expects valid input models to abide by their metamodel's uniqueness constraints. In return, a transformation should only produce valid target models. It naturally depends on how a transformation is implemented if the output model's OIDs are unique, and evidence must be given for this.

B.3.2. Encoding QVT-R Transformations

In Section 3.5.1 we presented the formal semantics of important QVT-R concepts encoded in CTT under Coq. This embedding of QVT-R programs into Coq has been encoded as a transformation program. We invoked the program to automatically translate the UML2RDBMS example transformation to logical expressions. For example, the top relation `Class2Table`, which is given in Listing B.1, is encoded as in Listing B.2.

Recursive Relations The *where* clause of the top `Class2Table` relation invokes a non-top relation `Attribute2Column`, which in turn calls three subordinate relations, of which two recursively call `Attribute2Column`. In QVT-R, there are no restrictions on what can be achieved through recursion,

```
Definition Top_Class2Table (uml : UML) (rdbms : RDBMS) : Prop
    :=
  forall p : UML.Package,
  exists s : RDBMS.Schema,
    Package2Schema uml rdbms p s→
  forall (cn : string) (prefix : string) (c : UML.Class),
    In c (UML.AllInstances_Class uml) ∧
    Some p = (UML.Resolve_Class_namespace uml c) ∧
    (UML.Project_Class_kind c) = UML.PERSISTENT ∧
    (UML.Project_Class_name c) = cn→
  exists t : RDBMS.Table,
    In t (RDBMS.AllInstances_Table rdbms) ∧
  exists (cl : RDBMS.Column) (k : RDBMS.Key),
    (RDBMS.Project_Table_name t) = cn ∧
    Some s = (RDBMS.Resolve_Table_schema rdbms t) ∧
    ⋮
    (RDBMS.Project_Key_name k) = (cn ++ "_pk")%string ∧
    In (Some cl) (RDBMS.Resolve_Key_column rdbms k) ∧
  (prefix = ""→ Attribute2Column uml c t prefix).
```

Listing B.2: Coq Encoding of Relation Class2Table

but inevitably there is a price to pay, for not all QVT-R transformations are guaranteed to terminate. By way of contrast, it is simply not possible to construct a program, e.g. a transformation, which does not terminate in Coq.

To marry QVT-R's unrestricted support for recursion, with Coq's more restricted form, the recursive `Attribute2Column` relation is encoded as a `Fixpoint` as follows.

```
Fixpoint Attribute2Column (c : UML.Class) (t : RDBMS.Table) ...
     : Prop :=
  (forall (an : string) ...,
  (fix PrimitiveAttribute2Column (l : list UML.Attribute) :
       Prop :=
    match l with ... end) (UML.Project_Class_attributes c)) ∧
  (forall (an : string) ...,
```

```
(fix ComplexAttribute2Column (l : list UML.Attribute) :
    Prop :=
  match l with ... end) (UML.Project_Class_attributes c)) ∧
match Project_Class_general c with
  | None ⇒ True
  | Some sc ⇒ Attribute2Column sc t prefix
end.
```

On each invocation of `Attribute2Column`, the principal argument `c` is guaranteed to be structurally smaller than it was last time, in virtue of the way that the relations between `UML.Class` and its neighbouring classes are encoded, i.e. as a set of mutually inductive types (rather than as record types), with explicit references to each other rather than implicit references via OIDs, i.e.

```
⋮
with Class : Set := Build_Class : Class_OID → Classifier →
  option Class → list Attribute → Class
with Attribute : Set := Build_Attribute : Attribute_OID →
    ModelElement → (Class + PrimitiveDataType) → Attribute
with PrimitiveDataType : Set := Build_PrimitiveDataType :
    PrimitiveDataType_OID → Classifier → PrimitiveDataType
⋮
```

B.4. Verification Process

In constructive type theory, proofs are carried out by constructing an inhabitant of a type that fulfills the specification. There is an analogy between a constructive proof and a program, which has been formulated as the Curry-Howard correspondence [CH88]. Whenever the specification 'asks' for an inhabitant of a type, we provide a function that generates an inhabitant for which we are able to prove that it possesses the required properties. A

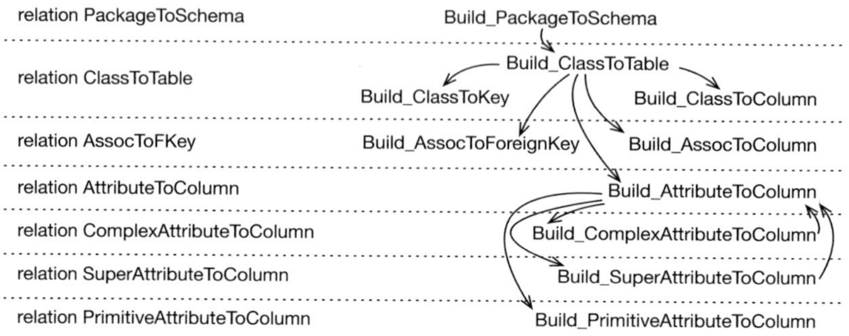

Figure B.2: UML2RDBMS relations vs. functions (arrows depict call dependencies).

verification process thus consists of two steps. First, we define the mapping functions that generate model elements in the target model. Second, we verify that the elements created in this manner do in fact possess the required properties.

B.4.1. Defining an Implementation

Implementing a transformation in a functional programming language is easiest done by recursing over the target model's (tree-like) containment structure and constructing the elements bottom-up. The same approach, first constructing the target elements and then updating their references, is pursued by ATL as well. However, the same QVT relation can instantiate objects of distinct types, located at different nodes in the tree.

We must therefore untangle the transformation logic by splitting up the implementation of a relation into separate functions, with each function creating objects of exactly one type of target class. For instance, when creating a target table in UML2RDBMS, the associated columns must first be created. Now, there are three relations that create columns, and since one of them also creates foreign keys, creating columns must be factored out across a number of different functions. The complete set of functions is shown in Figure B.2. Each function is accompanied by an iterative variant, recognisable by the prefix `Establish`. For relation `Class2Table`, we wrote the following function:

```
Function Build_Class2Table (uml : UML) (p : UML.Package) (c : UML.Class)
                           (prefix : string) : RDBMS.Table :=
  (RDBMS.Build_Table
    (* oid *) (RDBMS.Build_Table_OID ...)
    (* super *) (RDBMS.Build_ModelElement ...)
    (* columns *) (RDBMS.Build_Column ...) ::
      ((Establish_Attribute2Column c prefix) ++
       (Establish_Assoc2Column uml ...)))
    (* hasKey *) (Some RDBMS.Build_Key ...)).
```

For a certain type instantiated in the target model, we are obliged to guarantee that each object has a unique OID. For bijective relations we can reuse the OID from the source objects (these are contractually certified to be unique). However, this is no longer possible when an object maps to multiple objects of the same type in the target model. To avoid the clashing of OID values, a state monad for generating a series of natural numbers can help [Swi09].

The implementation of `Establish_Attribute2Column` follows the same structure as its counterpart relation. However, instead of returning `Prop`, it returns `list RDBMS.Column`; and instead of taking the conjunction of the encodings of the subordinates relations, it concatenates the lists of columns returned by the implementations of the subordination relations.

```
Fixpoint Establish_Attribute2Column ... : list RDBMS.Column :=
  ((fix Primitive... (l : list UML.Attribute) : list RDBMS.Column :=
    match l with ... end) (Project_Class_attributes c)) ++
  ((fix Complex... (l : list UML.Attribute) : list RDBMS.Column :=
      match l with ... end) (Project_Class_attributes c)) ++
  match Project_Class_general c with
```

```
  | None ⇒ nil
  | Some sc ⇒ Establish_Attribute2Column sc prefix
  end.
```

B.4.2. Verifying the Implementation

Coq requires us to prove that a manually written implementation abides by the generated specification. This again is a manual step, which leads to relatively straightforward but long proofs[2].

Uniqueness properties are retained by the transformation Associations can only be resolved when OIDs in source and target models are unique. We prove that instances of a type in the target metamodel retain the uniqueness property, provided that elements in the source model have unique OIDs, e.g., for class `Table`,

```
Hypothesis TableOIDsAreUnique:
  forall (uml : UML) (rdbms : RDBMS) (t1 t2 : RDBMS.Table),
  rdbms = Establish_Package2Schema (uml) ∧
  In t1 (AllInstances_Table rdbms) ∧
  In t2 (AllInstances_Table rdbms) ∧
  (Project_Table_OID_nat (Project_Table_oid t1)) =
  (Project_Table_OID_nat (Project_Table_oid t2)) → t1 = t2.
```

As useful corollaries, we can then show that containment relations preserve uniqueness properties. We mentioned above that, in more complex scenarios, a state monad is needed to guarantee uniqueness of OIDs. However, running proofs that involve monads is cumbersome. Hoare-style reasoning to prove uniqueness of numbers generated by a state monad in Coq is demonstrated by Swierstra [Swi09].

[2] Any sources discussed here can be accessed at `http://qvt.github.io/qvtr2coq`.

Bidirectional references are invertible Independently of the transformation, we can show that backward references are invertible. To give an example, for any `Table t` and `Schema s`, we are able to reveal that

```
Some s = (RDBMS.Resolve_Table_schema rdbms t) →
In t (RDBMS.Project_Schema_tables s)
```

Transformation theorem Equipped with these helping lemmas, we finally prove that the implementation satisfies the theorem from Definition 6. When dealing with non-recursive relations, each of the target constraints $C_T, i, 1 \leq i \leq k$ can be proven one after the other. The implementation makes regular use of list operations, thus, lemmas to lift applicator functions out of list operations are very useful. One example is lemma `in_flat_map` from Coq's standard library.

Recursive relations The proof of the recursive relation `Attribute2Column` requires the use of Coq's `fix` tactic. Fixing the bound variable `c` when

```
forall (c : UML.Class), ... , Attribute2Column c t prefix
```

is the current goal does two things. First, it asserts by means of a hypothesis that the current goal is inhabited. Second, it guards the hypothesis to ensure that it is only ever used with objects of `UML.Class` that are structurally smaller than the one it started with.

List of Figures

List of Tables

List of Listings

Acronyms

CIM	Computationally-Independent Model	28, 29
CMOF	Complete Meta-Object Facilities	33, 34, 232
COM	Component Object Model	29
CORBA	Common Object Request Broker Architecture	29, 263
CTT	Constructive Type Theory	294, 299
DSL	Domain-Specific Language	3, 5, 53, 80, 133, 152, 238, 242, 256
EBNF	Extended Backus-Naur Form	33
EJB	Enterprise Java Beans	29, 188, 221
EMF	Eclipse Modeling Framework	34, 44, 49, 151, 232, 233, 239, 244, 297
EMOF	Essential Meta-Object Facilities	33, 34, 232, 240, 297, 298
EOL	Epsilon Object Language	152, 180
EPL	Eclipse Public License	44
ETL	Epsilon Transformation Language	12, 15, 37, 149, 152, 178–180, 239, 241
FJ	Featherweight Java	65, 88, 95, 96, 271
GMF	Graphical Modeling Framework	3, 4
GMM4CT	Global Model Management for Composite Transformations	242
GPL	General-Purpose Language	40, 57, 79, 133, 151, 152, 249, 252, 259

GQM	Goal, Question, Metric	185, 186, 197, 199, 213, 308
GReAT	Graph Rewriting and Transformation	37
GT	Graph Transformations	37, 241
HEB	Hierarchical Edge Bundling	154, 248, 249
HOL	Higher-Order Logics	80, 246
ICMT	International Conference of Model Transformations	38, 127
IDE	Integrated Development Environment	39, 128, 153, 200, 204, 208, 249
IDL	Interface Description Language	263
IEEE	Institute of Electrical and Electronics Engineers	10, 66–68, 307
ISO	International Organization for Standardization	66, 67, 307
JavaEE	Java Platform, Enterprise Edition	29, 30
JET	Java Emitter Templates	38
JML	Java Modeling Language	265
LOC	Lines of Code	187, 190–192, 194, 195
LPG	LALR Parser Generator	106
M2M	Model-to-Model, a class of model transformations	34, 47, 106, 107, 111, 188, 210, 238

M2T	Model-to-Text, a class of model transformations	34, 35, 47, 106, 107, 111, 126, 188, 196, 210, 236, 238
MCC	Model Control Center	242
MDA	Model-Driven Architecture	26, 28–31
MDE	Model-driven Engineering	25–27, 30, 31, 34, 35, 69, 70, 243, 244, 250, 307
MDG	Module Dependency Graph	75, 76
MDSD	Model-driven Software Development	26, 27, 30, 204
MDSE	Model-driven Software Engineering	1, 3–5, 12, 25
MeCl	MergeClumps, a similarity metric	175–177, 212, 213, 216, 217, 224
MODELS	International Conference on Model Driven Engineering Languages and Systems	20, 158
MODU-LARITY	International Conference on Modularity, formerly AOSD	126
MOF	Meta-Object Facilities	33, 39, 85, 92, 135, 153, 165, 181, 233, 237, 248, 296
MPS	JetBrains Meta Programming System	233, 237
MQ	Modularization Quality	76, 169, 170, 175, 177, 213, 216–218, 224, 225
MTL	Model Transformation Language	252
MWE	Modeling Workflow Engine	111, 242, 244, 313

QPN	Queuing Petri Net	200, 201, 209, 247
QVT	Query/View/Transformation	7, 8, 16, 36–38, 42, 46, 89, 90, 101, 118, 120, 122, 124, 131, 132, 135, 138, 153, 241, 245, 246, 251, 263, 293, 294, 302, 307
QVTd	QVT Declarative, Eclipse implementation of QVT Relations	20, 46
QVT-O	QVT Operational Mappings	7–10, 12, 15, 17, 20–22, 36, 38–40, 42, 44, 50, 79, 80, 83, 86, 88, 89, 93, 94, 106–108, 110, 111, 120, 122, 124, 125, 127–131, 133, 135–139, 146, 149, 151, 154, 164, 166, 174, 177–181, 196, 200, 201, 204, 209, 210, 214, 220, 221, 235, 239, 240, 242, 249, 251, 258, 263, 271, 307, 308, 313
QVTo	Eclipse implementation of QVT Operational Mappings	6, 20–22, 39, 42, 79, 87, 107, 153, 154, 258, 307

QVT-OM	QVT Operational Modular Mappings	79, 85–89, 94, 97, 105, 107, 111, 178, 238, 239, 242, 281, 307, 313
QVTom	Eclipse implementation of QVT Operational Modular Mappings	20, 21, 106, 108, 242, 271
QVT-R	QVT Relations	15, 17, 18, 20, 36–38, 44–46, 53, 54, 65, 79, 80, 83, 112–117, 119–122, 124, 135, 137–139, 149, 151, 154, 178, 180, 237, 239, 240, 244–247, 250–252, 256, 262, 263, 293, 294, 296, 297, 299, 300, 313
RubyTL	Ruby Transformation Language	12, 154, 238, 242
SAT	Boolean Satisfiability Problem	265
SEFF	Service Effect Specification	217
SIL	Structural Information Language (probably), a proprietary file format by Bunch	173, 174, 313
SMT	Satisfiability Modulo Theories	64
SMTL	Scala Model Transformation Language	12
SQL	Structured Query Language	296

T2M	Text-to-Model transformation	34
TCF	Transformation Composition Framework	243
TGG	Triple Graph Grammars	37, 38, 53, 135, 136, 237, 308
TROPIC	Transformations on Petri Nets in Color	250
TTC	Transformation Tool Contest	38
UML	Unified Modeling Language	2, 3, 29, 30, 33, 92, 139, 233, 242, 248
UniTI	Universal Transformation Infrastructure	242
URI	Uniform Resource Identifier	39
VIATRA	VIsual Automated model TRAnsformations	12, 15, 37, 149, 152, 153, 178, 179, 181, 239, 241, 246, 249
VTCL	VIATRA Textual Command Language	246
VTL	Velocity Template Language	38
VTML	VIATRA Textual Metamodeling Language	153
XML	Extensible Markup Language	29
Xtend2m	Xtend Modular Mappings	20, 107, 108, 189, 242

Bibliography

[ASLS14] A. Anjorin, K. Saller, M. Lochau, and A. Schürr, "Modularizing Triple Graph Grammars Using Rule Refinement," in *Proceedings of the 17th International Conference on Fundamental Approaches to Software Engineering (FASE '14)*, S. Gnesi and A. Rensink, Eds., ser. Lecture Notes in Computer Science, vol. 8411, Springer, 2014, pp. 340–354, ISBN: 978-3-642-54803-1 (cit. on p. 237).

[Bas92] V. R. Basili, "Software Modeling and Measurement: The Goal/Question/Metric Paradigm," University of Maryland at College Park, College Park, MD, USA, Tech. Rep., 1992 (cit. on pp. 185, 197).

[BAT14] G. M. Bierman, M. Abadi, and M. Torgersen, "Understanding TypeScript," in *Proceedings of the 28th European Conference on Object-Oriented Programming (ECOOP '14), Uppsala, Sweden, July 28 - August 1, 2014*, R. Jones, Ed., ser. Lecture Notes in Computer Science, vol. 8586, Springer, 2014, pp. 257–281, ISBN: 978-3-662-44201-2 (cit. on pp. 235, 260).

[BC10] Y. Bertot and P. Castéran, *Interactive Theorem Proving and Program Development: Coq'Art The Calculus of Inductive Constructions*, 1st. Springer, 2010, ISBN: 3-642-05880-9, 978-3-642-05880-6 (cit. on pp. 17, 64, 65).

[BCK03] L. Bass, P. Clements, and R. Kazman, *Software Architecture in Practice*, 2nd ed. Boston, MA, USA: Addison-Wesley

Longman Publishing Co., Inc., 2003, ISBN: 0-321-15495-9 (cit. on p. 56).

[Bec08a] S. Becker, "Coupled Model Transformations," in *Proceedings of the 7th International Workshop on Software and Performance (WOSP '08)*, A. Avritzer, E. J. Weyuker, and C. M. Woodside, Eds., ACM, 2008, pp. 103–114 (cit. on p. 222).

[Bec08b] ——, "Coupled Model Transformations for QoS Enabled Component-Based Software Design," PhD thesis, University of Oldenburg, Germany, Mar. 2008 (cit. on p. 188).

[Bel06] M. Belaunde, "Transformation Composition in QVT," in *Proceedings of the 1st European Workshop on Composition of Model Transformations (CMT '06)*, ser. TR-CTI, Centre for Telematics and Information Technology, Univ. of Twente, Jun. 2006, pp. 39–46. [Online]. Available: `http://doc.utwente.nl/66171/` (cit. on pp. 235, 242).

[Bie10] M. Biehl, "Literature Study on Model Transformations," Embedded Control Systems, Royal Institute of Technology, Stockholm, Sweden, Tech. Rep. ISRN/KTH/MMK, Jul. 2010. [Online]. Available: `http://www.md.kth.se/~biehl/files/papers/mt.pdf` (cit. on p. 38).

[BKR09] S. Becker, H. Koziolek, and R. Reussner, "The Palladio Component Model for Model-Driven Performance Prediction," *Journal of Systems and Software*, vol. 82, no. 1, pp. 3–22, Jan. 2009 (cit. on p. 185).

[BL84] R. M. Burstall and B. W. Lampson, "A Kernel Language for Abstract Data Types and Modules," in *Proceedings of the International Symposium on Semantics of Data Types*, G. Kahn, D. B. MacQueen, and G. D. Plotkin, Eds., ser. Lecture Notes in Computer Science, vol. 173, Springer, 1984, pp. 1–50, ISBN: 3-540-13346-1 (cit. on p. 235).

[BLW05] P. Baker, S. Loh, and F. Weil, "Model-Driven Engineering in a Large Industrial Context - Motorola Case Study," in *Proceedings of the 8th International Conference on Model Driven Engineering Languages and Systems (MoDELS '05)*, L. C. Briand and C. Williams, Eds., ser. Lecture Notes in Computer Science, vol. 3713, Springer, 2005, pp. 476–491, ISBN: 3-540-29010-9 (cit. on pp. 3, 255).

[BN05] D. Beyer and A. Noack, "Clustering Software Artifacts Based on Frequent Common Changes," in *Proceedings of the 13th International Workshop on Program Comprehension (IWPC '05)*, IEEE Computer Society, 2005, pp. 259–268, ISBN: 0-7695-2254-8 (cit. on p. 248).

[BS12] J. C. Bradfield and P. Stevens, "Recursive Checkonly QVT-R Transformations with General when and where Clauses via the Modal Mu Calculus," in *Proceedings of the 15th International Conference on Fundamental Approaches to Software Engineering (FASE '12)*, J. de Lara and A. Zisman, Eds., ser. Lecture Notes in Computer Science, vol. 7212, Springer, 2012, pp. 194–208, ISBN: 978-3-642-28871-5 (cit. on pp. 245, 293).

[BS13] ——, "Enforcing QVT-R with mu-Calculus and Games," in *Proceedings of the 16th International Conference on Fundamental Approaches to Software Engineering (FASE '13)*, V. Cortellessa and D. Varró, Eds., ser. Lecture Notes in Computer Science, vol. 7793, Springer, 2013, pp. 282–296, ISBN: 978-3-642-37056-4 (cit. on pp. 245, 293).

[Bur14] E. Burger, *Flexible Views for View-based Model-driven Development*, ser. The Karlsruhe Series on Software Design and Quality; 14. Karlsruhe: KIT Scientific Publishing, 2014 (cit. on p. 234).

[BW08] A. D. Brucker and B. Wolff, "HOL-OCL: A Formal Proof Environment for UML/OCL," in *Proceedings of the 11th International Conference on Fundamental Approaches to Software Engineering (FASE '08)*, J. L. Fiadeiro and P. Inverardi, Eds., ser. Lecture Notes in Computer Science, vol. 4961, Springer, 2008, pp. 97–100, ISBN: 978-3-540-78742-6 (cit. on p. 246).

[Car97] L. Cardelli, "Type Systems," in *The Computer Science and Engineering Handbook*, A. B. Tucker, Ed., CRC Press, 1997, pp. 2208–2236, ISBN: 0-849-32909-4 (cit. on p. 63).

[CBBD09] E. Cariou, N. Belloir, F. Barbier, and N. Djemam, "OCL Contracts for the Verification of Model Transformations," *Electronic Communications of the EASST (ECEASST)*, vol. 24, 2009. [Online]. Available: `http://journal.ub.tu-berlin.de/index.php/eceasst/article/view/326` (cit. on p. 265).

[CBFB11] E. Cariou, C. Ballagny, A. Feugas, and F. Barbier, "Contracts for Model Execution Verification," in *Proceedings of the 7th European Conference on Modelling Foundations and Applications (ECMFA '11), Birmingham, UK, June 6 - 9, 2011*, R. B. France, J. M. Küster, B. Bordbar, and R. F. Paige, Eds., Springer, 2011, pp. 3–18. DOI: `10.1007/978-3-642-21470-7_2` (cit. on p. 265).

[CCGdL08] J. Cabot, R. Clarisó, E. Guerra, and J. de Lara, "An Invariant-Based Method for the Analysis of Declarative Model-to-Model Transformations," in *Proceedings of the 11th International Conference on Model Driven Engineering Languages and Systems (MODELS '08)*, ser. Lecture Notes in Computer Science, K. Czarnecki, I. Ober, J.-M. Bruel, A. Uhl, and M. Voelter, Eds., vol. 5301, Springer, 2008, pp. 37–52, ISBN:

978-3-540-87874-2. DOI: http://dx.doi.org/10.1007/978-3-540-87875-9_3 (cit. on p. 245).

[CGdL11] J. S. Cuadrado, E. Guerra, and J. de Lara, "Generic Model Transformations: *Write Once, Reuse Everywhere*," in *Proceedings of the 4th International Conference Theory and Practice of Model Transformations (ICMT '11)*, J. Cabot and E. Visser, Eds., ser. Lecture Notes in Computer Science, vol. 6707, Springer, 2011, pp. 62–77, ISBN: 978-3-642-21731-9. DOI: 10.1007/978-3-642-21732-6_5 (cit. on pp. 244, 264).

[CGdL12] ——, "Flexible Model-to-Model Transformation Templates: An Application to ATL," *Journal of Object Technology*, vol. 11, no. 2, pp. 1–28, 2012. DOI: 10.5381/jot.2012.11.2.a4 (cit. on p. 244).

[CGL14] J. S. Cuadrado, E. Guerra, and J. D. Lara, "Uncovering Errors in ATL Model Transformations Using Static Analysis and Constraint Solving," in *IEEE 25th International Symposium on Software Reliability Engineering (ISSRE '14), Naples, Italy, November 3-6, 2014*, To Appear, 2014 (cit. on pp. 247, 264).

[CH03] K. Czarnecki and S. Helsen, "Classification of Model Transformation Approaches," *OOPSLA Workshop on Generative Techniques in the Context of Model-Driven Architecture*, Oct. 2003. [Online]. Available: http://www.softmetaware.com/oopsla2003/czarnecki.pdf (cit. on p. 38).

[CH06] ——, "Feature-based Survey of Model Transformation Approaches," *IBM Systems Journal*, vol. 45, no. 3, pp. 621–646, 2006 (cit. on pp. 12, 38).

[CH88] T. Coquand and G. Huet, "The Calculus of Constructions," *Information and Computation*, vol. 76, no. 2-3, pp. 95–120,

Feb. 1988, ISSN: 0890-5401. DOI: 10.1016/0890-5401(88)90005-3 (cit. on pp. 65, 301).

[CIM14] J. S. Cuadrado, J. L. C. Izquierdo, and J. G. Molina, "Applying Model-driven Engineering in Small Software Enterprises," *Sci. Comput. Program.*, vol. 89, pp. 176–198, 2014. DOI: 10.1016/j.scico.2013.04.007 (cit. on p. 4).

[Cip95] B. Cipra, "How Number Theory Got the Best of the Pentium Chip," *Science*, vol. 267, no. 5195, p. 175, Jan. 1995, ISSN: 1095-9203. DOI: 10.1126/science.267.5195.175 (cit. on p. 60).

[CK01] M. V. Cengarle and A. Knapp, "A Formal Semantics for OCL 1.4," in *Proceedings of the 4th International Conference on The Unified Modeling Language, Modeling Languages, Concepts, and Tools (UML '01)*, M. Gogolla and C. Kobryn, Eds., ser. Lecture Notes in Computer Science, vol. 2185, London, UK: Springer, 2001, pp. 118–133, ISBN: 978-3-540-42667-7. DOI: 10.1007/3-540-45441-1_10 (cit. on pp. 17, 125).

[CLST10] D. Calegari, C. Luna, N. Szasz, and A. Tasistro, "A Type-Theoretic Framework for Certified Model Transformations," in *Proceedings of the 13th Brazilian Symposium on Formal Methods (SBMF '10)*, ser. Lecture Notes in Computer Science, J. Davies, L. Silva, and A. da Silva Simão, Eds., vol. 6527, Springer, 2010, pp. 112–127 (cit. on p. 297).

[CM06] J. S. Cuadrado and J. G. Molina, "A Plugin-Based Language to Experiment with Model Transformation," in *Proceedings of the 9th International Conference on Model Driven Engineering Languages and Systems (MoDELS '06)*, O. Nierstrasz, J. Whittle, D. Harel, and G. Reggio, Eds., ser. Lecture Notes in Computer Science, vol. 4199, Springer, 2006, pp. 336–350, ISBN: 3-540-45772-0 (cit. on p. 238).

[CM08] ——, "Approaches for Model Transformation Reuse: Factorization and Composition," in *Proceedings of the 1st International Conference Theory and Practice of Model Transformations (ICMT '08)*, A. Vallecillo, J. Gray, and A. Pierantonio, Eds., ser. Lecture Notes in Computer Science, vol. 5063, Springer, 2008, pp. 168–182, ISBN: 978-3-540-69926-2 (cit. on p. 238).

[CM09] ——, "Modularization of Model Transformations through a Phasing Mechanism," *Software and System Modeling*, vol. 8, no. 3, pp. 325–345, 2009. DOI: 10.1007/s10270-008-0093-0 (cit. on p. 238).

[CMSD04] E. Cariou, R. Marvie, L. Seinturier, and L. Duchien, "OCL for the Specification of Model Transformation Contracts," in *Proceedings of the Workshop OCL and Model Driven Engineering of the 7th International Conference on UML Modeling Languages and Applications (UML '04)*, O. Patrascoiu, Ed., University of Kent, Lisbon, Portugual, Oct. 2004, pp. 69–83 (cit. on p. 265).

[CMT06] J. S. Cuadrado, J. G. Molina, and M. M. Tortosa, "RubyTL: A Practical, Extensible Transformation Language," in *Proceedings of the Second European Conference on Model Driven Architecture - Foundations and Applications (ECMDA-FA '06)*, A. Rensink and J. Warmer, Eds., ser. Lecture Notes in Computer Science, vol. 4066, Springer, 2006, pp. 158–172, ISBN: 3-540-35909-5 (cit. on pp. 12, 238).

[CP92] W. Chu and S. Patel, "Software Restructuring by Enforcing Localization and Information Hiding," in *Proceedings of the 18th International Conference on Software Maintenance (ICSM '92)*, Nov. 1992, pp. 165–172. DOI: 10.1109/ICSM.1992.242546 (cit. on p. 248).

[CR00] K. Chen and V. Rajlich, "Case Study of Feature Location Using Dependence Graph," in *Proceedings of the IEEE 8th International Workshop on Program Comprehension (IWPC '00)*, 2000, pp. 241–249, ISBN: 0-769-50656-9 (cit. on p. 249).

[CR10] K. Chen and V. Rajlich, "Case Study of Feature Location Using Dependence Graph, after 10 Years," in *Proceedings of the IEEE 18th International Conference on Program Comprehension (ICPC '10)*, Jul. 2010, pp. 1–3. DOI: 10.1109/ICPC.2010.40 (cit. on p. 249).

[CR14] J. Cho and S. Ryu, "JavaScript Module System: Exploring the design space," in *Proceedings of the 13th International Conference on Modularity (AOSD '14), Lugano, Switzerland, April 22 - 26, 2014*, W. Binder, E. Ernst, A. Peternier, and R. Hirschfeld, Eds., ACM, 2014, pp. 229–240, ISBN: 978-1-4503-2772-5 (cit. on p. 260).

[CV08] M. Cimadamore and M. Viroli, "Integrating Java and Prolog through Generic Methods and Type Inference," in *Proceedings of the ACM Symposium on Applied Computing (SAC '08), Fortaleza, Ceara, Brazil, March 16-20, 2008*, R. L. Wainwright and H. Haddad, Eds., ACM, 2008, pp. 198–205, ISBN: 978-1-59593-753-7 (cit. on p. 263).

[CWWW13] Y. Cai, H. Wang, S. Wong, and L. Wang, "Leveraging Design Rules to Improve Software Architecture Recovery," in *Proceedings of the 9th International ACM SIGSOFT Conference on Quality of Software Architectures (QoSA '13)*, P. Kruchten, A. Koziolek, and R. L. Nord, Eds., ACM, 2013, pp. 133–142. DOI: 10.1145/2465478.2465480 (cit. on p. 267).

[DDH72] O. J. Dahl, E. W. Dijkstra, and C. A. R. Hoare, Eds., *Structured Programming*. London, UK, UK: Academic Press Ltd., 1972, ISBN: 0-122-00550-3 (cit. on p. 2).

[DGL+05] K. Duddy, A. Gerber, M. J. Lawley, K. Raymond, and J. Steel, "Declarative Transformation for Object-Oriented Models," in *Transformation of Knowledge, Information, and Data: Theory and Applications*, P. van Bommel, Ed., Idea Group Publishing, 2005, ch. 4, ISBN: 1-59140-529-7 (cit. on pp. 159, 248).

[Die07] S. Diehl, *Software Visualization: Visualizing the Structure, Behaviour, and Evolution of Software*. Springer, 2007, ISBN: 978-3-540-46504-1. DOI: 10.1007/978-3-540-46505-8 (cit. on pp. 71, 72, 248).

[Dij68] E. W. Dijkstra, "Letters to the Editor: Go to Statement Considered Harmful," *Commun. ACM*, vol. 11, no. 3, pp. 147–148, Mar. 1968, ISSN: 0001-0782. DOI: 10.1145/362929.362947 (cit. on p. 2).

[dLG09] J. de Lara and E. Guerra, "Formal Support for QVT-Relations with Coloured Petri Nets," in *Proceedings of the 12th International Conference on Model Driven Engineering Languages and Systems (MODELS '09)*, A. Schürr and B. Selic, Eds., ser. Lecture Notes in Computer Science, vol. 5795, Springer, 2009, pp. 256–270, ISBN: 978-3-642-04424-3 (cit. on pp. 245, 293).

[Dow97] M. Dowson, "The Ariane 5 Software Failure," *SIGSOFT Softw. Eng. Notes*, vol. 22, no. 2, p. 84, Mar. 1997, ISSN: 0163-5948. DOI: 10.1145/251880.251992 (cit. on p. 60).

[DYM+08] J. Dietrich, V. Yakovlev, C. McCartin, G. Jenson, and M. Duchrow, "Cluster Analysis of Java Dependency Graphs," in *Proceedings of the 4th ACM Symposium on Software Visualization (SoftVis '08)*, Ammersee, Germany: ACM, 2008, pp. 91–94, ISBN: 978-1-605-58112-5. DOI: 10.1145/1409720.1409735 (cit. on p. 210).

[ELL11] B. S. Everitt, S. Landau, and M. Leese, *Cluster Analysis*, 5th, B. Everitt, Ed., ser. Wiley Series in Probability and Statistics. Chichester, UK: Wiley Publishing, 2011, ISBN: 978-0-470-74991-3 (cit. on p. 74).

[EPS73] H. Ehrig, M. Pfender, and H. J. Schneider, "Graph-Grammars: An Algebraic Approach," in *Proceedings of the 14th Annual Symposium on Switching and Automata Theory (SWAT '73)*, IEEE Computer Society, 1973, pp. 167–180. DOI: 10.1109/SWAT.1973.11 (cit. on p. 53).

[Fav05] J.-M. Favre, "Languages evolve too! Changing the Software Time Scale," in *Proceedings of the 8th International Workshop on Principles of Software Evolution (IWPSE '05)*, IEEE Computer Society, 2005, pp. 33–44, ISBN: 0-7695-2349-8 (cit. on p. 4).

[FMRS07] C. Fuss, C. Mosler, U. Ranger, and E. Schultchen, "The Jury Is Still Out: A Comparison of AGG, Fujaba, and PROGRES," *ECEASST*, vol. 6, 2007 (cit. on p. 37).

[Fow10] M. Fowler, *Domain-Specific Languages*, 1st. Addison-Wesley Professional, 2010, ISBN: 978-0-321-71294-3 (cit. on pp. 32, 80).

[FW08] D. P. Friedman and M. Wand, *Essentials of Programming Languages*, 3rd. MIT Press, 2008, pp. I–XXII, 1–410, ISBN: 978-0-262-06279-4 (cit. on pp. 58, 61).

[Gar08] M. Garcia, "Formalization of QVT-Relations: OCL-based Static Semantics and Alloy-based Validation," in *Proceedings of the 2nd Workshop on MDSD Today*, P. Friese, S. Zambrovski, and F. Zimmermann, Eds., Shaker Verlag, Oct. 2008, pp. 21–30, ISBN: 978-3-832-27627-0 (cit. on pp. 245, 293).

[GdL12] E. Guerra and J. de Lara, “An Algebraic Semantics for QVT-Relations Check-only Transformations,” *Fundam. Inform.*, vol. 114, no. 1, pp. 73–101, 2012 (cit. on p. 245).

[GdLK+13] E. Guerra, J. de Lara, D. S. Kolovos, R. F. Paige, and O. M. dos Santos, “Engineering Model Transformations with transML,” *Software and System Modeling*, vol. 12, no. 3, pp. 555–577, 2013 (cit. on p. 243).

[Ger94] N. Gershon, “From Perception to Visualization,” in *Scientific Visualization - Advances and Challenges*, L. Rosenblum, R. Earnshaw, J. Encarnacao, H. Hagen, A. Kaufman, S. Klimenko, G. Nielson, F. Post, and D. Thalmann, Eds., Academic Press, 1994, pp. 129–139 (cit. on p. 71).

[GGKdL14] A. Garmendia, E. Guerra, D. S. Kolovos, and J. de Lara, “EMF Splitter: A Structured Approach to EMF Modularity,” in *Proceedings of the 3rd Workshop on Extreme Modeling (XM ’14) collocated with the 17th ACM/IEEE International Conference on Model Driven Engineering Languages and Systems (MODELS ’11), Valencia, Spain, September 29, 2014*, D. D. Ruscio, J. de Lara, and A. Pierantonio, Eds., ser. CEUR Workshop Proceedings, vol. 1239, CEUR-WS.org, Oct. 2014, pp. 22–31. [Online]. Available: `http://nbn-resolving.de/urn:nbn:de:0074-1239-2` (cit. on p. 233).

[GK10] J. Greenyer and E. Kindler, “Comparing Relational Model Transformation Technologies: Implementing Query/View/-Transformation with Triple Graph Grammars.,” *Software and System Modeling*, pp. 21–46, 2010 (cit. on p. 53).

[Gla01] R. L. Glass, “Loyal Opposition - Frequently Forgotten Fundamental Facts about Software Engineering,” *IEEE Software*, vol. 18, no. 3, pp. 112–111, 2001 (cit. on pp. 2, 14).

[Gol11] T. Goldschmidt, *View-based Textual Modelling*, ser. The Karlsruhe Series on Software Design and Quality; 6. Karlsruhe:

KIT Scientific Publishing, 2011, ISBN: 978-3-86644-642-7. [Online]. Available: http://dx.doi.org/10.5445/KSP/1000022234 (cit. on p. 234).

[GPT09] P. Guduric, A. Puder, and R. Todtenhoefer, "A Comparison between Relational and Operational QVT Mappings," in *Proceedings of the 6th International Conference on Information Technology: New Generations (ITNG '09)*, S. Latifi, Ed., IEEE Computer Society, 2009, pp. 266–271, ISBN: 978-0-7695-3596-8 (cit. on p. 37).

[GT03] P. A. Grubb and A. A. Takang, *Software Maintenance - Concepts and Practice*, 2nd. World Scientific, 2003, pp. I–XIX, 1–349, ISBN: 978-9-812-38426-3 (cit. on p. 67).

[GWS12] L. George, A. Wider, and M. Scheidgen, "Type-Safe Model Transformation Languages as Internal DSLs in Scala," in *Proceedings of the 5th International Conference Theory and Practice of Model Transformations (ICMT '12)*, Z. Hu and J. de Lara, Eds., Springer, 2012, pp. 160–175. DOI: 10.1007/978-3-642-30476-7_11 (cit. on p. 12).

[Har92] R. Harper, "Constructing Type Systems over an Operational Semantics," *Journal of Symbolic Computation*, vol. 14, no. 1, pp. 71–84, 1992, ISSN: 0747-7171. DOI: http://dx.doi.org/10.1016/0747-7171(92)90026-Z (cit. on p. 61).

[HB85] D. Hutchens and V. Basili, "System Structure Analysis: Clustering with Data Bindings," *IEEE Transactions on Software Engineering*, vol. SE-11, no. 8, pp. 749–757, Aug. 1985, ISSN: 0098-5589. DOI: 10.1109/TSE.1985.232524 (cit. on p. 248).

[HC01] G. T. Heineman and W. T. Councill, Eds., *Component-based Software Engineering: Putting the Pieces Together*. Boston, MA, USA: Addison-Wesley Longman Publishing Co., Inc., 2001, ISBN: 0-201-70485-4 (cit. on p. 59).

[HEET99] R. Heckel, G. Engels, H. Ehrig, and G. Taentzer, "Classification and Comparison of Module Concepts for Graph Transformation Systems," in *Handbook of Graph Grammars and Computing by Graph Transformations, Volume 2: Applications, Languages, and Tools*, H. Ehrig, G. Engels, H.-J. Kreowski, and G. Rozenberg, Eds. World Scientific, Oct. 1999, ch. 1, ISBN: 9-810-24020-1 (cit. on p. 236).

[Hel06] S. Helsen, "Model Transformations with QVT," in *Model-driven Software Development - Technology, Engineering, Management*. Pitman, 2006, ch. 10, pp. 203–222, ISBN: 978-0-470-02570-3 (cit. on p. 36).

[Hen94] F. Henglein, "Fundamentals of Type Inference Systems," Course notes, updated August 9, 2009, 1994, [Online]. Available: `http://typesatwork.imm.dtu.dk/material/TaW_Paper_TypeInferenceFundamentals.pdf` (cit. on p. 62).

[HGSS13] R. Hebig, H. Giese, F. Stallmann, and A. Seibel, "On the Complex Nature of MDE Evolution," in *Proceedings of the 16th International Conference on Model-Driven Engineering Languages and Systems (MODELS '13), Miami, FL, USA, September 29 - October 4, 2013*, A. Moreira, B. Schätz, J. Gray, A. Vallecillo, and P. J. Clarke, Eds., Springer, 2013, pp. 436–453. DOI: `10.1007/978-3-642-41533-3_27` (cit. on p. 69).

[HKA11] F. Heidenreich, J. Kopcsek, and U. Aßmann, "Safe Composition of Transformations," *Journal of Object Technology*, vol. 10, pp. 1–20, 2011 (cit. on p. 243).

[HKGV10] Z. Hemel, L. C. L. Kats, D. M. Groenewegen, and E. Visser, "Code Generation by Model Transformation: A Case Study in Transformation Modularity," *Software and System Modeling*, vol. 9, no. 3, pp. 375–402, 2010 (cit. on p. 238).

[HKV07] I. Heitlager, T. Kuipers, and J. Visser, "A Practical Model for Measuring Maintainability," in *Proceedings of the 6th International Conference on Quality of Information and Communications Technology (QUATIC '07)*, Washington, DC, USA: IEEE Computer Society, 2007, pp. 30–39, ISBN: 0-769-52948-8. DOI: 10.1109/QUATIC.2007.7 (cit. on p. 66).

[Hol97] C. M. Holloway, "Why Engineers Should Consider Formal Methods," NASA Langley Research Center, Tech. Rep. 20040105661, Oct. 1997. [Online]. Available: https://archive.org/details/nasa%5C_techdoc%5C_20040105661 (cit. on p. 60).

[HRW09] M. Herrmannsdoerfer, D. Ratiu, and G. Wachsmuth, "Language Evolution in Practice: The History of GMF," in *Revised Selected Papers of the 2nd International Conference on Software Language Engineering (SLE '09)*, M. van den Brand, D. Gasevic, and J. Gray, Eds., ser. Lecture Notes in Computer Science, vol. 5969, Springer, 2009, pp. 3–22, ISBN: 978-3-642-12106-7 (cit. on p. 4).

[HRW11] J. Hutchinson, M. Rouncefield, and J. Whittle, "Model-driven Engineering Practices in Industry," in *Proceedings of the 33rd International Conference on Software Engineering (ICSE '11)*, R. N. Taylor, H. Gall, and N. Medvidovic, Eds., ACM, 2011, pp. 633–642, ISBN: 978-1-4503-0445-0 (cit. on pp. 3, 26, 30, 255).

[HWG03] A. Hejlsberg, S. Wiltamuth, and P. Golde, *C# Language Specification*. Boston, MA, USA: Addison-Wesley Longman Publishing Co., Inc., 2003, ISBN: 0-321-15491-6 (cit. on p. 181).

[HWRK11] J. Hutchinson, J. Whittle, M. Rouncefield, and S. Kristoffersen, "Empirical Assessment of MDE in Industry," in *Pro-*

ceedings of the 33rd International Conference on Software Engineering (ICSE '11), R. N. Taylor, H. Gall, and N. Medvidovic, Eds., ACM, 2011, pp. 471–480, ISBN: 978-1-4503-0445-0 (cit. on pp. 3, 26, 30, 255).

[IdFF07] R. Ierusalimschy, L. H. de Figueiredo, and W. C. Filho, "The Evolution of Lua," in *Proceedings of the 3rd ACM SIGPLAN History of Programming Languages Conference (HOPL-III), San Diego, California, USA, 9-10 June 2007*, B. G. Ryder and B. Hailpern, Eds., ACM, 2007, pp. 1–26 (cit. on p. 260).

[IEE06] IEEE Computer Society, "International Standard for Software Engineering – Software Life Cycle Processes – Maintenance," *ISO/IEC 14764(E) and IEEE Std 14764-2006*, pp. 1–46, Sep. 2006, Revision of IEEE Std 1219-1998. DOI: `10.1109/IEEESTD.2006.235774` (cit. on pp. 10, 66–68).

[IEE90] ——, "IEEE Standard Glossary of Software Engineering Terminology," *IEEE Std 610.12-1990*, pp. 1–84, Dec. 1990. DOI: `10.1109/IEEESTD.1990.101064` (cit. on p. 66).

[IPW01] A. Igarashi, B. C. Pierce, and P. Wadler, "Featherweight Java: A Minimal Core Calculus for Java and GJ," *ACM Trans. Program. Lang. Syst.*, vol. 23, no. 3, pp. 396–450, 2001 (cit. on pp. 65, 88, 95, 96).

[JAB+06] F. Jouault, F. Allilaire, J. Bézivin, I. Kurtev, and P. Valduriez, "ATL: A QVT-like Transformation Language," in *Companion to the 21th Annual ACM SIGPLAN Conference on Object-Oriented Programming, Systems, Languages, and Applications, (OOPSLA '06)*, P. L. Tarr and W. R. Cook, Eds., ACM, 2006, pp. 719–720, ISBN: 1-595-93491-X (cit. on pp. 12, 151).

[JCP08] A. Jedlitschka, M. Ciolkowski, and D. Pfahl, "Reporting Experiments in Software Engineering," in *Guide to Advanced Empirical Software Engineering*, F. Shull, J. Singer, and D. I.

Sjøberg, Eds., New York, NY, USA: Springer, 2008, ch. 8, pp. 201–228, ISBN: 978-1-848-00043-8 (cit. on p. 185).

[JGB11] C. Jeanneret, M. Glinz, and B. Baudry, "Estimating Footprints of Model Operations," in *Proceedings of the 33rd International Conference on Software Engineering (ICSE '11)*, Waikiki, Honolulu, HI, USA: ACM, 2011, pp. 601–610, ISBN: 978-1-4503-0445-0. DOI: 10.1145/1985793.1985875 (cit. on pp. 154, 155, 249).

[JM01] N. J. Juzgado and A. M. Moreno, *Basics of Software Engineering Experimentation.* Kluwer Academic Publishers, 2001, pp. I–XX, 1–395, ISBN: 978-0-792-37990-4 (cit. on p. 199).

[Jr73] J. H. M. Jr., "Types are Not Sets," in *Conference Record of the ACM Symposium on Principles of Programming Languages (POPL '73), Boston, Massachusetts, USA, October 1973*, P. C. Fischer and J. D. Ullman, Eds., ACM Press, 1973, pp. 120–124. DOI: 10.1145/512927.512938 (cit. on p. 64).

[KAF+08] D. Keim, G. Andrienko, J.-D. Fekete, C. Görg, J. Kohlhammer, and G. Melançon, "Visual Analytics: Definition, Process, and Challenges," in *Information Visualization*, A. Kerren, J. T. Stasko, J.-D. Fekete, and C. North, Eds., Berlin, Heidelberg: Springer, 2008, pp. 154–175, ISBN: 978-3-540-70955-8. DOI: 10.1007/978-3-540-70956-5_7 (cit. on p. 72).

[Kau63] A. F. Kaupe Jr., "A Note on the Dangling else ALGOL 60," *Commun. ACM*, vol. 6, no. 8, pp. 460–462, Aug. 1963, ISSN: 0001-0782. DOI: 10.1145/366707.367585 (cit. on p. 60).

[KB04] C. Kaner and W. P. Bond, "Software Engineering Metrics: What Do They Measure and How Do We Know?" In *Proceedings of the IEEE 10th International Software Metrics*

Symposium (METRICS '04), Sep. 2004, pp. 1–12 (cit. on p. 175).

[KCPT11] M. Kezadri, B. Combemale, M. Pantel, and X. Thirioux, "A Proof Assistant Based Formalization of components in MDE," in *8th International Symposium on Formal Aspects of Component Software (FACS '11)*, University of Oslo, Norway, Sep. 2011 (cit. on p. 245).

[KE00] R. Koschke and T. Eisenbarth, "A Framework for Experimental Evaluation of Clustering Techniques," in *Proceedings of the 8th International Workshop on Program Comprehension (IWPC '00)*, IEEE Computer Society, 2000, pp. 201–210, ISBN: 0-7695-0656-9 (cit. on p. 176).

[KGBH10] L. Kapová, T. Goldschmidt, S. Becker, and J. Henss, "Evaluating Maintainability with Code Metrics for Model-to-Model Transformations," in *Proceedings of the 6th International Conference on the Quality of Software Architectures: Research into Practice - Reality and Gaps (QoSA '10)*, ser. LNCS, Prague, Czech Republic: Springer, 2010, pp. 151–166, ISBN: 3-642-13820-9, 978-3-642-13820-1. DOI: 10.1007/978-3-642-13821-8_12 (cit. on p. 247).

[KKEM10] D. A. Keim, J. Kohlhammer, G. Ellis, and F. Mansmann, *Mastering the Information Age - Solving Problems with Visual Analytics*. Eurographics Association, 2010, pp. 1–168, ISBN: 978-3-905-67377-7 (cit. on pp. 71, 72).

[KKS07] F. Klar, A. Königs, and A. Schürr, "Model Transformation in the Large," in *Proceedings of the 6th Joint Meeting of the European Software Engineering Conference and the ACM SIGSOFT International Symposium on Foundations of Software Engineering (ESEC/SIGSOFT-FSE '07)*, I. Crnkovic and A. Bertolino, Eds., ACM, 2007, pp. 285–294, ISBN: 978-1-595-93811-4 (cit. on p. 237).

[Kle06] A. Kleppe, "MCC: A Model Transformation Environment," in *Proceedings of the Second European Conference on Model Driven Architecture - Foundations and Applications (ECMDA-FA '06)*, A. Rensink and J. Warmer, Eds., ser. Lecture Notes in Computer Science, vol. 4066, Springer, 2006, pp. 173–187, ISBN: 3-540-35909-5 (cit. on p. 242).

[Kle09] ——, *Software Language Engineering: Creating Domain-specific Languages Using Metamodels*. Addison Wesley, Pearson Education, 2009, ISBN: 978-0-321-55345-4 (cit. on pp. 32, 34, 35).

[KMS+08] D. A. Keim, F. Mansmann, J. Schneidewind, J. Thomas, and H. Ziegler, "Visual Analytics: Scope and Challenges," in *Visual Data Mining*, S. J. Simoff, M. H. Böhlen, and A. Mazeika, Eds., Berlin, Heidelberg: Springer, 2008, pp. 76–90, ISBN: 978-3-540-71079-0. DOI: 10.1007/978-3-540-71080-6_6 (cit. on pp. 72, 131).

[KPP08] D. S. Kolovos, R. F. Paige, and F. Polack, "The Epsilon Transformation Language," in *Proceedings of the 1st International Conference Theory and Practice of Model Transformations (ICMT '08)*, A. Vallecillo, J. Gray, and A. Pierantonio, Eds., ser. Lecture Notes in Computer Science, vol. 5063, Springer, 2008, pp. 46–60, ISBN: 978-3-540-69926-2 (cit. on pp. 12, 37, 152).

[KR12] S. Kang and S. Ryu, "Formal Specification of a JavaScript Module System," *SIGPLAN Not.*, vol. 47, no. 10, pp. 621–638, Oct. 2012, ISSN: 0362-1340 (cit. on p. 235).

[Krä11] J.-P. Krämer, "Stacksplorer – Understanding Dynamic Program Behavior," Diploma Thesis, RWTH Aachen University, Jan. 2011 (cit. on p. 249).

[Kru11] S. Kruse, "On the Use of Operators for the Co-Evolution of Metamodels and Transformations," in *Proceedings of the 2nd International Workshop on Models and Evolution (ME '11) collocated with the 14th ACM/IEEE International Conference on Model Driven Engineering Languages and Systems (MODELS '11)*, Wellington, New Zealand, 2011 (cit. on p. 154).

[KSW+13] A. Kusel, J. Schönböck, M. Wimmer, G. Kappel, W. Retschitzegger, and W. Schwinger, "Reuse in Model-to-Model Transformation Languages: Are we there yet?" English, *Software and Systems Modeling (SoSyM)*, pp. 1–36, 2013, ISSN: 1619-1366. DOI: `10.1007/s10270-013-0343-7`. [Online]. Available: `http://dx.doi.org/10.1007/s10270-013-0343-7` (cit. on pp. 236, 261).

[Kur07] I. Kurtev, "State of the Art of QVT: A Model Transformation Language Standard," in *Proceedings of the 3rd International Symposium on Applications of Graph Transformations with Industrial Relevance (AGTIVE '07)*, A. Schürr, M. Nagl, and A. Zündorf, Eds., ser. Lecture Notes in Computer Science, vol. 5088, Springer, 2007, pp. 377–393, ISBN: 978-3-540-89019-5 (cit. on p. 36).

[KvBJ06] I. Kurtev, K. van den Berg, and F. Jouault, "Evaluation of Rule-based Modularization in Model Transformation Languages Illustrated with ATL," in *Proceedings of the 2006 ACM Symposium on Applied Computing (SAC), Dijon, France, April 23-27, 2006*, H. Haddad, Ed., ACM, 2006, pp. 1202–1209, ISBN: 1-59593-108-2 (cit. on pp. 161, 248, 266).

[KvBJ07] I. Kurtev, K. van den Berga, and F. Jouault, "Rule-based Modularization in Model Transformation Languages illustrated with ATL," *Sci. Comput. Program.*, vol. 68, no. 3, pp. 138–154, 2007 (cit. on pp. 161, 248, 266).

[KW07] E. Kindler and R. Wagner, "Triple Graph Grammars: Concepts, Extensions, Implementations, and Application Scenarios," Software Engineering Group, Department of Computer Science, University of Paderborn, Paderborn, Germany, Tech. Rep. TR-RI-07-284, Jun. 2007, p. 75 (cit. on pp. 53, 135).

[KWB03] A. G. Kleppe, J. Warmer, and W. Bast, *MDA Explained: The Model Driven Architecture: Practice and Promise*. Boston, MA, USA: Addison-Wesley Longman Publishing Co., Inc., 2003, ISBN: 0-321-19442-X (cit. on p. 29).

[LDGR04] M. Lawley, K. Duddy, A. Gerber, and K. Raymond, "Language Features for Re-use and Maintainability of MDA Transformations," in *Proceedings of the OOPSLA Workshop on Best Practices for Model-Driven Software Development*, 2004 (cit. on pp. 157, 161, 248).

[LK14] K. Lano and S. Kolahdouz-Rahimi, "Model-Transformation Design Patterns," *Software Engineering, IEEE Transactions on*, vol. PP, no. 99, 2014, To Appear, ISSN: 0098-5589. DOI: 10.1109/TSE.2014.2354344 (cit. on p. 266).

[LKP+12] K. Lano, S. Kolahdouz-Rahimi, I. Poernomo, J. Terrell, and S. Zschaler, "Correct-by-Construction Synthesis of Model Transformations using Transformation Patterns," *Software and Systems Modeling (SoSyM)*, pp. 1–35, 2012, ISSN: 1619-1366. DOI: 10.1007/s10270-012-0291-7 (cit. on p. 294).

[LW90] S.-S. Liu and N. Wilde, "Identifying Objects in a Conventional Procedural Language: An example of data design recovery," in *Proceedings of the 16th International Conference on Software Maintenance (ICSM '90)*, Nov. 1990, pp. 266–271. DOI: 10.1109/ICSM.1990.131371 (cit. on p. 248).

[Mar04] R. Marvie, "A Transformation Composition Framework for Model Driven Engineering," IRCICA, University of Lille

1, France, Tech. Rep. LIFL 2004-n10, Nov. 2004. [Online]. Available: http://www2.lifl.fr/~marvie/pubs/RT2004-10.pdf (cit. on p. 243).

[Mar96] R. Martin, "Granularity," *C++ Report*, vol. 8, no. 10, pp. 57–62, Nov. 1996, ISSN: 1040-6042. [Online]. Available: http://www.objectmentor.com/resources/articles/granularity.pdf (cit. on p. 221).

[MB07] O. Maqbool and H. A. Babri, "Hierarchical Clustering for Software Architecture Recovery," *IEEE Transactions on Software Engineering*, vol. 33, no. 11, pp. 759–780, 2007 (cit. on pp. 76, 161).

[MC13] N. Macedo and A. Cunha, "Implementing QVT-R Bidirectional Model Transformations Using Alloy," in *Fundamental Approaches to Software Engineering*, ser. Lecture Notes in Computer Science, V. Cortellessa and D. Varró, Eds., vol. 7793, Springer, 2013, pp. 297–311, ISBN: 978-3-642-37056-4. DOI: 10.1007/978-3-642-37057-1_22 (cit. on pp. 245, 293).

[McC04] S. McConnell, *Code Complete: A Practical Handbook of Software Construction*, 2nd ed. Redmond, WA, USA: Microsoft Press, 2004, ISBN: 0735619670, 9780735619678 (cit. on p. 57).

[Mes14] D. Messinger, "Automatic Clustering for Software Architecture Recovery with Bunch," in *Seminar: Big Data, Architecture and Performance*, Best Paper Award by the SDQ Chair, Computer Science Faculty, Karlsruhe Institute of Technology, Germany, Feb. 2014 (cit. on p. 77).

[Mey97] B. Meyer, *Object-Oriented Software Construction*, 2nd. Prentice-Hall, 1997, ISBN: 0-136-29155-4 (cit. on pp. 55, 57).

[MFV+05] P.-A. Muller, F. Fleurey, D. Vojtisek, Z. Drey, D. Pollet, F. Fondement, P. Studer, and J.-M. Jézéquel, "On Executable

Meta-Languages Applied to Model Transformations," in *Model Transformations In Practice Workshop*, Montego Bay, Jamaica, Oct. 2005. [Online]. Available: http://hal.inria.fr/inria-00000381 (cit. on pp. 12, 152).

[Mit02] B. S. Mitchell, "A Heuristic Search Approach to Solving the Software Clustering Problem," PhD thesis, Drexel University, 2002 (cit. on p. 220).

[Mit86] J. C. Mitchell, "Representation Independence and Data Abstraction," in *Proceedings of the 13th ACM SIGACT-SIGPLAN Symposium on Principles of Programming Languages (POPL '86)*, St. Petersburg Beach, Florida: ACM, 1986, pp. 263–276. DOI: 10.1145/512644.512669 (cit. on p. 64).

[MKK11] P. Meier, S. Kounev, and H. Koziolek, "Automated Transformation of Component-Based Software Architecture Models to Queueing Petri Nets," in *Proceedings of the 19th International Symposium on Modeling, Analysis Simulation of Computer and Telecommunication Systems (MASCOTS '11)*, IEEE, Jul. 2011, pp. 339–348. DOI: 10.1109/MASCOTS.2011.23 (cit. on pp. 184, 200).

[MM01] B. S. Mitchell and S. Mancoridis, "Comparing the Decompositions Produced by Software Clustering Algorithms Using Similarity Measurements," in *Proceedings of the IEEE International Conference on Software Maintenance (ICSM '01)*, IEEE Computer Society, 2001, pp. 744–753 (cit. on p. 176).

[MM06] B. S. Mitchell and S. Mancoridis, "On the Automatic Modularization of Software Systems Using the Bunch Tool," *IEEE Transactions on Software Engineering*, vol. 32, no. 3, pp. 193–208, 2006 (cit. on pp. 21, 75, 76, 157).

[MM08] ——, "On the Evaluation of the Bunch Search-based Software Modularization Algorithm," *Soft Computing*, vol. 12, no. 1, pp. 77–93, 2008 (cit. on pp. 175, 176).

[MMCG99] S. Mancoridis, B. S. Mitchell, Y. Chen, and E. R. Gansner, "Bunch: A Clustering Tool for the Recovery and Maintenance of Software System Structures," in *Proceedings of the IEEE International Conference on Software Maintenance (ICSM '99)*, IEEE Computer Society, 1999, pp. 50–59 (cit. on pp. 75, 76).

[Mor73] J. H. Morris Jr., "Protection in Programming Languages," *Commun. ACM*, vol. 16, no. 1, pp. 15–21, Jan. 1973, ISSN: 0001-0782. DOI: 10.1145/361932.361937 (cit. on p. 64).

[MRB07] A. MacCormack, J. Rusnak, and C. Baldwin, "The Impact of Component Modularity on Design Evolution: Evidence from the Software Industry," *Harvard Business School Technology & Operations Mgt. Unit Research Paper*, vol. No. 08-038, 2007 (cit. on p. 59).

[Mül01] R. Müller, *The Concept of Model: Definitions and Types*, [Online]. Available: http://www.muellerscience.com/ENGLISH/Theconceptofmo-del.definitions.htm, 2001 (cit. on p. 31).

[NNH05] F. Nielson, H. R. Nielson, and C. Hankin, *Principles of Program Analysis*, 2nd. Springer, 2005, pp. I–XXI, 1–452, ISBN: 978-3-540-65410-0 (cit. on p. 70).

[OAO06] G. K. Olsen, J. Aagedal, and J. Oldevik, "Aspects of Reusable Model Transformations," in *Proceedings of the 1st European Workshop on Composition of Model Transformations (CMT '06)*, ser. TR-CTI, URL: doc.utwente.nl/66171/, Centre for Telematics and Information Technology, Univ. of Twente, Jun. 2006, pp. 21–26 (cit. on p. 236).

[Obj03] Object Management Group, *Model Driven Architecture – Specifications, Version 1.0.1*, Jun. 2003. [Online]. Available: http://www.omg.org/cgi-bin/doc?omg/03-06-01 (cit. on pp. 28, 29).

[Obj11] ——, *MOF 2.0 Query/View/Transformation, version 1.1*, Jan. 2011. [Online]. Available: http://www.omg.org/spec/QVT/1.1/PDF/ (cit. on pp. 7, 36, 42, 46, 92, 115, 118, 123, 131, 135, 214, 240, 245, 294).

[Obj12] ——, *Object Constraint Language (OCL), Version 2.3.1*, Jan. 2012. [Online]. Available: http://www.omg.org/spec/OCL/2.3.1/ (cit. on p. 42).

[Obj14] ——, *Meta-Object Facility – Core Specification, Version 2.4.2*, Jan. 2014. [Online]. Available: http://www.omg.org/spec/MOF/ISO/19508/ (cit. on pp. 33, 232).

[OGS09] D. Oberle, S. Grimm, and S. Staab, "An Ontology for Software," in *Handbook on Ontologies*, ser. International Handbooks on Information Systems, 2nd, Springer, 2009, pp. 383–402, ISBN: 978-3-540-70999-2 (cit. on p. 34).

[Par72] D. L. Parnas, "On the Criteria To Be Used in Decomposing Systems into Modules," *Communications of the ACM*, vol. 15, no. 12, pp. 1053–1058, 1972 (cit. on pp. 15, 55, 59).

[Pau12] C. Paulin-Mohring, "Introduction to the Coq Proof-Assistant for Practical Software Verification," in *Tools for Practical Software Verification*, ser. Lecture Notes in Computer Science, B. Meyer and M. Nordio, Eds., vol. 7682, Springer, 2012, pp. 45–95, ISBN: 978-3-642-35745-9. DOI: 10.1007/978-3-642-35746-6_3 (cit. on p. 294).

[Pau93] ——, "Inductive Definitions in the System Coq - Rules and Properties," in *Proceedings of the Conference on Typed Lambda Calculi and Applications (TLCA '93)*, ser. Lecture Notes in Computer Science, M. Bezem and J. F. Groote, Eds., vol. 664, Springer, 1993, pp. 328–345, ISBN: 3-540-56517-5 (cit. on p. 65).

[Per82] A. J. Perlis, "Epigrams on Programming," *SIGPLAN Notices*, vol. 17, no. 9, pp. 7–13, 1982 (cit. on pp. xiii, 270).

[Pie02] B. C. Pierce, *Types and Programming Languages.* MIT Press, 2002, pp. I–XXI, 1–623, ISBN: 978-0-262-16209-8 (cit. on pp. 63, 102).

[Pie04] ——, *Advanced Topics in Types and Programming Languages.* The MIT Press, 2004, ISBN: 0-262-16228-8 (cit. on pp. 64, 81).

[PM11] C. Picard and R. Matthes, "Coinductive Graph Representation: the Problem of Embedded Lists," *ECEASST*, vol. 39, 2011 (cit. on p. 298).

[Poe08] I. Poernomo, "Proofs-as-Model-Transformations," in *Proceedings of the 1st International Conference on Model Transformation (ICMT '08)*, ser. Lecture Notes in Computer Science, A. Vallecillo, J. Gray, and A. Pierantonio, Eds., vol. 5063, Springer, 2008, pp. 214–228, ISBN: 978-3-540-69926-2 (cit. on pp. 113, 294).

[PPH05] D. Pilone, N. Pitman, and D. Heymann-Reder, *UML 2.0 in a Nutshell*, 1st. O'Reilly Media, Inc., 2005, ISBN: 978-0-596-00795-7 (cit. on p. 232).

[Rat13] C. Rathfelder, *Modelling Event-Based Interactions in Component-Based Architectures for Quantitative System Evaluation*, ser. The Karlsruhe Series on Software Design and Quality; 10. Karlsruhe: KIT Scientific Publishing, 2013, ISBN: 978-3-86644-969-5. [Online]. Available: `http://dx.doi.org/10.5445/KSP/1000032232` (cit. on p. 214).

[RC93] L. Rising and F. Calliss, "An Experiment Investigating the Effect of Information Hiding on Maintainability," in *Proceedings of the 12th Annual International Phoenix Conference on*

Computers and Communications (IPCCC '93), Mar. 1993, pp. 510–516. DOI: 10.1109/PCCC.1993.344523 (cit. on p. 12).

[Ren06] A. Rentschler, "Model-To-Text Transformation Languages," in *Seminar: Modellgetriebene Software-Entwicklung Architekturen, Muster und Eclipse-basierte MDA*, S. Becker, J. Happe, H. Koziolek, K. Krogmann, M. Kuperberg, and R. Reussner, Eds., ser. Karlsruhe Reports in Informatics, Best Paper Award by the SDQ Chair, Computer Science Faculty, University of Karlsruhe, Germany, 2006, pp. 98–129. [Online]. Available: http://digbib.ubka.uni-karlsruhe.de/volltexte/documents/2918 (cit. on p. 38).

[Reu01] R. H. Reussner, *Parametrisierte Verträge zur Protokolladaption bei Software-Komponenten*. Logos Verlag, Berlin, 2001, ISBN: 978-3-89722-783-5 (cit. on pp. 59, 60).

[Rey83] J. C. Reynolds, "Types, Abstraction and Parametric Polymorphism," in *Proceedings of the IFIP 9th World Computer Congress (IFIP Congress '83)*, R. E. A. Mason, Ed., 1983, pp. 513–523, ISBN: 0-444-86729-5 (cit. on p. 63).

[Rey98] ——, *Theories of Programming Languages*. Cambridge University Press, 1998, pp. I–XII, 1–500, ISBN: 978-0-521-59414-1 (cit. on p. 61).

[RKSK13] C. Rathfelder, B. Klatt, K. Sachs, and S. Kounev, "Modeling Event-based Communication in Component-Based Software Architectures for Performance Predictions," *Journal of Software and Systems Modeling (SoSyM)*, pp. 1–27, Mar. 2013, ISSN: 1619-1366. DOI: 10.1007/s10270-013-0316-x. [Online]. Available: http://dx.doi.org/10.1007/s10270-013-0316-x (cit. on p. 214).

[RNHR13] A. Rentschler, Q. Noorshams, L. Happe, and R. Reussner, "Interactive Visual Analytics for Efficient Maintenance of

Model Transformations," in *Proceedings of the 6th International Conference on Model Transformation (ICMT '13), Budapest, Hungary*, K. Duddy and G. Kappel, Eds., ser. Lecture Notes in Computer Science, Acceptance Rate (Full Paper): 20.7%, vol. 7909, Berlin–Heidelberg–New York: Springer, Jun. 2013, pp. 141–157, ISBN: 978-3-642-38882-8. DOI: 10.1007/978-3-642-38883-5_14 (cit. on pp. 18, 127, 163).

[RRLB09] J. E. Rivera, D. Ruiz-González, F. López-Romero, and J. M. Bautista, "Wires* : A Tool for Orchestrating Model Transformations," in *XIV Jornadas de Ingeniería del Software y Bases de Datos (JISBD 2009), San Sebastián, Spain, September 8-11, 2009*, A. Vallecillo and G. Sagardui, Eds., 2009, pp. 158–161, ISBN: 978-84-692-4211-7 (cit. on p. 243).

[RRMB08] R. Romeikat, S. Roser, P. Müllender, and B. Bauer, "Translation of QVT Relations into QVT Operational Mappings," in *Proceedings of the 1st International Conference Theory and Practice of Model Transformations (ICMT '08)*, A. Vallecillo, J. Gray, and A. Pierantonio, Eds., ser. Lecture Notes in Computer Science, vol. 5063, Springer, 2008, pp. 137–151, ISBN: 978-3-540-69926-2 (cit. on p. 263).

[RS14] A. Rentschler and P. Sterner, "Interactive Dependency Graphs for Model Transformation Analysis," in *Joint Proceedings of MODELS '13 Invited Talks, Demonstration Session, Poster Session, and ACM Student Research Competition co-located with the 16th International Conference on Model Driven Engineering Languages and Systems (MODELS '13), Miami, USA, September 29 - October 4, 2013*, Y. Liu and S. Zschaler, Eds., ser. CEUR Workshop Proceedings, vol. 1115, CEUR-WS.org, Jan. 2014, pp. 36–40 (cit. on pp. 20, 21).

[RWN+14a] A. Rentschler, D. Werle, Q. Noorshams, L. Happe, and R. Reussner, "Designing Information Hiding Modularity for Model Transformation Languages," in *Proceedings of the 13th International Conference on Modularity (AOSD '14), Lugano, Switzerland, April 22 - 26, 2014*, Acceptance Rate: 35.0%, New York, NY, USA: ACM, Apr. 2014, pp. 217–228, ISBN: 978-1-450-32772-5. DOI: 10.1145/2577080.2577094 (cit. on pp. 17, 20).

[RWN+14b] ——, "Remodularizing Legacy Model Transformations with Automatic Clustering Techniques," in *Proceedings of the 3rd Workshop on the Analysis of Model Transformations co-located with the 17th International Conference on Model Driven Engineering Languages and Systems (AMT@MODELS 2014), Valencia, Spain, September 29, 2014*, B. Baudry, J. Dingel, L. Lucio, and H. Vangheluwe, Eds., ser. CEUR Workshop Proceedings, vol. 1277, CEUR-WS.org, 2014, pp. 4–13 (cit. on pp. 19, 21).

[Sal09] K. A. Saleh, *Software Engineering*. J Ross Publishing, 2009, ISBN: 978-1-932-15994-3 (cit. on p. 200).

[SBC+13] G. M. K. Selim, F. Büttner, J. R. Cordy, J. Dingel, and S. Wang, "Automated Verification of Model Transformations in the Automotive Industry," in *Proceedings of the 16th International Conference on Model-Driven Engineering Languages and Systems (MODELS '13), Miami, FL, USA, September 29 - October 4, 2013*, A. Moreira, B. Schätz, J. Gray, A. Vallecillo, and P. J. Clarke, Eds., Springer, 2013, pp. 690–706. DOI: 10.1007/978-3-642-41533-3_42 (cit. on p. 265).

[SBPM09] D. Steinberg, F. Budinsky, M. Paternostro, and E. Merks, *EMF: Eclipse Modeling Framework 2.0*, 2nd. Addison-Wesley Professional, 2009, ISBN: 0-321-33188-5 (cit. on pp. 34, 232, 297).

[Sch95] A. Schürr, "Specification of Graph Translators with Triple Graph Grammars," in *Proceedings of the 20th International Workshop on Graph-Theoretic Concepts in Computer Science (WG '94)*, E. W. Mayr, G. Schmidt, and G. Tinhofer, Eds., ser. Lecture Notes in Computer Science, vol. 903, Springer, 1995, pp. 151–163, ISBN: 3-540-59071-4 (cit. on pp. 53, 135).

[Sel03] B. Selic, "The Pragmatics of Model-Driven Development," *IEEE Software*, vol. 20, no. 5, pp. 19–25, 2003 (cit. on p. 31).

[SG12] E. Syriani and J. Gray, "Challenges for Addressing Quality Factors in Model Transformation," in *Proceedings of the IEEE Fifth International Conference on Software Testing, Verification and Validation (ICST '12)*, G. Antoniol, A. Bertolino, and Y. Labiche, Eds., IEEE, 2012, pp. 929–937, ISBN: 978-1-4577-1906-6 (cit. on p. 266).

[SGCH01] K. J. Sullivan, W. G. Griswold, Y. Cai, and B. Hallen, "The Structure and Value of Modularity in Software Design," *SIGSOFT Softw. Eng. Notes*, vol. 26, no. 5, pp. 99–108, Sep. 2001, ISSN: 0163-5948 (cit. on p. 79).

[SGdL14] J. Sánchez Cuadrado, E. Guerra, and J. de Lara, "A Component Model for Model Transformations," *IEEE Transactions on Software Engineering*, vol. PP, no. 99, 2014, To Appear, ISSN: 0098-5589. DOI: 10.1109/TSE.2014.2339852 (cit. on p. 244).

[SKK+10] J. Schönböck, G. Kappel, A. Kusel, W. Retschitzegger, W. Schwinger, and M. Wimmer, "Catch Me If You Can - Debugging Support for Model Transformations," in *Models in Software Engineering, Workshops and Symposia at MODELS '09*, ser. Lecture Notes in Computer Science, Springer, 2010, pp. 5–20, ISBN: 978-3-642-12260-6 (cit. on p. 250).

[SMDM05] A. Shokoufandeh, S. Mancoridis, T. Denton, and M. Maycock, "Spectral and Meta-heuristic Algorithms for Software Clustering," *Journal of Systems and Software*, vol. 77, no. 3, pp. 213–223, 2005 (cit. on p. 161).

[SP07] R. Sindhgatta and K. Pooloth, "Identifying Software Decompositions by Applying Transaction Clustering on Source Code," in *Proceedings of the 31st Annual International Computer Software and Applications Conference (COMPSAC '07)*, IEEE Computer Society, 2007, pp. 317–326, ISBN: 978-0-7695-2870-0 (cit. on p. 248).

[SR99] M. Siff and T. W. Reps, "Identifying Modules via Concept Analysis," *IEEE Transactions on Software Engineering*, vol. 25, no. 6, pp. 749–768, 1999 (cit. on p. 248).

[ST12] M. Shtern and V. Tzerpos, "Clustering Methodologies for Software Engineering," *Adv. Soft. Eng.*, vol. 2012, 1:1–1:1, Jan. 2012, ISSN: 1687-8655. DOI: 10.1155/2012/792024 (cit. on pp. 73, 176).

[Sta73] H. Stachowiak, *Allgemeine Modelltheorie [General Model Theory]*. Springer Verlag, Wien, 1973, ISBN: 3-211-81106-0 (cit. on p. 31).

[Ste10] P. Stevens, "Bidirectional Model Transformations in QVT: Semantic Issues and Open Questions," *Software and System Modeling*, vol. 9, no. 1, pp. 7–20, 2010 (cit. on pp. 37, 245).

[Ste12] P. Sterner, "Statische Code-Analyse von Modelltransformationen," Diploma Thesis, Computer Science Faculty, Karlsruhe Institute of Technology, Germany, Nov. 2012 (cit. on p. 128).

[Ste13] P. Stevens, "A Simple Game-theoretic Approach to Checkonly QVT Relations," *Software and System Modeling*, vol. 12, no. 1, pp. 175–199, 2013 (cit. on pp. 245, 293).

[Str08] M. Strecker, “Modeling and Verifying Graph Transformations in Proof Assistants,” *Electr. Notes Theor. Comput. Sci.*, vol. 203, no. 1, pp. 135–148, 2008 (cit. on p. 245).

[SV06] T. Stahl and M. Voelter, *Model-Driven Software Development: Technology, Engineering, Management*. John Wiley & Sons, 2006, ISBN: 978-0-470-02570-3 (cit. on pp. 25–27).

[Swi09] W. Swierstra, “A Hoare Logic for the State Monad,” in *Theorem Proving in Higher Order Logics*, ser. Lecture Notes in Computer Science, S. Berghofer, T. Nipkow, C. Urban, and M. Wenzel, Eds., vol. 5674, Springer, 2009, pp. 440–451, ISBN: 978-3-642-03358-2. DOI: 10.1007/978-3-642-03359-9_30 (cit. on pp. 303, 304).

[SZ93] A. Schill and M. Zitterbart, “A System Framework for Open Distributed Processing,” *J. Network Syst. Manage.*, vol. 1, no. 1, pp. 71–93, 1993 (cit. on p. 29).

[Szy02] C. Szyperski, *Component Software: Beyond Object-Oriented Programming*, 2nd. Boston, MA, USA: Addison-Wesley Longman Publishing Co., Inc., 2002, ISBN: 0-201-74572-0 (cit. on p. 59).

[Szy92] C. A. Szyperski, “Import is Not Inheritance - Why We Need Both: Modules and Classes,” in *Proceedings of the European Conference on Object-Oriented Programming (ECOOP ’92)*, O. L. Madsen, Ed., ser. Lecture Notes in Computer Science, vol. 615, Springer, 1992, pp. 19–32, ISBN: 3-540-55668-0 (cit. on pp. 57, 58).

[TB02] J. Tilly and E. M. Burke, *Ant - The Definitive Guide: Complete build management for Java*. O’Reilly, 2002, pp. I–XVIII, 1–269, ISBN: 978-0-596-00184-1 (cit. on p. 244).

[TC10] G. Tamura and A. Cleve, “A Comparison of Taxonomies for Model Transformation Languages,” *Paradigma*, vol. 4, no.

1, pp. 1–14, Mar. 2010. [Online]. Available: http://hal.inria.fr/inria-00488765 (cit. on p. 38).

[TEV10] A. Telea, O. Ersoy, and L. Voinea, "Visual Analytics in Software Maintenance: Challenges and Opportunities," in *International Symposium on Visual Analytics Science and Technology (EuroVAST '10)*, J. Kohlhammer and D. Keim, Eds., Bordeaux, France: Eurographics Association, 2010, pp. 75–80, ISBN: 978-3-905-67374-6. DOI: 10.2312/PE/EuroVAST/EuroVAST10/075-080 (cit. on p. 72).

[The12] The Coq Development Team, *The Coq Proof Assistant, Reference Manual, Version 8.4*, 2012. [Online]. Available: http://coq.inria.fr/refman (cit. on pp. 17, 64, 65).

[The13] The Eclipse Foundation, *Xtend User Guide, Version 2.5.0*, Dec. 2013. [Online]. Available: http://www.eclipse.org/xtend/documentation/ (cit. on p. 53).

[THER09] A. Telea, H. Hoogendorp, O. Ersoy, and D. Reniers, "Extraction and Visualization of Call Dependencies for Large C/C++ Code Bases: A Comparative Study," in *Proceedings of the 5th IEEE International Workshop on Visualizing Software for Understanding and Analysis (VISSOFT '09)*, IEEE, Sep. 2009, pp. 81–88. DOI: 10.1109/VISSOF.2009.5336419 (cit. on p. 248).

[TSG+11] J. B. Tolosa, O. Sanjuán-Martínez, V. García-Díaz, B. C. P. G-Bustelo, and J. M. C. Lovelle, "Towards the Systematic Measurement of ATL Transformation Models," *Softw., Pract. Exper.*, vol. 41, no. 7, pp. 789–815, 2011 (cit. on p. 247).

[TV11] J. Troya and A. Vallecillo, "A Rewriting Logic Semantics for ATL," *Journal of Object Technology*, vol. 10, pp. 1–29, 2011 (cit. on p. 245).

[Tze01] V. Tzerpos, "Comprehension-driven Software Clustering," PhD thesis, University of Toronto, 2001 (cit. on pp. 73, 76).

[UHV09] Z. Ujhelyi, Á. Horváth, and D. Varró, "A Generic Static Analysis Framework for Model Transformation Programs," Budapest Univ. of Technology and Economics, Tech. Rep., Jun. 2009 (cit. on p. 246).

[UHV12] ——, "Dynamic Backward Slicing of Model Transformations," in *Proceedings of the 5th International Conference on Software Testing, Verification and Validation (ICST '12)*, IEEE, 2012, pp. 1–10, ISBN: 978-0-7695-4670-4. DOI: 10.1109/ICST.2012.80 (cit. on p. 246).

[VAB+07] B. Vanhooff, D. Ayed, S. V. Baelen, W. Joosen, and Y. Berbers, "UniTI: a unified transformation infrastructure," in *Proceedings of the 10th International Conference on Model Driven Engineering Languages and Systems (MODELS '07)*, G. Engels, B. Opdyke, D. C. Schmidt, and F. Weil, Eds., ser. Lecture Notes in Computer Science, vol. 4735, Springer, 2007, pp. 31–45, ISBN: 978-3-540-75208-0 (cit. on p. 242).

[vALvB08] M. van Amstel, C. Lange, and M. van den Brand, "Metrics for Analyzing the Quality of Model Transformations," in *ECOOP Workshop on Quantitative Approaches in Object-Oriented Software Engineering (ECOOP-QAOOSE '08)*, vol. 12, 2008, pp. 41–51 (cit. on p. 247).

[Van10] B. Vanhooff, "Loosely Coupled Transformation Chains. How to Enable Transformation Reuse with Traceability Information," Berbers, Yolande (supervisor), PhD thesis, Informatics Section, Department of Computer Science, Faculty of Engineering Science, Apr. 2010, p. 196. [Online]. Available: https://lirias.kuleuven.be/handle/123456789/262244 (cit. on p. 242).

[Var06] D. Varró, "Model Transformation by Example," in *Proceedings of the 9th International Conference on Model Driven Engineering Languages and Systems (MoDELS '06)*, O. Nierstrasz, J. Whittle, D. Harel, and G. Reggio, Eds., ser. Lecture Notes in Computer Science, vol. 4199, Springer, 2006, pp. 410–424, ISBN: 3-540-45772-0 (cit. on p. 261).

[vAvB11] M. van Amstel and M. G. J. van den Brand, "Model Transformation Analysis: Staying Ahead of the Maintenance Nightmare," in *Proceedings of the 4th International Conference on Theory and Practice of Model Transformations (ICMT '11)*, ser. LNCS, Zürich, Switzerland: Springer, 2011, pp. 108–122, ISBN: 978-3-642-21731-9 (cit. on pp. 209, 247, 249).

[VB07] D. Varró and A. Balogh, "The Model Transformation Language of the VIATRA2 Framework," *Sci. Comput. Program.*, vol. 68, no. 3, pp. 214–234, 2007 (cit. on pp. 12, 152).

[vDVW07] A. van Deursen, E. Visser, and J. Warmer, "Model-Driven Software Evolution: A Research Agenda," in *CSMR Workshop on Model-Driven Software Evolution (MoDSE '07)*, D. Tamzalit, Ed., Amsterdam, The Netherlands, Mar. 2007, pp. 41–49. [Online]. Available: `http://swerl.tudelft.nl/twiki/pub/Main/TechnicalReports/TUD-SERG-2007-006.pdf` (cit. on p. 69).

[VGB+12] A. Vallecillo, M. Gogolla, L. Burgueño, M. Wimmer, and L. Hamann, "Formal Specification and Testing of Model Transformations," in *12th International School on Formal Methods for the Design of Computer, Communication, and Software Systems (SFM '12)*, M. Bernardo, V. Cortellessa, and A. Pierantonio, Eds., ser. LNCS, vol. 7320, Springer, 2012, pp. 399–437, ISBN: 978-3-642-30981-6 (cit. on p. 126).

[Voe10] M. Voelter, "Architecture As Language," *IEEE Software*, vol. 27, no. 2, pp. 56–64, 2010 (cit. on pp. 3, 30).

[Voe11] ——, "Language and IDE Modularization and Composition with MPS," in *Generative and Transformational Techniques in Software Engineering IV, International Summer School,*

GTTSE 2011, Braga, Portugal, July 3-9, 2011. Revised Papers, R. Lämmel, J. Saraiva, and J. Visser, Eds., Springer, 2011, pp. 383–430. DOI: 10.1007/978-3-642-35992-7_11. [Online]. Available: http://dx.doi.org/10.1007/978-3-642-35992-7_11 (cit. on p. 237).

[Voe13] ——, *DSL Engineering: Designing, Implementing and Using Domain-Specific Languages*, January 23 2013. CreateSpace Independent Publishing Platform, 2013, ISBN: 978-1-481-21858-0. [Online]. Available: http://dslbook.org (cit. on pp. 32, 34).

[VR11] A. Vieira and F. Ramalho, "A Static Analyzer for Model Transformations," in *Proceedings of the 3rd International Workshop on Model Transformation with ATL (MtATL '11)*, ser. CEUR Workshop Proceedings, vol. 742, CEUR-WS.org, Jun. 2011, pp. 75–88 (cit. on p. 247).

[VVE+06] D. Varró, S. Varró-Gyapay, H. Ehrig, U. Prange, and G. Taentzer, "Termination Analysis of Model Transformations by Petri Nets," in *Proceedings of the 3rd International Conference on Graph Transformations (ICGT '06)*, Natal, Rio Grande do Norte, Brazil, September 17-23: Springer, 2006, pp. 260–274 (cit. on p. 246).

[Wag08] D. Wagelaar, "Composition Techniques for Rule-Based Model Transformation Languages," in *Proceedings of the 1st International Conference on Theory and Practice of Model Transformation (ICMT '08)*, A. Vallecillo, J. Gray, and A. Pierantonio, Eds., ser. Lecture Notes in Computer Science, vol. 5063, Springer, 2008, pp. 152–167, ISBN: 978-3-540-69926-2 (cit. on p. 241).

[WHK13] E. Willink, H. Hoyos, and D. Kolovos, "Yet Another Three QVT Languages," in *Proceedings of the 6th International Conference on Model Transformation (ICMT '13)*, ser. Lecture Notes in Computer Science, K. Duddy and G. Kappel, Eds., vol. 7909, Springer, Jun. 2013, pp. 58–59, ISBN: 978-3-642-38882-8. DOI: 10.1007/978-3-642-38883-5_8 (cit. on pp. 36, 46).

[WHR+13] J. Whittle, J. Hutchinson, M. Rouncefield, H. Burden, and R. Heldal, "Industrial Adoption of Model-Driven Engineering: Are the Tools Really the Problem?" In *Proceedings of the 16th International Conference on Model-Driven Engineering Languages and Systems (MODELS '13)*, A. Moreira, B. Schätz, J. Gray, A. Vallecillo, and P. J. Clarke, Eds., ser. Lecture Notes in Computer Science, vol. 8107, Springer, 2013, pp. 1–17, ISBN: 978-3-642-41532-6 (cit. on pp. 4, 13, 30, 157, 255).

[Wig97] T. A. Wiggerts, "Using Clustering Algorithms in Legacy Systems Remodularization," in *Proceedings of the 4th Working Conference on Reverse Engineering (WCRE '97)*, IEEE, 1997, pp. 33–43 (cit. on p. 74).

[WKK+09] M. Wimmer, G. Kappel, A. Kusel, W. Retschitzegger, J. Schoenboeck, and W. Schwinger, "Right or Wrong? – Verification of Model Transformations using Colored Petri Nets," in *Proceedings of the 9th OOPSLA Workshop on Domain-Specific Modeling (DSM 2009)*, Helsinki Business School, Orlando, Oct. 2009 (cit. on pp. 245, 247).

[WKK+12a] M. Wimmer, G. Kappel, A. Kusel, W. Retschitzegger, J. Schönböck, and W. Schwinger, "Fact or Fiction - Reuse in Rule-Based Model-to-Model Transformation Languages," in *Proceedings of the 5th International Conference Theory and Practice of Model Transformations (ICMT '12)*, Z. Hu and J. de Lara, Eds., ser. Lecture Notes in Computer Science, vol. 7307, Springer, 2012, pp. 280–295, ISBN: 978-3-642-30475-0 (cit. on p. 236).

[WKK+12b] M. Wimmer, G. Kappel, A. Kusel, W. Retschitzegger, J. Schönböck, W. Schwinger, D. S. Kolovos, R. F. Paige, M. Lauder, A. Schürr, and D. Wagelaar, "Surveying Rule Inheritance in Model-to-Model Transformation Languages," *Journal of Object Technology*, vol. 11, no. 2, pp. 1–46, 2012 (cit. on pp. 209, 236).

[WKS+09a] M. Wimmer, G. Kappel, J. Schoenboeck, A. Kusel, W. Retschitzegger, and W. Schwinger, "A Petri Net Based Debugging Environment for QVT Relations," in *Proceedings of the 2009 IEEE/ACM 24th International Conference on Automated Software Engineering (ASE '09)*, IEEE, 2009, pp. 3–14, ISBN: 978-0-7695-3891-4. DOI: 10.1109/ASE.2009.99 (cit. on p. 250).

[WKS+09b] M. Wimmer, A. Kusel, J. Schönböck, G. Kappel, W. Retschitzegger, and W. Schwinger, "Reviving QVT Relations: Model-Based Debugging Using Colored Petri Nets," in *Proceedings of the 12th International Conference on Model Driven Engineering Languages and Systems (MODELS '09)*, ser. Lecture Notes in Computer Science, A. Schürr and B. Selic, Eds., vol. 5795, Springer, 2009, pp. 727–732 (cit. on p. 250).

[WM14] E. D. Willink and N. Matragkas, "QVT Traceability: What does it really mean?" The Eclipse Foundation, Tech. Rep., 2014. [Online]. Available: http://www.eclipse.org/mmt/qvt/docs/ICMT2014/QVTtraceability.pdf (cit. on p. 124).

[WPXZ11] J. Wang, X. Peng, Z. Xing, and W. Zhao, "An Exploratory Study of Feature Location Process: Distinct Phases, Recurring Patterns, and Elementary Actions.," in *Proceedings of the 27th IEEE International Conference on Software Maintenance (ICSM '11)*, Washington, DC, USA: IEEE Computer

Society, 2011, pp. 213–222, ISBN: 978-1-457-70663-9 (cit. on pp. 199, 208).

[WT04] Z. Wen and V. Tzerpos, "An Effectiveness Measure for Software Clustering Algorithms," in *Proceedings of the 12th International Workshop on Program Comprehension (IWPC '04)*, IEEE Computer Society, 2004, pp. 194–203, ISBN: 0-7695-2149-5 (cit. on p. 176).

[WT05] ——, "Software Clustering based on Omnipresent Object Detection," in *Proceedings of the 13th International Workshop on Program Comprehension (IWPC '05)*, IEEE Computer Society, 2005, pp. 269–278, ISBN: 0-7695-2254-8 (cit. on p. 248).

[WVD10] D. Wagelaar, R. Van Der Straeten, and D. Deridder, "Module Superimposition: A Composition Technique for Rule-based Model Transformation Languages," English, *Software and Systems Modeling (SoSyM)*, vol. 9, pp. 285–309, 3 2010, ISSN: 1619-1366. DOI: `10.1007/s10270-009-0134-3` (cit. on pp. 240, 241).

[Zsc14] S. Zschaler, "Towards Constraint-Based Model Types: A Generalised Formal Foundation for Model Genericity," in *Proceedings of the 2nd Workshop on View-Based, Aspect-Oriented and Orthographic Software Modelling (VAO '14)*, ser. VAO '14, York, United Kingdom: ACM, 2014, 11:11–11:18, ISBN: 978-1-4503-2900-2. DOI: `10.1145/2631675.2631678`. [Online]. Available: `http://doi.acm.org/10.1145/2631675.2631678` (cit. on p. 264).

All web sites were last retrieved on March 12, 2015.

The Karlsruhe Series on Software Design and Quality

Edited by Prof. Dr. Ralf Reussner // ISSN 1867-0067

Band 1 **Steffen Becker**
Coupled Model Transformations for QoS Enabled Component-Based Software Design. 2008
ISBN 978-3-86644-271-9

Band 2 **Heiko Koziolek**
Parameter Dependencies for Reusable Performance Specifications of Software Components. 2008
ISBN 978-3-86644-272-6

Band 3 **Jens Happe**
Predicting Software Performance in Symmetric Multi-core and Multiprocessor Environments. 2009
ISBN 978-3-86644-381-5

Band 4 **Klaus Krogmann**
Reconstruction of Software Component Architectures and Behaviour Models using Static and Dynamic Analysis. 2012
ISBN 978-3-86644-804-9

Band 5 **Michael Kuperberg**
Quantifying and Predicting the Influence of Execution Platform on Software Component Performance. 2010
ISBN 978-3-86644-741-7

Band 6 **Thomas Goldschmidt**
View-Based Textual Modelling. 2011
ISBN 978-3-86644-642-7

Die Bände sind unter www.ksp.kit.edu als PDF frei verfügbar oder als Druckausgabe bestellbar.

The Karlsruhe Series on Software Design and Quality

Edited by Prof. Dr. Ralf Reussner // ISSN 1867-0067

Band 7 **Anne Koziolek**
Automated Improvement of Software Architecture Models for Performance and Other Quality Attributes. 2013
ISBN 978-3-86644-973-2

Band 8 **Lucia Happe**
Configurable Software Performance Completions through Higher-Order Model Transformations. 2013
ISBN 978-3-86644-990-9

Band 9 **Franz Brosch**
Integrated Software Architecture-Based Reliability Prediction for IT Systems. 2012
ISBN 978-3-86644-859-9

Band 10 **Christoph Rathfelder**
Modelling Event-Based Interactions in Component-Based Architectures for Quantitative System Evaluation. 2013
ISBN 978-3-86644-969-5

Band 11 **Henning Groenda**
Certifying Software Component Performance Specifications. 2013
ISBN 978-3-7315-0080-3

Band 12 **Dennis Westermann**
Deriving Goal-oriented Performance Models by Systematic Experimentation. 2014
ISBN 978-3-7315-0165-7

Die Bände sind unter www.ksp.kit.edu als PDF frei verfügbar oder als Druckausgabe bestellbar.

The Karlsruhe Series on Software Design and Quality

Edited by Prof. Dr. Ralf Reussner // ISSN 1867-0067

Band 13 **Michael Hauck**
Automated Experiments for Deriving Performance-relevant Properties of Software Execution Environments. 2014
ISBN 978-3-7315-0138-1

Band 14 **Zoya Durdik**
Architectural Design Decision Documentation through Reuse of Design Patterns. 2014
ISBN 978-3-7315-0292-0

Band 15 **Erik Burger**
Flexible Views for View-based Model-driven Development. 2014
ISBN 978-3-7315-0276-0

Band 16 **Benjamin Klatt**
Consolidation of Customized Product Copies into Software Product Lines. 2015
ISBN 978-3-7315-0368-2

Band 17 **Andreas Rentschler**
Model Transformation Languages with Modular Information Hiding. 2015
ISBN 978-3-7315-0346-0

Die Bände sind unter www.ksp.kit.edu als PDF frei verfügbar oder als Druckausgabe bestellbar.